Political Forgiveness

Political Forgiveness

P. E. D I G E S E R

Cornell University Press / Ithaca and London

First published 2001 by Cornell University Press

Printed in the United States of America

Library of Congress Cataloging-in-Publication Data
Digeser, Peter.
    Political forgiveness/P.E. Digeser.
      p. cm.
    Includes bibliographical references and index.
    ISBN 0-8014-3810-1 (alk. paper)
    1. Political ethics. 2. Pardon. 3. Religion and politics. 4.
Forgiveness. I. Title.
JA79 .D54 2001
172—dc21
                                        00-011685

Cornell University Press strives to use environmentally
responsible suppliers and materials to the fullest extent
possible in the publishing of its books. Such materials
include vegetable-based, low-VOC inks and acid-free
papers that are recycled, totally chlorine-free, or partly
composed of nonwood fibers. Books that bear the logo of the
FSC (Forest Stewardship Council) use paper taken from
forests that have been inspected and certified as meeting the
highest standards for environmental and social responsibility.
For further information, visit our website at
www.cornellpress.cornell.edu.

Cloth printing   10 9 8 7 6 5 4 3 2 1

FSC FSC Trademark © 1996 Forest Stewardship Council A.C.
    SW-COC-098

To My Nieces and Nephews

Sometimes it is better to ask forgiveness for something that is already done than to ask permission.

Contents

Acknowledgments

I OWE an enormous debt to those who read and commented on this manuscript. They include Jackie Colby, Beth Digeser, Henry Digeser, Richard Flathman, David Mapel, Dan Philpott, and, of course, Tom Schrock. I forgive them all for placing me in their debt. I would also like to thank the University of California and my colleagues for their continued support. A great deal of the manuscript was written during my sabbatical in 1998.

Much of chapter 7 was published in "Forgiveness and Politics: Dirty Hands and Imperfect Procedures," *Political Theory* 26 (1998) and appears with the permission of Sage Publications, Inc.

P. E. D.

Santa Barbara, California

Political Forgiveness

Introduction

ALL THEORIZING begins with the particular, the con-
crete, the obvious stuff that appears before our noses. As an engagement
in theorizing, this book is no different. It is occasioned by political actors
who, in their official and unofficial capacities, have come to believe that
forgiveness can be a political concept: high and low officials of Chile,
Argentina, South Korea, Japan, Germany, and the United States asking
their victims and their countries for forgiveness; the South African Truth
and Reconciliation Commission putting its faith in truth and the capacity of a people to forgive in order to aid in the peaceful transformation of
a regime; a president of the United States publicly asking to be forgiven
for telling lies about a sordid sexual relationship. In addition, forgiveness also plays a more mundane but no less significant role when
domestic and international institutions deal with crushing financial
debts or when criminals appeal to the legal system and their victims for
forgiveness. In other words, forgiveness has become part of our public
life in such a way that we may wonder what exactly forgiveness means,
how it is connected to other political ideas and concepts, and whether it
is a practice that ultimately coheres with important political commitments and values. When we become curious about forgiveness in this
way, we are on the road to theorizing. That is to say, paradoxically, we
are attempting to understand that which we may never have suspected
that we didn't understand.

The attempt to understand forgiveness theoretically can, of course, be
driven by a variety of motives. With more or less missionary zeal, the
theoretician may aspire to improve or transform the world; or, as an
agent of the *zeitgeist*, the theorist may seek to clarify and map out the
meanings and political uses of forgiveness; or she may simply be dissat-

isfied with the ordinary understandings of forgiveness and wonder whether a more rigorous, political conceptualization is possible. This book is motivated by the last concern. It is not intended as a call to action, as a report on the present state of the practice of forgiving, or as an assessment of the acceptability of a particular act of forgiveness.[1] Instead, it seeks to redescribe our ordinary understanding of forgiveness in the hopes of rendering it compatible with a vision of politics that emphasizes action over motivation and the ability of people to receive their due. It is not a blueprint for political activity. It is, however, an argument in favor of incorporating forgiveness into our theories about politics.

Undoubtedly, many theorists who aspire to provide practical advice and many practitioners who desire to be told what to do may not find this motive sufficient for all this scribbling.[2] Nevertheless, one can be skeptical of the grander aspirations of theory and still believe that it is possible for theory to do more than engage in a complex cartography of practice. Here, the underlying assumption is that there is something dissatisfying about the ordinary understandings of forgiveness and their employment in politics. In general, this type of dissatisfaction motivates all efforts to theorize. In this particular case, our usual accounts of forgiveness are philosophically dissatisfying because they rarely qualify as accounts. Despite the ease with which we bestow or withhold forgiveness, we rarely attend to the concept itself. This is not to say that practitioners of forgiveness don't know what they are doing when they forgive (or don't forgive); rather, they don't know how much they don't know about the concept. This shouldn't be surprising, for our practical activities ordinarily require a great deal of know-how but rarely much reflection: competent speakers do not need to be able to recite the rules of grammar in order to be competent speakers. Theorizing forgiveness, then, is an attempt to think about something we rarely think about.

A second dissatisfaction with our ordinary understandings of forgiveness is that even a cursory reflection on the concept reveals that it is used in a variety of contexts and for different purposes. A priest may provide it as part of a sacrament, a Pecksniff may use it as a weapon, a judge may offer it as a way to relieve a financial burden, a politician may raise it as a way to heal a nation or garner partisan advantage, or a

1. For one such survey, see Shriver 1995; for a recent discussion of the problems of bringing forgiveness into politics, see Minow 1998.

2. This view of theorizing is very much influenced by the work of Michael Oakeshott, particularly his compact account offered in the first section of *On Human Conduct* (1975).

spouse may express it in the hope of reconciliation. This diversity raises the question whether there exist competing conceptions of forgiveness. For some theoreticians, this diversity may ignite a desire to establish an essential conception that would warrant his or her ability to judge true from false or central from subsidiary performances of forgiveness. The rich, complex character of practice, however, may be dissatisfying without licensing the position of the theoretician as umpire. The theorist may seek instead to bestow a greater level of coherence to a particular conception of forgiveness than is found in practice.

A final dissatisfaction I have with many commonsensical understandings of forgiveness is that they are so burdened with psychological and religious assumptions that their connection to politics is occluded. Obviously, others may see these "burdens" as the heart of forgiveness and argue that if anything has to be changed, it is the unwillingness of political theorists to be open to its psychological and religious characteristics. Nevertheless, I will argue that a secular, performative notion of forgiveness, one that takes as its cue the practices of forgiving debts and pardoning criminals, can be compatible with a politics that places a high value on justice (receiving what is due) and action (as opposed to motive).

In light of the motivation behind this project, I explore forgiveness as a political concept rather than analyze particular cases. Although I use the South African Truth and Reconciliation Commission on occasion to illustrate certain features of and problems with political forgiveness, my primary concern is to obtain a clear view of the concept of political forgiveness and its relationship to other ideas. Moving from the rich, concrete character of practice to the desiccated, abstract world of theory, however, should not be taken as rejection of practical life or as failure of theory. Rather, the present book is driven both by curiosity toward one aspect of human activity and a desire to understand the conditions invoked when responding to moral wrongs and unbearable debts. Understanding these conditions requires positioning political forgiveness within such concepts as justice, responsibility, self-disclosure, vicarious action, and pardoning. From this constellation of ideas the political character of forgiveness will become clearer.

Chapter 1 begins the investigation by setting out arguments against understanding forgiveness as a political concept. To address those criticisms, I assert that the practices of pardoning and financial forgiveness provide a glimpse of what I call political forgiveness. My interpretation of those practices, however, is not uncontroversial. Nevertheless, such practices do provide an entrance to a conception of forgiveness that is already part of political life. More specifically, they suggest a conception of forgiveness in which to forgive means to release what is owed, either financially or morally. For my purposes, theorizing this conception of forgiveness entails elucidating its conditions or prerequisites. Elucidating the conditions of political forgiveness reveals that the concept requires a relationship between at least two parties in which the appropriate party relieves a debt through appropriate signs or utterances. In addition, political forgiveness assumes that the success of this release does not depend on the emotional or internal states of the forgiver, but it does imply that the victim or creditor not receive what is due. A final attribute of political forgiveness is that it settles past claims and invites a restoration of a valued political relationship through the reinstatement of civic and moral equality or of the status quo ante.

As conceived of here, the idea of political forgiveness is not the only understanding of forgiveness, and in fact it differs in significant ways from ordinary, interpersonal conceptions of forgiveness. Those conceptions tend to rely heavily on the connection between forgiveness and the removal of resentment or other negative feelings. In general, they contend that if victims have not either freed themselves from those negative feelings or made a sincere commitment to do so, then forgiveness is an empty gesture. In contrast, chapter 1 argues that political forgiveness is an illocutionary act of self-disclosure. As an act of what Michael Oakeshott calls self-disclosure, what counts in political forgiveness are not motives or sentiments but whether the actor is pursuing a desired end by publicly subscribing to a set of moral practices and rules. As an illocutionary act, the rules governing its use require that the successful performance of political forgiveness have what J. L. Austin calls "uptake," as well as "take effect." Unlike ordinary, resentment- or sentiment-based conceptions of forgiveness, political forgiveness is necessarily public: an audience must receive and understand both the message that the debt has been forgiven and the invitation to restore a relationship. In other words, these features further condition the idea of political forgiveness.

This idea of political forgiveness presents a number of theoretical challenges, the most significant of which is the claim that the theoretical space for forgiveness is fully occupied by rectificatory justice—the form of justice that seeks to correct voluntary and coercive exchanges between parties. If it is good to receive what is due, as justice implies, and it is always possible to obtain justice, then how could forgiveness of what is due ever be justified? Much of chapter 2 explores the possibility that injustice is intractable and that the good of receiving what is due may be balanced by other values. If these claims are plausible, then rectificatory justice may neither be complete nor trump all other concerns. If rectificatory justice has its limitations, then political forgiveness may be able to supplement justice. If it can be balanced against other goods, then perhaps the good of forgiveness can moderate a relentless pursuit of justice. Rectificatory justice, in other words, doesn't preclude the consideration of political forgiveness. However, in setting out the relationship between justice and political forgiveness, it is also important that the latter not exclude the former. Even if justice can be incomplete and overridden by other goods, it still retains a degree of urgency such that political forgiveness cannot justifiably and completely supplant or displace its pursuit. Political forgiveness is dependent on the demands of justice being addressed and at least minimally satisfied.

Having carved out the meaning of and a space for political forgiveness, in chapter 3 I consider its point or purpose. Built into the idea of political forgiveness is an illocutionary purpose that entails the release of debts. Consequently, part and parcel of political forgiveness is the achievement of a state of reconciliation such that the released debt can no longer serve as the basis for future claims. Both rectificatory justice and political forgiveness are ways to settle the past such that it no longer legitimately haunts the future. The ability of political forgiveness to achieve a reconciliatory state cannot be accomplished by simply letting the matter drop or officially forgetting the problem through an unconditional amnesty. More strongly, situations may exist in which justice cannot be fully met, and the only path available to a reconciliatory state is through political forgiveness. Political forgiveness has an additional effect insofar as it initiates a process of reconciliation in which the transgressor's civic position is restored or the debtor's financial position is renewed. By forgiving a transgressor or debtor, victims and creditors send a message to others to invite a process of reconciliation. Unlike the first effect, the effects of the invitation are not as certain. The process of restoring civic friendship may never take off, despite the issuing of the invitation. But the ability of political forgiveness to issue such an invitation is not an insignificant attribute.

In chapter 4, I begin to consider who has authority to forgive and whether that authority can be lost or transferred. The authority to engage in political forgiveness depends on more than just one's status as victim or creditor; it can also depend on the nature of the debt and the severity of the wrong. Some wrongs may be so severe that they preclude the possibility for minimally meeting the requirements for rectificatory justice and, hence, for political forgiveness. For example, wrongs that result in the obliteration of an individual's personhood are politically unforgivable. In other cases, even if the victim has survived, she or he may have no authority to release the transgressor from the debt or to initiate the restoration of civic or moral equality. If the minimal demands of justice have not been met, the transgressor should not and perhaps cannot be politically forgiven.

Unlike the forgiveness of wrongs, no financial debt is unforgivable in principle. Viewing the forgiveness of financial debt as a form of political forgiveness, however, raises the problem of whether the authority to forgive may be lost to a third party. What I call vicarious forgiveness is justifiable in the case of financial debts, as long as an authoritative mechanism can establish the extent of the debt and whether the debt is "crushing." In these cases, a party such as a court may be legitimately empowered to forgive a debt on behalf of the creditors. It is, however, more difficult to justify the vicarious forgiveness of moral wrongs. Assuming a highly individualized sense of what it means to be wronged and to suffer an injustice, I claim that third parties can acquire a right to forgive only if that right is explicitly or implicitly transferred. In a system that values individuality, no authoritative mechanism ensures that transgressors warrant forgiveness.

Although the analysis in the rest of the book concentrates on moral wrongs and the relationship between citizens and governments, it is not intended to rule out the possibility that other kinds of debts and other political actors could be forgiven. This concentration, however, emphasizes the political nature of these concerns and makes the analysis somewhat more manageable. In chapter 5, the philosophical problem of wronged groups, including governments, is explored. For governments to be wronged, they must possess significant interests that can be set back by others. I argue that governments can be wronged (and, hence, can forgive) to the extent that their interest in protecting and cultivating the interests of their citizens is violated. Although this second-order interest may be set back in any number of ways, chapter 5 focuses on crime as a form of public wrong and, not surprisingly, the authority to pardon as a form of forgiveness. A crime, then, can be understood not merely as a wrong to a particular person or persons but as a wrong to the political association. The remainder of chapter 5 addresses Kathleen Dean Moore's arguments to the contrary.

If governments can forgive wrongs, can they also be forgiven? Chapter 6 explores the central assumption that must be made in order to answer this question affirmatively: namely, that governments are morally culpable. To structure the argument, I turn to recent theories of individual and group responsibility. I conclude that the most parsimonious account of governmental responsibility is to treat governments *as if* they were moral agents. In other words, governments may be held morally responsible for what they do because there are good reasons to treat them *as if* they were blameworthy. One central reason in favor of this treatment is that it provides a degree of moral cover for those who serve in government. The relationship between officials and the government, then, can be seen as a principal/agent relationship in which the officials are the actual actors, but the government is responsible. Nevertheless, this form of argument has important limitations. For example, if officials exceed their authority or if the basic rules, laws, and procedures of the government are unjust, then the officials are themselves responsible for their actions. Governmental responsibility, then, extends as far as it is reasonable to protect citizens in their official capacities. Just and nearly just governments are responsible for the wrongs done by officials carrying out their duties. Unjust governments cannot be politically forgiven because they are not responsible for the actions of their officers. More, however, can be said about the scope of this responsibility. Chapter 6 also considers the spillover of governmental responsibility to citizens and the question of historical responsibility for past wrongs. In the former case, I claim that citizens can be responsible for governmental wrongs if they possess the requisite knowledge and freedom to prevent or resist those wrongs. In the latter case, the scope of governmental responsibility does extend to past wrongs as long as the government's identity does not change. Both of these positions raise difficult issues affecting whether citizens may appropriately forgive a government that has wronged them.

Because unjust governments are not culpable, chapter 7 considers the case of wrongs committed by a nearly just government. This chapter argues that there are at least two kinds of wrongs against which nearly just governments cannot guarantee: wrongs that result from dirty hands and from imperfect procedures. In the case of dirty hands, an official does wrong in the hope of doing good. The problem raised by dirty hands is that it is impossible for those who have done wrong to receive their due (e.g., punishment) without creating another injustice. Despite this impasse, I argue that wronged citizens should not forgive such officials. This judgment is based on the inherent dangers posed by appeals to necessity to do wrong and the skepticism that citizens should exhibit to those appeals. In contrast, political forgiveness may be appropriate for wrongs that result from imperfect procedures. Although reform can certainly address many imperfections, there is no guarantee that all imperfections can be remedied. Citizens who value the operation of a nearly just government, and have received some satisfaction for their demands of justice, should be willing to forgive or forget the unfortunate results of procedural imperfections. Governments can be forgiven, but not all governmental wrongs are forgivable.

In chapter 8, the discussion of whether citizens should forgive the wrongs of other citizens begins by considering the lesser offenses that trouble the ordinary politics of democracies (e. g., insults, lies, misrepresentations, negative advertisements). In many of these cases, it is possible for the aggrieved party to receive what is due—an apology, a straightening out of the record, a promise not to do it again. In instances where what is owed can be delivered, there is nothing to forgive. Political forgiveness, however, could play a role if the offense could not be fully redressed. The more difficult problem is when the wrong is criminal in nature. Here, I maintain that because the crime injures not only the individual victim but also the political association, the individual victim's decision to forgive is separable from the government's decision to pardon. Additional difficulties arise when considering whether citizens may forgive other citizens who are implicated in the wrongdoings of a previous unjust regime or a just government. Because justice requires a public acknowledgment of who did what to whom, in neither case is it evident that it will always be possible or desirable to satisfy the minimal demands of justice. If the demands of justice are not met to some degree, political forgiveness cannot be granted without supplanting those demands. In the case of collaboration, a strong argument may be made that if justice cannot be minimally addressed, forgiveness cannot take place.

In summary, the first half of the book elucidates the concept of political forgiveness and establishes its relationship to justice, reconciliation, and authority. This understanding of political forgiveness is wide enough to accommodate the release of both monetary and moral debts. In addition, it is clear that the meaning of political forgiveness is parasitic on the notion of justice as receiving one's due. Without a notion of rectificatory justice and something being due, there would be no notion of political forgiveness. Connecting political forgiveness to the release of what is due supports a fairly modest notion of political reconciliation. Assuming that those who forgive have the authority to do so, political forgiveness can achieve a state of reconciliation and initiate a reconciliatory process that should be conditioned by meeting minimal demands of justice.

In contrast, the second half of the book explores the ways in which political forgiveness of wrongs structures the relationships between governments and citizens and among citizens themselves. Political forgiveness takes what can be called a *many to one* form when a group seeks to forgive an individual. For this form of political forgiveness to make sense, groups must be capable of being wronged and of having the authority to forgive. Governments, I argue, exercise this form of forgiveness when they pardon individuals (chapter 5). In addition, political forgiveness takes a *one to many* form when an individual forgives the group. This kind of forgiveness is plausible only if groups can bear moral responsibility (chapter 6). Not all groups as groups, however, are capable of such responsibility. Because nearly just governments can bear moral responsibility for wrongs they commit, individual citizens have the power to forgive publicly those regimes under certain conditions (chapter 7). A third relationship of forgiveness, or *one to one* forgiveness, is between individuals. In the relationship between citizens, one individual may forgive another for both lesser offenses and more severe crimes (chapter 8). The final relationship consists of a group forgiving a group (or *many to many* forgiveness) and is considered only very briefly in these pages. As the analysis of groups shows, all kinds of groups can be wronged, harmed, or offended. Very few, however, can actually engage in political forgiveness for the group itself. Consequently, because one group has wronged another group, for example, a group called "a government" has violated the rights of a minority group, the situation may look like an opportunity for a *many to many* form of forgiveness. However, because no one in the wronged group is officially authorized to forgive for all of the members of the group or for the group itself, the situation could actually be nothing more than an opportunity for individuals to forgive the offending group (*one to many* forgiveness). One of the few situations in which both parties have the standing to forgive and be forgiven as groups would be wrongs done by nearly just governments to other nearly just governments. This relationship raises problems of defining the character of the international system that would bring the analysis too far afield for consideration here.

The idea of political forgiveness will not satisfy those who believe that forgiveness should only be about our highest aspirations for harmony and reconciliation. For these critics, political forgiveness may be a disappointing, middling concept that still spins in the orbit of justice. Nor will political forgiveness satisfy those who hold that justice is the only appropriate response to moral wrongs and financial debts. From their perspective, the problem with political forgiveness is that it requires victims and creditors to release their claims to what is due. Finally, this conception of forgiveness will not be acceptable to those who believe that it is best to just drop or forget intractable problems. For victims who just want to get on with their lives and are tired of relentless demands for justice, political forgiveness is still too demanding because it requires finding out publicly who did what to whom.

To those with the highest hopes for forgiveness, political forgiveness doesn't render politics all sweetness and light. It presumes that unforgivable acts exist and that receiving one's due remains an important but not necessarily the most important good. For lovers of rectificatory justice, political forgiveness can address situations in which the limits of justice are reached. In addition, it may secure ends otherwise unattainable through a strict concern for what is due, for example, exercising the virtue of generosity, securing peace, or establishing order. Finally, for those who are tired of the relentless concern with past wrongs, political forgiveness provides a way to publicly acknowledge what had happened, establish a state of reconciliation, and initiate a process of reconciliation. In all of these cases, the value of political forgiveness only makes sense if the ends that it assumes, achieves, and helps to secure are of value. Political forgiveness is only of importance if the political relationships that it may restore are themselves worthy of concern and respect.

I

Political Forgiveness

All of the terms invoked by President Clinton in the past week revolve around the Christian terms of forgiveness and sin. As a Christian I am told not to judge Mr. Clinton, for I, too, am a sinner.

However, this Christian idea of mercy has no place in the United States' secular government and its prescribed proceedings. There is no such thing as political forgiveness. While the Bible instructs me to forgive President Clinton, it does not tell me to refrain from the political judgment that he is unworthy to hold the most respected office in the world.

—LETTER TO THE EDITOR of the *New York Times*, September 15, 1998

The Case against Forgiveness

The act of forgiving belongs to a peculiar set of performances that releases people from their past actions.[1] In a world in which what is done at one moment cannot be undone the next, forgiving relieves the burdens created by wrongful actions and unbearable debts. In relieving those burdens, forgiveness presents the opportunity to start afresh or reestablish a relationship of moral equality between victim and trans-

---

1. Thus, forgiving belongs in the company of but is distinguishable from such ideas as forgetting, excusing, justifying, and condoning. Although we may forgive and then forget, forgiving is not forgetting. Forgiving requires recalling and understanding the past, whereas forgetting involves letting go of the past. Forgiving can also be distinguished from excusing and justifying. When we excuse, we say that a wrong was done, but the actor offering the excuse was not fully responsible. When we justify an action, we imply that the

gressor. These qualities point to its potential value in politics. Given that few, if any, political relationships start with a clean slate, and that even the best regimes cannot guarantee against injustice, forgiving can be viewed not only as a generous act but also as an integral part of instituting and maintaining a political life.

On the other hand, freeing the present from the past is not always a good thing. Those who deny, cover up, disavow, or evade their wrongful acts seek unfairly to abate the burdens of history. For anyone even minimally familiar with the abuse and manipulation of history, detaching the present from the past is frequently part of more vicious, brutal actions. Any practice, including forgiveness, that releases us from the past carries the risk of not taking seriously harms done. In addition, forgiveness would appear to be a rather soft-headed, unrealistic way to respond to anything political. It could be argued that those who have suffered wrongs perpetrated by governments or other political actors should petition, appeal, lobby, protest, conduct civil disobedience, or when things get bad enough, rebel or use violence against those who have acted wrongly—but never forgive.

From a certain perspective, there seems to be something deeply irrational about forgiveness, particularly if rationality is understood as a way to connect available means to desired ends. For example, if what we truly want is to be paid back, to receive compensation, to seek revenge, or to punish those who have harmed us, then forgiving does not get us there. Nevertheless, one could argue that an act of forgiveness does not abandon all ends, and so it may not be necessarily irrational. After all, an act of forgiveness may enhance a reputation for generosity, serve as an expression of concern, permit one's debtors to start again and acquire new debt, or serve the cause of peace. Still, even if the charge of irrationality does not stick, there is something queer about forgiveness.

One way to account for our reluctance to think seriously about forgiveness in politics is to consider its relationship to justice. If we start with Justinian's broad view of justice as "the constant and perpetual will to render everyone his due" (Miller 1987, 260), then forgiving is releas-

---

actor did perform the action but no wrong was involved (Austin 1961, 124). In contrast, when we forgive, there is an injured party, victim, or creditor, and a perpetrator, wrongdoer, or debtor. Finally, condoning is similar to excusing; there is an admission that something was done. It differs from excusing in the sense that we acquiesce to an action that we may even see as wrong (e.g., condoning immoral behavior [Haber 1991, 59–60]).

ing what is due. With this understanding in hand, the fundamental problem with forgiveness comes into view: whether it is in financial matters or after we have been wronged, receiving our due is extremely important to us. In a competition with justice, forgiveness does not appear to stand a chance. This perspective is particularly true in political theory, where forgiveness can be easily squeezed out of consideration if we suppose that justice trumps all other concerns and that it is always possible to redress injustice adequately.

Although far from universally endorsed, these not-unfamiliar assumptions come close to what Judith Shklar called the "normal model of justice" (Shklar 1990, 15–28). This model effectively closes out a theoretical rationale for forgiveness: If it is a good thing (and one of the most important things) to receive what is due, and if it is always possible to make good on the claims of justice, what place could forgiveness have? More strongly, one could argue that within these assumptions, forgiveness essentially short-circuits justice and leaves victims with less than is their due. In order to open a space for a conception of political forgiveness, it will be necessary to challenge the assumptions of the normal model of justice.

The problem with forgiveness in politics is not solely a question of its relationship with justice. Even if it were possible to discern a theoretically compelling account of that relationship, the idea of political forgiveness could be rejected on the grounds that it was sectarian. Given the significance of forgiveness to Christianity, the concept comes freighted with theological baggage. Because of these religious roots, some would argue that a public conception of forgiveness would violate an understanding of politics that had to tolerate a wide diversity of beliefs and religious perspectives. For others, because the concept of forgiveness is inseparable from the teachings of Jesus (or from the Judeo-Christian tradition), a nonreligious vision of forgiveness would be nothing more than a pale imitation of the true thing. Marius Schoon directly raised the former objection after he "came home one day to find the flesh and bones of his wife and six-year-old daughter spread over the floor by a South African security bomb." In response to Archbishop Tutu's Truth and Reconciliation Commission (TRC), Schoon objected "bitterly to what he call[ed] 'the imposition of a Christian morality of forgiveness' " (Ash 1997, 36). The letter to the *Times* editor, quoted at the beginning of this chapter, takes a less strident but still critical stance against political forgiveness: because of its religious connotations, forgiveness is appropriate in private, but not as a way to conduct politics.

Nevertheless, one may discern a nonreligious conception of forgiveness and still find objectionable overtones if it were imported into politics. One of these overtones may be the dream of universal reconciliation. This dream is clearly associated with Christianity but is not exclusively Christian. For Albert Camus, the connection between forgiveness and a dangerous utopian wish for ultimate reconciliation was expressed in the writings of Saint-Just. Prior to the Terror in the French Revolution, Saint-Just believed that because the roots of crime and criminality could be eradicated, the state should find offenders weak instead of guilty. Saint-Just "dreamed of a republic of forgiveness which would recognize that though the fruits of crime are bitter, its roots are nevertheless tender" (Camus 1956, 124). The eventual realization that the roots were tougher, that harmony did not reign, and that unity was a difficult thing to achieve led Saint-Just not to revise his theory of criminality but to seek out more fervently "factions" who, "by their very actions," denied unity. To save the republic of forgiveness a few weeds had to be pulled, and more heads needed to be pruned. For Camus, the republic of forgiveness's utopian hope for harmony and unity helped fuel the Terror: "Absolute virtue is impossible, and the republic of forgiveness leads, with implacable logic, to the republic of the guillotine" (124).[2]

As Timothy Garton Ash notes, drawing on the work of Isaiah Berlin, when taken in "the extreme, the reconciliation of all with all is a deeply illiberal idea" (Ash 1997, 37). If "liberalism means living with unresolvable conflicts of values and goals," then the dream of forgiveness as a universal solution to differences may not only be unreasonable but also undesirable. We may not only sacrifice or usurp important values like self-respect or the rights of the victim to achieve such a soaring form of reconciliation, but certain acts and actions may also be unforgivable. A

---

2. Almost immediately after the liberation of France, Albert Camus and the Catholic writer François Mauriac debated the merits of forgiving those who had collaborated with the Nazis. Mauriac argued that although some of the worst collaborators should be punished, "it was the task of the Republic to offer 'fallen' citizens the opportunity to redeem themselves: it was precisely by refusing to write off any human being as irredeemable that the Republic would establish its own moral legitimacy and durably distinguish itself from the totalitarian and authoritarian regimes it fought" (quoted in Sa'adah 1992, 107). In contrast, Camus argued that forgiveness was a dictate of private morality and "would be as fatal to the Republic as hatred" (quoted ibid., 106). He was more willing to support retroactive laws to punish in the name of political justice. Anne Sa'adah notes that Charles de Gaulle engaged in a mixed strategy that punished some but also created a political myth of unanimous support for the Resistance that exonerated many. Camus' *The Rebel*, published some years after this debate, shows his enduring distrust for forgiveness in politics.

politics that does not recognize the limited purposes of political forgiveness may generate its own forms of injustice.

Friedrich Nietzsche found the whole idea of forgiveness objectionable. From his perspective, forgiving is a matter of the weak making a virtue out of necessity. Because they cannot avenge themselves, they call their weakness "forgiveness" (Nietzsche [1887] 1956, 181). In contrast, more noble types have no need to forgive. They see the resentment that is connected to forgiveness as a poison that they must purge as quickly as possible through an instantaneous, perhaps violent, reaction (173). Nietzsche recommends forgetting instead of forgiving. As an example, he presents Mirabeau, "who lacked all memory for insults and meanness done him, and who was unable to forgive because he had forgotten" (173). Forgiveness that is linked to resentment is either a form of weakness or is unnecessary. Far from trying to recover an alternative vision of forgiveness, Nietzsche calls for its abandonment.[3]

Obviously, if political forgiveness is to make sense, then an adequate response must be made to Nietzsche's critique. For if forgiveness in general is indefensible, then political forgiveness will certainly be as well. One characteristic of forgiveness that the Nietzschean critique raises is the connection between forgiveness and resentment. Indeed, the view that forgiveness requires either a change of heart or the expression of a commitment to eradicating one's resentment to the wrongdoer dominates most philosophical discussions of forgiveness. Bishop Butler, for example, argued that forgiveness required an injured party to eliminate

---

3. Nietzsche's reason for avoiding resentment, hence also for avoiding forgiveness, is not that resentment has bad effects but that resentment itself is unhealthy and even herd-like. It is a soured attitude toward the world and life, one that is exacerbated by forgiving. He argues that cultivating an ethic of forgiveness also cultivates our feelings of resentment. But he also seems to see forgiveness as part and parcel of a dulled conventionality. In *Twilight of the Idols*, Nietzsche claims,

> We find nothing easier than being wise, patient, superior. We drip with the oil of forbearance and sympathy, we are absurdly just, we forgive everything. For that very reason we ought to discipline ourselves a little; for that very reason we ought to *cultivate* a little emotion, a little emotional vice from time to time. It may be hard for us; and among ourselves we may perhaps laugh at the appearance we thus present. But what of that! We no longer have any other mode of self-overcoming available to us: this is *our* asceticism, *our* penance. (Nietzsche [1888] 1968, 94)

While Nietzsche's critique picks up the degree to which forgetting is conceptually distinguishable from forgiving, Martha Minow sees forgiveness as sliding all too easily into forgetting (Minow 1998, 15–17, 118). Her portrayal of vengeance as endorsing "too much memory" and forgiveness as permitting "too much forgetting" is an attempt to steer a response to mass atrocities that falls between these two poles.

such resentment. He believed that although resentment is a socially useful sentiment, it could become excessive and destructive.[4] Others have echoed this theme and argued that forgiveness conceptually requires either a commitment to the process of eliminating resentment (Haber 1991, 7) or the actual elimination of it.[5]

One of the few authors to have discussed forgiveness in the context of political theory also makes a tight conceptual connection between forgiveness and a particular sentiment. According to Hannah Arendt, the story of forgiveness begins with the teachings of Jesus of Nazareth. She believed that Jesus' use of forgiveness is important because unlike the scribes and Pharisees at the time, he claimed that it was not the sole prerogative of God. Humans could and should forgive one another for their sins and debts. Forgiveness, in this view, is quickly assimilated to our personal relationships and our capacity to love one another. Although Arendt saw forgiveness as an authentic secular and political concept extraordinarily important to human action, she concluded that it has "always been deemed unrealistic and inadmissible in the public realm." She thought that its ostensibly private character arose from either its "religious context" or from "the connection with love attending its discovery." Because love destroys the space or distance people need between each other to create the plurality of politics, the relationship, for Arendt, was nonpolitical (1958, 242–43). Nevertheless, Arendt does suggest a way out of the problem. If we can have respect for one another, which is analogous to love, then we may have the requisite motive for forgiveness. Drawing on Kant, Arendt argued that unlike love, respect requires distance[6] and, she believed, would permit us to forgive the actor for the actor's sake. Nevertheless,

4. Butler wrote that resentment against vice and wickedness "is one of the common bonds by which society is held together; a fellow-feeling which each individual has in behalf of the whole species as well as of himself" (Butler [1726] 1847, 81, 95).

5. Golding 1984–85, 134; Govier 1999, 65; Hampton 1988b, 157; Holmgren 1993, 341; McGary 1989, 347; Minow 1998, 15–20; North 1987, 506; Roberts 1995, 289. The view of forgiveness that requires the removal of resentment can be seen as part of a more general understanding of forgiveness that is linked to the presence or absence of particular feelings or sentiments. For Jeffrie Murphy, "It is more illuminating—more loyal to the actual texture of our moral lives—to think of forgiveness as overcoming a variety of negative feelings that one might have toward a wrongdoer—resentment, yes, but also such feelings as anger, hatred, loathing, contempt, indifference, disappointment or even sadness" (Murphy 1998, 89). In contrast, the success of political forgiveness spins free of any particular sentiments on the part of the creditor/victim or debtor/transgressor.

6. Arendt maintains that respect "is a regard for the person from the distance which the space of the world puts between us, and this regard is independent of qualities which we may admire or of achievements which we may highly esteem" (Arendt 1958, 243).

despite the opportunities implied by respect, she once again closed down the possibility for a public or political form of forgiveness given what she saw as "the modern loss of respect."[7] Without respect, we are apparently thrown back to forgiveness being tied to love, rendering it unpolitical. On Arendt's account, forgiveness in the modern world has become an inherently private relationship because it is cultivated in the sentiment of love.

The connection between particular sentiments (resentment or love) and forgiveness raises two hurdles for considering a notion of political forgiveness. The first is a Nietzschean critique and suggests that the sentiment of resentment is itself a sour, life-denying response to the world, and because forgiveness is linked to resentment, it too is objectionable. The second hurdle is that if a particular sentiment is conceptually linked to forgiveness, then the notion of political forgiveness is incompatible with an understanding of politics that focuses more on the content of our actions than on the character of our motivations. In the conception of politics that I use throughout this book, politics is more a matter of civil behavior than appropriate sentiment. The plausibility of this conception of politics turns on the difficulty of truly knowing the feelings that motivate an action. Any number of sentiments can motivate the same action, and what lurks in the heart of the individual may never be adequately brought to the surface. In light of the difficulties of understanding our "true" motivations, appropriate political conduct cannot rest on possession of the appropriate sentiments.[8] This "agency-based" theory of politics shies away from advancing a particular form of politics as soulcraft or demanding particular feelings in order to guarantee stability and the maintenance of political life. It takes agents as it finds them.

Obviously, those who argue that politics must entail soulcraft, and that appropriate action follows only when appropriate motives are nurtured and recognized, deeply contest this assumption. For those who make this

7. Brian Weiner (1996) argues that Arendt overcame these objections and saw forgiveness as integral to politics.

8. This assumption follows Oakeshott's discussion in *On Human Conduct*. Not being able to get to our "true" motives does not mean that other individuals are entirely opaque to us. We may quite easily be able to discern their intentions in terms of what they are after, but we may never really know whether they are really doing it out of spite or love, for example. For Oakeshott, motive is "not an antecedent drive or tendency or disposition to choose one action (or one kind of action) in preference to another, but an agent's sentiment in choosing and performing the actions he chooses and performs. Thus, while the 'intention' of an action is the action itself understood in terms of the imagined and wished-for outcome the agent means to procure in choosing and performing it, the 'motive' of an action is the action itself considered in terms of the sentiment or sentiments in which it is chosen and performed" (Oakeshott 1975, 71–72).

case, taking agents as one finds them tends to mean reducing human beings to the lowest common denominator (e.g., rationally self-interested egoists) and depriving political institutions of the educational and developmental mechanisms necessary for sustaining moderate, democratic governance. In contrast, from the perspective of an agency theory of politics, the soulcraft requirements of a sentiment-based politics rest on a contestable moral psychology that is deeply intrusive and potentially tyrannical.

My purpose here, however, is not to settle or even address this debate. Instead, by assuming an understanding of politics that emphasizes action over sentiment, it would appear that forgiveness is necessarily a nonpolitical act. If an unbreakable connection exists between forgiveness and particular sentiments (such as the removal of resentment), then forgiveness may simply not cohere with this conception of politics.

Hence, the discussion of political forgiveness begins with a set of problems, constraints, and objections, some of which are quite significant. To theorize political forgiveness, it appears necessary to discern the appropriate relationship between justice and forgiveness, formulate a conception of forgiveness that is not dependent on a set of religious commitments, detach that conception from a utopian hope for an ultimate form of reconciliation, address its potentially troublesome connection with resentment, and, finally, see if it can cohere with an agency-based conception of politics. Obviously, not every understanding of politics would see these concerns as problems that need to be overcome. Nevertheless, they are significant challenges for conceiving political forgiveness from the perspective adopted here. To make sense of these challenges and to arrive at an idea of political forgiveness, one would hope to rely on the theoretic equipment provided by political theory. Unfortunately, this literature, with a few exceptions, has ignored the concept of forgiveness. This signals either an opportunity to break new ground or the possibility that political theorists have not considered the notion of forgiveness, for good reason. Consequently, it may be helpful to start with some practices that appear to be political uses of forgiveness. By abstracting from those practices, one can theorize a conception of political forgiveness.

A Starting Point

Perhaps it is because of the dangers and limitations discussed above that forgiveness has been so infrequently practiced by political actors and institutions and largely ignored by political philosophers. Nevertheless, at a practical level, one can still glimpse practices of forgiveness in the establishment of truth commissions, in the offering of authoritative apologies, in the handling of unbearable financial debt, and in the executive prerogative to issue pardons. Whether or not these practices suggest a greater role for forgiveness, they do at least suggest that forgiveness is not entirely precluded from public life. More important, they provide a starting point.

Unfortunately, this starting point is controversial. If we focus on the forgiveness of financial debt (involving individuals, states, corporate entities, or international actors) and the pardoning of a criminal as cases where we can glimpse political forgiveness in the practical world, we are quickly informed by a number of theoreticians and philosophers that these are not proper instances of forgiveness. It has been argued, in the case of the "forgiveness" of financial debt, that this is a subsidiary use of the term and, in the case of pardoning, that it is a conceptual error to conflate "financial debt" with forgiveness (Downie 1965, 132; Haber 1991, 60–62; Moore 1989, 193).[9] Nevertheless, we should not be discouraged by these assessments, for they are the logical outcome of general theories of forgiveness with which we need not begin.

In considering what a conception of political forgiveness would look like, it is useful to learn from and draw on practices of forgiveness already current in the public realm. Because it is neither unusual nor exceptional to view pardoning and the forgiveness of financial debt as forms of forgiveness, we can identify something called political forgiveness as sharing the characteristics of these two activities. By abstracting a notion of political forgiveness from these practices, we may discern a conception of forgiveness broader and more general than simply pardons and financial debt. The question then becomes whether this conception can meet the criticisms set out above (which I believe it can) and then consider how it would mediate various political relationships. Pardons and financial debts point to the plausibility of a conception of political forgiveness.

In theorizing political forgiveness, however, my concern is not with trying to understand this or that pardon by an executive or act of forgiveness by a creditor. Instead, it entails discerning what must be the case for political forgiveness to be a coherent, intelligible concept. Sifting through the

9. Some theorists on forgiveness have distinguished between core and peripheral uses of the term (Haber 1991, 32–33; Lang 1994, 116, n. 6). In doing so, they have claimed that when we talk about a tennis racket being forgiving or forgiving a breach of etiquette or a debt, we are using peripheral or metaphorical uses of the word, the core understanding of forgiveness being the forgiveness of wrongs. (In chapter 5, I respond more thoroughly to the claim that pardoning cannot be forgiveness.)

enormous number of characteristics that may be associated with pardoning and financial forgiveness can give us some idea of what to look for in discerning the conditions of political forgiveness. Although some of those characteristics, such as the presence of an official stamp on a particular bureaucratic form or the ripping up of an IOU, are not going to be particularly useful, it is nevertheless possible to discern a set of conditions that identify political forgiveness. First, political forgiveness presupposes a relationship between at least two parties: in the case of pardon, offenders and the state, and in the case of financial forgiveness, creditors and debtors. Second, the relationship between these parties implies a moral, legal, or financial debt owed by one to the other. In the case of the offender, the debt is created by a criminal act, and in the case of financial debt, it is created by borrowing and lending money. Third, forgiveness, in these instances, depends on the appropriate person having the authority to forgive. Only an authorized governmental official may pardon a criminal of the debt owed to the larger association. In the case of financial debt, the creditor is normally thought to have the right to forgive, but this right is not exclusive and may be taken up by a third party. Fourth, that authority must convey the appropriate signs and utterances to those who are being forgiven. A creditor cannot forgive a debt by simply forming an intention do so or by telling just anybody. Rather, the forgiveness of the debt must be conveyed to those who are in debt. Fifth, the emotional or internal states of the forgivers are largely irrelevant to the act of forgiving. Although executives may feel quite happy about pardoning an offender, their happiness is irrelevant to the success of the pardon. Similarly, creditors may feel bad about the state of affairs a debtor has gotten into and that may be a reason to forgive, but the success of forgiving the debt does not depend on the sentiments of the creditors. Sixth, it is generally the case that it is a good thing for criminals to serve time and financial debts to be repaid. There is a presumption that receiving one's due is important and that, although forgiving financial debts and providing pardons may be performed for little or no reason, a case must be made for not pushing for one's "just deserts." In other words, political forgiveness relieves what is due and is done for reasons.

Finally, public forgiveness invites the restoration of the relationship of the parties involved and fully resolves the debts of the past. By fully forgiving a debt, the financial relationship between the creditor and the debtor is brought back to the status quo ante. What has been forgiven should not serve as the basis for future claims. By pardoning a criminal, the state restores the offender to public life and grants him his freedom.

The value of forgiveness is that it settles the past and opens possibilities for the future.

What is immediately apparent about these conditions is that many of them play no role in other, very ordinary ways in which individuals forgive each other. Jack may find himself forgiving Jill for no reason in particular, except that he thinks it is a good thing to forgive others. Jill may forgive Jack for what he said, even though Jack never hears that he has been forgiven—suggesting that the message of forgiveness can be an entirely personal affair. Indeed, she may find that forgiving in her "heart of hearts" is the only true form of forgiveness. Finally, Jack may forgive Jill for bumping into him on a train platform, even though he will never see her again. In other words, the characteristics that we frequently associate with interpersonal or nonpolitical forms of forgiveness differ from the assumptions set out above. In theorizing political forgiveness these differences must be kept in mind. Whatever we assume about political forgiveness may not and probably does not hold in cases of nonpolitical or nonpublic forms of forgiveness.

Perhaps the most striking difference between the conditions of political forgiveness and religious or personal uses of forgiveness is that the success of the former does not require an examination into the sentiments of the forgiver. The idea that those sentiments are irrelevant to the success of political forgiveness runs headlong into ordinary uses of the word that are intimately linked to the removal or attempted removal of resentment. The first question, then, is whether political forgiveness is forgiveness if it doesn't require the removal or the presence (as for Arendt) of any particular motive. In arguing that political forgiveness requires only a form of civil behavior and not a particular attitude, one may not only be able to discern a form of forgiveness that is compatible with an agency-based conception of politics but also respond to the Nietzschean critique linking forgiveness with resentment.

Resentment and Forgiveness

Because of the importance of the sentiment of resentment to many philosophical analyses of forgiveness, considering how political forgiveness swings free of that particular feeling helps focus the more general discussion of whether forgiveness could stand independently of any sentiment. In general, sentiment-based conceptions of forgiveness rest on two claims. The first is that individuals can work on themselves to remove resentment, anger, loathing, contempt; the second is that this kind of self-fashioning is necessary because these sentiments are unhealthy, tend to spark inappropriate actions, or have other unfortunate consequences. One way to understand the first claim is to say that human beings are capable of choosing or altering the sentiment in which to act. Michael Oakeshott calls this capability *self-enactment* (Oakeshott 1975, 76–77). Self-enactment involves the "demands that an agent makes upon himself" to act on particular sentiments and not others. We engage in self-enactment when we do whatever we are doing joyfully, spitefully, fearfully, generously, greedily, and so on. Self-enactment does not involve establishing what particular action to perform but rather the sentiment to adopt when performing it. This, of course, is not the same as assuming that human beings can simply generate whatever sentiment they "want," although it does assume that they can work on themselves to cultivate a certain set of feelings toward the world. At the very least, this idea implies that if humans are capable of simultaneously feeling resentful and generous they can be motivated by one sentiment and not the other.

Because a sentiment-based vision of forgiveness rests so heavily on self-enactment, it is possible for forgiveness to be a largely internal, private matter. Jack can forgive his tormentors sotto voce even though no one else knows that Jack has done so. In fact, he may have had no contact with his tormentors (perhaps they are dead), or perhaps Jack always treated them with respect, despite the anger he possessed. It is possible for Jack to forgive privately in this instance, where forgiveness entails working on his feelings of resentment and anger. The point of forgiveness in such cases usually goes beyond the argument that this sentiment is itself inappropriate or unhealthy. The claim is frequently made that the sentiment of resentment erodes our confidence in the forgiver's ability to act appropriately in the future. As Bishop Butler noted, resentment can become a very destructive sentiment if not properly regulated. By removing resentment we lose the motivation to exact revenge against a transgressor. The elimination of resentment guarantees peace into the future. This characterization is plausible, for we do tend to "have more confidence . . . in a man whose subscriptions to his obligations seem to be made in good faith rather than fear" (Oakeshott 1975, 77). Similarly, we could have less faith in a forgiver who still feels anger in his heart.

The view that forgiveness and the removal of resentment are connected is fairly standard, but it is not the only account. Under an alternative view, forgiveness is so tightly linked to resentment that the two terms are inseparable.

Forgive! How many will say, "forgive," and find
A sort of absolution in the sound
To hate a little longer!
                    Tennyson, [1860] 1969, 1098

From Nietzsche's perspective, forgiveness is an expression of resentment. We resent a world in which injustice is intractable. We resent an existence in which not all harm can be repaired and where not all wrongs can be rectified. Forgiveness is the culmination of cultivating our resentment by finding someone or something responsible for our situation. We need to know exactly who did what to whom. Forgiveness cultivates resentment, since victims must calculate how much they are owed by their oppressors and tormentors. A practice of forgiveness stirs the fetid pot of resentment, then enables the victim to take on a mantle of moral superiority and lord it over those who have wronged her: my willingness to forgive, despite the injury that has been done, reveals just how much better I am than you. It is no accident, Nietzsche might say, that victims must work so hard at forgiving, for forgiving thrives on the very feelings that it claims to counteract. All of those who seek to forgive and yet keep alive the crimes of the past must stir the pot of resentment. Better, Nietzsche believed, simply to forget.

Unlike the standard vision of forgiveness, then, a Nietzschean reading sees forgiveness not as eliminating anger and resentment but as keeping it at a slow boil. Only by so doing can one adopt a guise of moral superiority by constantly overcoming the injustices that one suffers. From the Nietzschean perspective, resentment lurks within the heart of forgiveness.[10] Despite enormous differences, both the ordinary and Nietzschean accounts link the sentiment of resentment to forgiveness.

Disconnecting Political Forgiveness and Resentment

To understand how political forgiveness could swing free of resentment, it is useful to consider the notion of promising. Just as Jill may promise to do

---

10. In responding to the Nietzschean position, Joram Haber argues, "If we take the Übermensch to be the paradigm of the moral personality, then resentment will never be justified, because other people simply do not matter" (Haber 1991, 84). In contrast, Haber argues that we ought to feel resentment against those who have injured us. Not to do so displays a lack of self-respect. For Haber, the problem is not with resentment per se but with misplaced or excessive resentment. But does Nietzsche argue that resentment is unjustified because others aren't worthy of being resented? A more challenging reading of Nietzsche sees him as arguing not that resentment must be sloughed off because others don't matter but that resentment is a problem because others matter greatly. What lies behind resentment is not a claim of self-respect (as Haber argues) but a claim that others are Evil and oneself is Good (Nietzsche [1887]

something despite the contempt, generosity, kindness, or pity she feels, I argue that Jack may forgive generously, condescendingly, insultingly, or even (if this argument works) resentfully. Successful promising requires living up to the prevailing conventions of or conditions for performing this act. The motivations behind a promise may vary significantly. Consequently, Jill cannot say that her promise to meet Jack was any less of a promise because she made it contemptuously. In contrast to *self-enactment*, promising is a public act of *self-disclosure* in which the promisers pursue an intended goal under the rules that govern its practice.[11] The success of this act is independent of its motivations. Similarly, I am arguing that political forgiveness is also an exercise of self-disclosure. Its success depends not on the sentiments that may motivate it but on whether one lives up to the public rules that govern its practice.

The distinction between self-disclosure and self-enactment and the difference between choosing to perform an action and choosing the motivations by which to act emphasize an alternative moral psychology, one that resists seeing actions as necessarily connected to the presence of certain sentiments. From this alternative perspective, human beings are quite capable of having all sorts of desires, beliefs, and judgments without acting on them. In fact, virtues such as self-control, civil-

---

1956, 173). Nietzsche does not deny that when one is wronged, one will feel anger (expressed in an "instantaneous reaction," which could be interpreted as an exhibition of self-respect), but he sees resentment as a form of cultivated or nursed anger. If resentment is this kind of stoked, controlled burn for past injuries, then those who connect it to self-respect need to explain why it is so important to keep this fire burning and what other consequences fueling the flames may have. Why does self-validation require keeping anger alive? Finally, for Nietzsche, forgiveness is not about extinguishing the flames or "repressing" resentment but about stoking them enough to allow a display of superiority and "goodness" when forgiving.

11. "Self-disclosure," Oakeshott maintains, "is (briefly) choosing satisfactions to pursue and pursuing them; its compunction is, in choosing and acting, to acknowledge and subscribe to the conditions intimated or declared in a practice of moral intercourse" (Oakeshott 1975, 76). It may seem strange to call this "self-disclosure" when acting on your chosen sentiments (what Oakeshott calls self-enactment) would be more appropriately described as disclosing or revealing something that is hidden. Nevertheless, it is possible to talk about disclosing an identity by acting in a public space according to rules over which one has no immediate control. To some extent, Oakeshott's notion of self-disclosure resembles Hannah Arendt's conception of political action. In contrast to Arendt, Oakeshott does not see it as a purely political act and probably admits a greater degree of authorial control over identity. Nonetheless, like Arendt, Oakeshott also finds self-disclosure to be a risky business that reveals one's identity. For all adventures in self-disclosure are hazardous, necessarily "immersed in contingency," and "liable to frustration, disappointment, and defeat" (Oakeshott 1975, 73).

ity, manners, self-possession, unflappability, and imperturbability, as well as vices such as hypocrisy, two-facedness, insincerity, and phoniness all postulate a capacity to feel one way and act another. In other words, it is plausible to presume that not all sentiments issue in actions and that not all actions reflect our sentiments. Resentful feelings need not issue in action.

Nevertheless, we certainly are not surprised when particular sentiments issue in action, and we generally presume some connection between feelings and actions. We do judge people, in part, by the sentiments they adopt when they go about their business. We admire virtuous sentiments and recoil from vicious ones. We also have more confidence that noble sentiments tend to result in noble actions rather than ignoble ones. All of this favors viewing political forgiveness as necessarily linked to the removal of resentment. However, to say that only the heart can guarantee appropriate action is to assume that a heart, once transformed, cannot rekindle the flames of resentment. If we find this assumption implausible, assuming instead that self-enactment may be ongoing and that we must often work assiduously to keep resentment down, then the position begins to look no better than a self-disclosive vision of forgiveness, one in which we may have to work continually at being civil to our transgressors.

The larger difficulty associated with the sentiment-based view concerns our inability to see clearly into the recesses of the human heart. This opacity leads to the presumption that the act of forgiving itself, not the sentiments behind it, should count in politics. Oakeshott, for example, suggested that "our concern with the sentiment in which the action of another is performed is limited by a recognition of our hardly avoidable ignorance and by the conviction that in ordinary human intercourse a man's choices of what to do and the compunction they exhibit matter more than the sentiment in which he makes them. In respect of motive it is appropriate that we should take our fellows as we find them" (Oakeshott 1975, 77). If the elimination of resentment is key, we may simply never know whether a victim has actually and successfully forgiven her transgressor.[12] Given its inherently public character, politics need not focus on the forms of self-enactment linked to forgiveness. It is far better, Oakeshott suggests, to place more emphasis on the self-disclosive aspects of action.

---

12. This problem does not arise in Joram Haber's theory of forgiveness, in which forgiveness requires not the elimination of resentment but a commitment to work on eliminating it (Haber 1991).

But is a form of forgiveness that is disconnected from resentment still forgiveness? Certain features of ordinary forgiveness support the plausibility of seeing political forgiveness as forgiveness. For example, a victim may forgive even though she does not feel resentment (Dressler 1990, 1467). Jack may have promised to send an article to Jill but then forgot all about it. Jill need not resent Jack for the breaking of the promise to be a wrong or to forgive Jack. When Jack remembers the broken promise, he may feel bad, even if Jill doesn't, and he may consequently apologize. It is possible to forgive even without resentment entering the scene. Similarly, if France forgives part of the debt that Honduras owes, France does so without even raising the problem of resentment. This, I believe, is the easiest response to the connection Nietzsche insists ties resentment to forgiveness.

For non-Nietzscheans who see forgiveness as inextricably bound to the elimination of resentment, the situation discussed above is either of peripheral interest or is illustrative of a kind of moral failing. On the one hand, they could argue, significant moral wrongs are rarely felt without resentment. On the other hand, an absence of resentment indicates a failure to take oneself seriously, a failure of self-respect. Forgiving a wrong when there is no resentment is a moral short circuit.

It is true that interpersonal forgiving without resentment is probably an exceptional situation. Nevertheless, it does show that forgiving is intelligible without the presence of resentment. As for claiming that victims not only do but also should feel resentment, it would seem that this move generates the very problem of which Nietzsche complained: if there is no resentment, then there should be. Forgiveness then becomes caught up in the cultivation of resentment. The idea of cultivating resentment, however, is peculiar if the notion of political forgiveness can be deployed not only by individuals but also by institutions and governments. If one does not believe that resentment is necessary in order to forgive, however, neither the possibility of institutional forgiveness is, prima facie, puzzling nor does Nietzsche's response threaten.

Putting Nietzsche to the side, the more interesting problem for conceptualizing a view of political forgiveness that swings free of resentment is not whether one can forgive in the absence of resentment but whether political forgiveness can make sense in the presence of resentment.[13] Under most ordinary understandings of forgiveness, this is impossible unless one is committed to working on the elimination of resentment. But it is not far-

13. This is not an issue when we consider whether institutions or governments can be forgiven, insofar as they do not have feelings (except metaphorically), but it is an issue in the context of what it means for individual citizens to engage in political forgiveness.

fetched to think that one could forgive without dispelling or attempting to eliminate this sentiment. Although not a political act and found in a work of fiction, an example of this possibility is provided by Anthony Trollope in *The Vicar of Bullhampton*. In that novel, the miller, Jacob Brattle, forgives his daughter for becoming a prostitute. Toward the end of the book, he says to his family, " 'I will bring myself to forgive her. That it won't stick here,' and the miller struck his heart violently with his open palm, 'I won't be such a liar as to say. For there ain't no good to lie. But there shall be never a word about it more out o' my mouth,—and she may come to me again as a child' " (Trollope [1870] 1988, 474–75). What is interesting about this excerpt is the degree to which Brattle understands forgiveness as a form of self-disclosure. The success of forgiving his daughter depends on his willingness to say nothing more about the matter. If he did, then his daughter would have cause to question whether he truly had forgiven her.[14]

In contrast, under a sentiment-based vision of forgiveness, Brattle's speech indicates that he has not "really" forgiven his daughter. Because the sentiment of resentment is still present in his heart, and he has not even pledged to work on himself to eliminate that resentment, true forgiveness eludes him. This kind of description has advantages, chiefly that it offers a clear explanation for why one would forgive: to eliminate one's resentment. For if a desire to change our feelings does not explain why political actors would engage in political forgiveness, to what do we turn? In the case of Jacob Brattle, the end that is served by forgiving his daughter is a reconciliation with the past and a restoration of their

14. Of course, this is not the only interpretation of what is going on here. An alternative reading is that although the miller *says*, "It won't stick here," he seems to be a man whose heart will eventually melt toward his daughter. Brattle is a fairly ambiguous character. Trollope portrays him as something of a vengeful, akratic man who "brooded over injuries done to him,—injuries real or fancied,—till he taught himself to wish that all who hurt him might be crucified for the hurt they did to him. He never forgot, and he never wished to forgive." Nevertheless, "He would almost despise himself, because when the moment for vengeance did come, he would abstain from vengeance. He would dismiss a disobedient servant with curses which would make one's hair stand on end, and would hope within his heart of hearts that before the end of the next week the man with his wife and children might be in the poorhouse. When the end of the next week came, he would send the wife meat, and would give the children bread, and would despise himself for doing so" (Trollope [1870] 1988, 34–35). Trollope's portrayal of the miller raises a number of interesting questions in moral psychology, one of which is whether the sentiments of civility might follow the commitment to act civilly. It may be the case that people acquire the right feelings because they act the right way just as much as they act the right way because they have the right feelings. If it is possible that the elimination of resentment occurs because people are behaving in a forgiving manner, that may add to the case for political forgiveness but does not mean we forgive only when the resentment has disappeared.

relationship, not the end of resentment. Similarly, political forgiveness is not about clearing the victim's heart of resentment. Rather, it entails clearing a debt that the transgressor or debtor owes to the victim or the creditor. Focusing on the self-disclosive character of political forgiveness highlights its necessarily public, even generous character. Political forgiveness can be understood as an action that forgives a debt, reconciles the past, and invites the restoration of the civil and moral equality of transgressors and their victims or the restoration of a relationship between creditors and debtors to the status quo ante. Consequently, political forgiveness can only make sense if we believe that the public relationship between the parties is worthy of respect and repair.[15]

Political Forgiveness as an Illocutionary Act

By detaching political forgiveness from resentment and understanding it as an act of self-disclosure, the public character of political forgiveness is illuminated. Political forgiveness cannot be done sotto voce, as is the case for ordinary forgiveness. But what, then, is required for political forgiveness to be successful? I postulate that a party must convey the message of forgiveness with the appropriate standing through the appropriate signs or utterances. Postponing the discussion of who has authority to forgive and who can be forgiven, one could argue that the appropriate signs and utterances for political forgiveness are rather straightforward. They would entail uttering or conveying the words "forgive" or "pardon" in the appropriate context. The locutions associated with forgiveness must have a certain force to them in order to be successful. Using J. L. Austin's terminology, we can say that political forgiveness must not only be a locutionary act but also an illocutionary act. Something must not only be said or somehow conveyed, but what is said must have the effect of releasing the debtor or the transgressor from the debt. In contrast, ordinary forgiveness or forms of forgiveness that require self-enactment need not even be locutionary acts.

---

15. Still, critics may argue that this kind of reconciliation of the past and the restoration of a valued relationship will never happen unless "real" changes occur in the emotions of the participants. The response to this criticism turns on the alternative moral psychology mentioned above, namely that citizens can feel one way and act another. In addition, political forgiveness does yield a particular state of reconciliation in which the past can no longer serve as the basis for legitimate claims into the future (see chapter 3). Finally, there is nothing to suggest that by acting in a particular way, one's sentiments aren't changed. As mentioned above, in footnote 14, the sentiments of civility may follow from civil actions.

Following Austin, the successful performance of an illocutionary act necessitates not only that they have "uptake" but that they "take effect."[16] The requirement of uptake is that the locution is heard and properly understood. This also implies an audience exists to whom the locution is addressed and that audience correctly understands the meaning of one's utterance: there is no promise if Jill or anyone else doesn't understand what Jack had said. In contrast, as we saw earlier, uptake does not appear to be necessary for ordinary forgiveness; it is perfectly intelligible to understand Jack forgiving his tormentors sotto voce. If one sees forgiveness as freeing oneself of resentment, then a successful act of forgiveness does not require an utterance or any communication.

In contrast, uptake is a necessary feature of political forgiveness. If the debtor or the criminal does not get the message that they've been released from their debts, then something has gone wrong. Indeed, the recipients of the forgiving act must understand that their debt has been forgiven for the forgiving act to be successful. The actions of a jailer, who releases a criminal without informing her that she has been pardoned, may just as easily be interpreted as corruption, a setup, or a mistake. This further specification of what "uptake" entails flows from both its public, political character and from the purposes of forgiveness, namely settling the past and restoring a valued political relationship. If the recipient fails to receive the message, the full political character of the act cannot be realized and the possibilities for restoration are abridged. Consequently, political forgiveness cannot be enacted if the party to be forgiven is absent or dead. In the latter case, it is impossible. Understanding political forgiveness through Austin's conditions of speech acts presents us with its first important limitation.[17]

For an illocutionary act to "take effect," Austin claims that it must have certain nonphysical consequences (Austin 1962, 117). Once again, senti-

16. A third feature of illocutionary acts, one that is not essential for their success, is that they invite a response or a sequel (Austin 1962, 117).

17. The problem of whether the dead can forgive (see chapter 4) may be raised by questioning whether anyone other than the victim can forgive a wrong. Can someone acquire the authority on behalf of the dead to forgive the living? Very briefly, the answer is that only the victim has a right to forgive, unless that right has somehow been transferred to another. The problem of whether the dead can be forgiven points to the problem of why the recipient of forgiveness must receive the message in order for political forgiveness to be successful. To prevent political forgiveness from being used as a surreptitious mechanism to proclaim the guilt of someone who cannot defend herself, the recipient of forgiveness must receive and understand the message.

ment-based conceptions of forgiveness need not result in any changes in the world, particularly if the offender is dead or the victim always treated the offender respectfully. In contrast, the central effect of political forgiveness is to release debtors or transgressors from what they owe. This effect is the internal point or purpose to political forgiveness. When political forgiveness is successful, it necessarily achieves this goal. This is what John Searle would call the illocutionary point of political forgiveness (Searle and Vanderveken 1985, 13–15) and what places it in conflict with the demands of justice.

Behabitive, Exercitive, or Commissive?

At the end of *How to do Things with Words*, Austin identifies five distinct types of utterances according to their illocutionary force: "verdictives," "exercitives," "commissives," "behabitives," and "expositives" (Austin 1962, 150–64). Austin admits that these categories are fairly rough. Still, Joram Haber, in what is one of the best philosophical accounts of the ordinary use of forgiveness, has argued that the locution "I forgive you" is a behabitive. Can political forgiveness be classified in the same way? According to Austin, "Behabitives include the notion of reaction to other people's behavior and fortunes and of attitudes and expressions of attitudes to someone else's past conduct or imminent conduct" (160). Austin's examples of behabitives include apologizing, thanking, deploring, welcoming, and protesting. Further, he notes, "In the field of behabitives, besides the usual liability to infelicities, there is a special scope for insincerity" (161).

Taking up this idea, Haber argues that in functioning as a behabitive, the locution "I forgive" is less a *report* on one's feelings (i.e., that one has overcome one's resentment), and more an *expression* of feeling (Haber 1991, 29–31). This distinction is important because it suggests that even the ordinary use of forgiveness need not be seen as an indication that one has eliminated resentment but rather as an expression of a commitment to eliminate it. Haber argues that when forgiveness is seen in this light, it is possible to continue to harbor resentment and still forgive. As a behabitive, unsuccessful forgiveness is also connected to sincerity—in this case, a sincere willingness to work on oneself and eliminate resentment. For Haber, if someone "should give up his effort at a later time, then—and only then—can we say his forgiveness was infelicitous, inasmuch as he has at that time breached his commitment to overcome resentment" (51).

In seeing ordinary forgiveness as a behabitive, Haber is asking what one is doing by performing a linguistic act of forgiving. In framing the question in this manner, he is not claiming that uttering or communicating forgiveness is the only way to forgive. While locutions involving forgiveness can have illocutionary effect, and are behabitives, not all acts of forgiveness need to be locutions. Haber notes that whereas a couple may marry by uttering the appropriate words (a performative utterance), getting married can also be accomplished, in many places, by living together long enough (Haber 1991, 40). Similarly, Jack may forgive Jill through a performative utterance or "by having the requisite attitude, independent of any verbal expression" (40). Jack may successfully forgive sotto voce, but when he does so "out loud," it is a behabitive.

Although Haber's analysis may capture a good many ways in which we utter forgiveness, it doesn't preclude the possibility of political forgiveness, nor does it encompass the forgiveness of financial debt or the pardoning of criminals. Although these activities may be seen as reactions to the behavior of others (behabitives), they also appear to entail a decision in favor of a course of action (an exercitive) and a commitment to a certain course of action on the part of the speaker (a commissive). In fact, Austin classifies pardoning as an exercitive that entails "the giving of a decision in favour of or against a certain course of action, or advocacy of it. It is a decision that something is to be so, as distinct from a judgement that it is so" (Austin 1962, 155). But the line between exercitives and commissives is not entirely clear insofar as "many exercitives . . . do in fact commit one to a course of action. . . . The connexion between an exercitive and committing oneself is as close as that between meaning and implication" (156). In any case, the notion of political forgiveness envisioned here need not be classified as a behabitive. Instead of sincerity, political forgiveness rests on authority, and instead of being an expression of feeling, it is a commitment to release one's debts.

Promising and Forgiving

The understanding of political forgiveness offered above also conflicts with R. S. Downie's analysis of forgiveness. According to Downie, the analogy with promising would be an inappropriate way to understand forgiveness:

> It is true that forgiving is like promising in that to say "I forgive you" is to raise certain expectations which may or may not be fulfilled. But if the expectations are not fulfilled in the case of promising it is still true that a promise has been given, although a false one, whereas if they are not ful-

filled in the case of forgiving we do not allow that there has been forgiveness at all. (Downie 1965, 131)

In other words, when Jack fails to meet the expectations created by his promise to Jill, Jill doesn't say that no promise was made (unless she is saying it bitterly). Rather, she would more likely say that Jack had broken his promise. In contrast, when Jill says that she forgives Jack but then berates him later for being wronged by him, Jack would probably conclude that she hadn't forgiven him. Downie is arguing that in the case of forgiveness, unlike the case of promising, if the appropriate, expected behavior is not forthcoming then we usually say that one has not forgiven. A kind of retrospective judgment exists that is part of forgiving but is not part of promising.[18]

In nonpolitical, ordinary conceptions of forgiveness, Downie's argument does point to an important distinction between promising and forgiving. In political forgiveness, however, the contrast is less clear. In the cases of forgiving a financial debt or in pardoning a criminal, it is not evident that conveying the message that one's debt has been forgiven or that one's crime has been pardoned do require the kind of retrospective judgment Downie claims. In other words, further expectations need not be met (other than there being uptake) in order to say that one has been relieved of the debt or released from the punishment. An individual who has received a full pardon, but remains in prison for his crimes, is likely to complain that he is being held unjustly, not that no pardon was given. It is, of course, conceivable that such an individual could eventually complain with some bitterness that no real pardon was given, but this may be no different from Jill's complaining that Jack's broken promise was merely a promise in name only. In both cases, the capacity of the individual to act appropriately is being attacked. Whether forgiveness was given or whether a promise was made is not in dispute.

Similarly, international monetary institutions and nation-states have some authority to restructure and forgive international debts. If, after such debt forgiveness, a nation still found its creditors (whose claims had been forgiven) knocking at its door, it would probably complain that those creditors had not upheld the authoritative forgiveness of debt. It is unlikely that its first impulse would be to deny that the debt had been forgiven. Thus, disappointing the expectations created by an act of

18. Consequently, Downie concludes that forgiveness cannot be a performative: uttering the words is neither necessary nor sufficient for forgiveness.

financial forgiveness need not automatically call into question whether forgiveness had been granted. In this theorization, political forgiveness operates much like the practice of promising. Although it goes beyond promising by inviting third-party responses to restore a relationship, political forgiveness could be seen as a kind of promise regarding the treatment of the past that requires a particular sort of future behavior on the part of the forgiver.

Other Effects of Political Forgiveness

The illocutionary effect of political forgiveness releases debtors and transgressors from their debts. The act of political forgiveness, however, can also have other effects. In a conventional way, the granting of forgiveness invites an expression of gratitude or appreciation on the part of the person being forgiven.[19] A financial or moral debt that once weighed down a transgressor or debtor has now been lifted. This response, of course, is not necessary for the success of the illocutionary act, and receiving such gratitude need not be a motive for the forgiver. In addition, political forgiveness can evoke certain reconciliatory effects. The discussion of these effects is the primary concern of chapter 3. I assert that, on the one hand, political forgiveness can be part of a *process* of reconciliation that involves the restoration of trust and civility. As part of this process, it neither guarantees nor secures a resulting state of reconciliation in which civic friendship is created or restored. On the other hand, political forgiveness is also part and parcel of a *state* of reconciliation. Political forgiveness ultimately entails a settlement with the past such that it should no longer serve as a basis for legitimate claims into the future. This state of reconciliation is not a grand vision of harmony or unity but a settling of past debts so that they do not haunt the future.

Political Forgiveness as a Result

Aside from having a set of illocutionary effects, could political forgiveness itself be an effect? In mapping out the uses of apology in various social relationships, Nicholas Tavuchis explains that, "the singular achievement of apologetic discourse paradoxically resides in its capacity to effectively eradicate the consequences of the offense by evoking the

19. This kind of conventional response to an illocutionary speech act is what Austin calls "a response or sequel." He further notes that "illocutionary acts invite by convention a response or sequel . . ." which "may be 'one-way' or 'two-way': thus we may distinguish arguing, ordering, promising, suggesting, and asking to, from offering, asking whether you will, and asking 'Yes or no?' " (Austin 1962, 117).

unpredictable faculty of forgiveness" (Tavuchis 1991, viii). Elsewhere, Tavuchis notes that an authentic apology (a genuine display of regret) warrants forgiveness, and he likens it to the middle term of a moral syllogism in which the end is forgiveness (20). One problem with this formulation is that the claims that forgiveness can be "evoked" and that it is unpredictable are somewhat at odds with the claim that forgiveness can be warranted or, more strongly, that it can be understood as the conclusion of a moral syllogism. In the former cases, forgiveness is a potential effect of an apology over which the victim still has some discretion. The offender may apologize, but the victim may quite easily refuse to grant forgiveness. In the latter cases, forgiveness moves closer to a duty or to a conventional sequel to an authentic apology. In this case, when the offender apologizes, the expectation is that forgiveness will be forthcoming.

Whichever account is correct in ordinary, sentiment-based conceptions of forgiveness, it becomes clear in later chapters that political forgiveness is not a perfect duty and that, at best, it may be evoked by a set of conditions. This is not to say that political forgiveness should be understood as unpredictable. For although victims and creditors retain a fair amount of discretion over when to engage in this kind of forgiveness, there are limits to its exercise. At times, it is inappropriate to engage in political forgiveness. Political forgiveness can be understood as an illocutionary effect. But with the exception of certain situations involving crushing financial debts, forgiveness should not be seen as an effect triggered by a set of circumstances or as a conclusion to a moral syllogism.

Responding to Criticisms of Forgiveness

Three general implications follow from seeing political forgiveness as an illocutionary act. The first is that political forgiveness need not be tarred with resentment, as suggested by the Nietzschean critic, because political forgiveness swings free of any particular sentiment. Successful political forgiveness is determined not by the feelings of the victims but by whether the act has uptake and takes effect. The illocutionary, self-disclosive aspects of political forgiveness circumvent the Nietzschean critique.

Second, emphasizing the self-disclosive character of forgiveness may also help address the criticism that forgiveness is essentially a Christian concept. Forgiveness does play a central role in Christianity—so central, in fact, that Arendt believed Jesus discovered "the role of forgiveness in the realm of human affairs" (Arendt 1958, 238). For her, "The fact that [Jesus] made this discovery in a religious context and articulated it in religious language is no reason to take it any less seriously in a strictly secular sense" (238; see also Haber 1991, 7–8). But whether we can take it seriously in a nonreligious sense depends on there being just such a sense. Does political forgiveness as an illocutionary act of self-disclosure rest on uniquely or exclusively Christian precepts or assumptions? If, for example, the only reason to forgive was that one should emulate God or follow divine command, it would in fact seem to have a religious nature. Likewise, if the only acceptable procedure for forgiving required following what was written in a sacred text, then the claim of exclusivity might hold. In contrast, the purposes of erasing debts and restoring a valued political relationship imply that the reasons why and the manner in which one forgives in politics are defined neither by Christian nor by other religious precepts and beliefs. To some degree they may be compatible with one another, but the conditions of political forgiveness do not require subscription to a particular set of religious beliefs.

Third, the idea of political forgiveness appears compatible with an agency-based conception of politics. Because it does not rest on the elimination of particular sentiments nor is rooted in a particular religious tradition, it evokes a politics in which actions are more important than sentiments. This feature of political forgiveness emerges most clearly in the conditions that are necessary for its success. To summarize, these include (1) the existence of a relationship between at least two parties in which (2) there is a debt owed to one party by the other (3) that is relieved by a party with appropriate standing, (4) conveying the appropriate signs or utterances, (5) whose success does not depend on the emotional or internal states of the forgivers, (6) even though it is generally thought good to receive what is due because (7) the effect of inviting the restoration of the offender or the debtor is somehow also thought to be good. What is conspicuous by its absence is the need for the victim or creditor to free themselves of or acquire a particular sentiment in order to forgive politically.

Of the criticisms with which this chapter began, what remains to be addressed are the relationships between political forgiveness and justice and between political forgiveness and reconciliation. To take the concept of forgiveness seriously in political theory, the concept of justice must not completely occupy the field. In addition, we must consider whether political forgiveness is a dangerous, utopian ideal or an important component in political reconciliation.

2

Political Forgiveness and Justice

A few years ago I learned, in a letter to our common friend
Hety S. . . . that Améry called me "the forgiver." I consider this neither insult
nor praise but imprecision. I am not inclined to forgive, I never forgave our
enemies of that time, nor do I feel I can forgive their imitators in Algeria,
Vietnam, the Soviet Union, Chile, Argentina, Cambodia, or South Africa,
because I know no human act that can erase a crime; I demand justice, but I
am not able, personally, to trade punches or return blows.

—Primo Levi, *The Drowned and the Saved*, 137

Justice

The idea of political forgiveness will be stillborn if justice and forgiveness
stand in opposition to one another and if the demands of justice trump
all other concerns. The discussion of justice seems to confirm the first
claim: where justice requires the receipt of what is due, forgiveness
releases what is due. The plausibility of the second claim is considered in
the discussion of the "normal model" of justice. What needs to be noted
here, however, is that justice is a complex concept with a variety of meanings. To be more precise about the nature of the conflict between justice
and forgiveness, we need to be more precise about the meaning of justice.
For example, in the *Nichomachean Ethics*, Aristotle's distinction between
general (or universal) and particular justice, and within the latter, his distinction between distributive and rectificatory (or corrective) justice,

reveals ways in which political forgiveness conflicts with and may conform to the demands of justice. General justice includes whatever "produces and maintains happiness and its parts for a political community" (Aristotle, *Nichomachean Ethics*, 1129b, 15–20). If an act of political forgiveness also serves the greater good, then it is not obvious that (general) justice and forgiveness necessarily conflict. In addition, forgiveness would seem to be only obliquely connected to distributive justice, which establishes the authoritative distribution of burdens and benefits.[1] Forgiveness seems unconnected to deciding what constitutes a relevant reason for distributing a good, unless a regime sought to reward or punish those who were forgiving or unforgiving.

In contrast, political forgiveness appears to conflict more directly with corrective or rectificatory forms of particular justice. Unlike distributive justice, rectificatory justice seeks to bring the parties back to the original conditions of a voluntary transaction (e.g., getting them to live up to their contracts, pledges, agreements) or, back to the original distribution when one party has not consented to the "transaction" (e.g., in cases of theft, fraud, bodily injury, or murder). In rectificatory justice, parties either recompense each other or one is "made whole" by an authoritative body. These corrections are always made with a view to the original conditions of a voluntary transaction or, more generally, to the authoritative distribution of benefits and burdens. Consequently, such corrections may entail punishment—or reform, in the case of institutions that have done wrong—as well as restitution. Rectificatory justice is consummated when the parties receive what is owed them. As Primo Levi noted, justice is needed, not forgiveness, when one has been unjustly treated; and what justice demands is some mixture of punishment (or institutional reform or transformation) and compensation.[2]

---

1. The problem of distributing punishment is taken up in the discussion of rectificatory justice later in this chpater.

2. With one brief exception (the restorative model of justice), this book brackets the role of compensation or restitution in responses to wrongs. This is not because the pursuit of compensation or restitution is less important than the nonfinancial or symbolic elements of rectificatory justice (e.g., truth-telling, apologies, imprisonment) but because a full discussion of the financial elements would require explaining how felt wrongs can be converted into monetary claims and how their adequacy should be judged. Consequently, the argument made later—that injustice is intractable—is not based on whether compensation or restitution can be adequate. Nothing in this analysis, however, precludes political forgiveness from releasing the transgressor from whatever compensation or restitution is owed. Obviously, this caveat does not apply to financial cases where the debt is already framed in monetary terms.

Political forgiveness, then, is an intervention in the moral economy of rectificatory justice. It applies to cases of financial debt as easily as to cases of moral wrong.[3] From the perspective of the debtor or the transgressor, to forgive is to relieve a debt that is owed. From the perspective of the creditor or the victim, it means that which was due is annulled. But why describe this as "an intervention" in the moral economy of justice? For the simple reason that by erasing what was due, forgiveness annuls or supersedes the demands of justice.[4] The implication of this erasure is that forgiveness has some degree of independence from rectificatory justice. Consequently, while it may make sense to say that an act of forgiveness was just or unjust from the perspective of general justice, we cannot talk about whether it is just to forgive from the perspective of rectificatory justice.

But this analysis seems to overstate the conflict between rectificatory justice and forgiveness in a couple of ways. First, the discussion of justice indicates that from the very start, political forgiveness is deeply dependent on the concept of rectificatory justice. For without justice and the concept of something being "due," it would be conceptually impossible to talk of freeing someone of their due. To put this another way, it is entirely possible to have a set of social practices in which one either receives or extracts what is due without the practice of releasing what is due; the concept of justice can make sense without forgiveness. It is not possible, however, to conceive of a practice of releasing debts without the notion of there being something due. Political forgiveness does not make sense unless a well-developed conceptualization of rectificatory justice already exists. This conceptual linkage, however, does not mean that in any given instance of forgiving, the demands of justice must be met. It merely means that forgiveness can only be meaningful or significant against the backdrop of justice.

Second, the conflict seems overstated in the sense that while it is true that forgiveness annuls what is due, such an annulment is always within the power of the creditor or the victim. There is no real conflict here because creditors and victims have a right to enjoy and not a duty to

---

3. A similar breadth can also be found within the Christian conception of forgiveness. Consider, for example, the two versions of the Lord's Prayer, in Luke and Matthew. In Luke (11:4), God is petitioned to forgive us our sins as we forgive those who trespass against us. In Matthew (6:12), God is asked to forgive us our debts as we forgive our debtors. In the latter case, forgiveness was apparently linked to "financial matters and involves the annulment of the obligation to repay what is owed" (Louw 1993, 232).

4. Erasing that debt requires fully and publicly understanding its character. Consequently, political forgiveness should not be mistaken for forgetting.

claim what is owed. Forgiveness, then, is consistent with a central feature of what it means to hold a right to a debt, namely that the right need not be exercised.

Although this formulation is largely correct, and in chapter 4 I consider whether victims and creditors possess an exclusive right to forgive, a fundamental conflict between forgiveness and justice is still present. This conflict turns on the good of justice. In very rough terms, there is something extraordinarily valuable about having debts repaid, victims made whole, and transgressors punished. Perhaps these assessments are based on the assumption that rectificatory justice has all sorts of wonderful effects: a practice of paying debts can encourage the generation of credit and commerce; the expectation that victims will be compensated can make us more careful in our activities and projects; the punishment of transgressors can be seen as a matter of fairness or as necessary to prevent future transgressions. Perhaps these assessments are based on an overwhelming deontological sense of what is right. Or, finally, the importance of rectificatory justice in political life may be grounded in the public conception of citizens as equal, independent sources of values. In any case, our sense of justice is so powerful that it is difficult to see how we could settle for anything less—and yet, that is what forgiveness appears to ask.

Forgiveness is easily marginalized as a political concept because of the good of justice. If, in addition, injustice can be always be rectified, then the space for political forgiveness is diminished even further. This additional assumption is not unusual in political theory and, as Judith Shklar points out, is the key feature of what she calls (and criticizes as) the normal model of justice. The central idea of this model is that, given sufficient resources and enough planning, injustice can be effectively swept away from just institutions. We need not suffer institutions that do wrong, and once just institutions and rules are up and running, injustice will be nothing more than "a surprising abnormality" (Shklar 1990, 17). It is always possible, in other words, to institute arrangements and practices that can produce a just state of affairs. With a view to rectificatory justice, this does not mean that injustices won't happen but that when things do go wrong, there is always an adequate remedy.

If justice is an extremely important political good that conflicts with forgiveness, and the demands for justice can always be satisfied, then political forgiveness is of marginal theoretical significance. There are, however, at least three ways to carve out some theoretical space for forgiveness. The first is to argue, against what has been heretofore claimed, that the conflict between forgiveness and justice can be resolved. The second is to argue that rectificatory justice may not be complete. And the third is to argue that the pursuit of justice shouldn't always have priority—that the good of fully receiving one's due can be occasionally trumped, displaced, or abridged by political forgiveness.

The restorative justice movement offers one prominent model that appears to reconcile forgiveness with justice. This model, which is briefly considered below, does not portray the choice between justice and forgiveness as a choice between competing values. Advocates of restorative justice tend to see no tension between these terms. Nevertheless, despite the apparent lack of tension, the restorative model still retains the core conflict between forgiveness and rectificatory justice. This conflict does not make an appearance in this model only because its advocates focus on a general conception of justice. What initially looks like a way to reconcile political forgiveness and rectificatory justice does not ultimately do so.

A second and potentially more successful way to carve out some theoretical space for political forgiveness is to claim that the normal model does not hold—that, on occasion, rectificatory justice cannot be fully met. If justice is incomplete, then there may be occasions when justice is carried out as fully as is possible and yet some element of injustice, some "remainder," resists being swept away. If such remainders exist, then political forgiveness may be an appropriate response to the intractability of injustice.

Finally, some space for political forgiveness can be cleared by rejecting the view of justice as necessarily trumping all other values. In theorizing political forgiveness, I assume that justice retains its powerful call in politics, but I also warn against always heeding that call completely. Given the great value attributed to it, political forgiveness should never entirely trump justice. Consequently, the burden of justification rests on those who would seek to abridge or forestall the pursuit of justice in public life. As the case of pardoning shows, the demands of rectificatory justice have a degree of priority, but it need not be a lexical priority; that is, we need not satisfy justice as fully as possible before forgiving. Political forgiveness may occasionally abridge but never completely displace the claims of justice.

Restorative Justice

Although it goes by a number of names—reconciliation, peacemaking, redress, republican criminal justice—restorative justice is a response to the perceived inadequacies of current practices of criminal law in many nations—practices that are seen as ignoring the victim, turning crime into a matter that can be handled only by the state, and relying on a brutal but ineffective system of incarceration (Braithwaite 1996, 15–17, 27–28; Van Ness 1989). Very broadly, advocates of restorative justice seek to remedy these defects by restoring to the victim and to the community the losses that result from crime, by reconciling the transgressor to the victim and the community, and by achieving these goals through the active participation of all the parties involved.[5] At most, under this model, the state is a watchdog or a guarantor so that the rights of the parties are not violated in the process of reconciliation. Moreover, the state should exercise the power to incarcerate only in the few cases where it would protect the community (Braithwaite 1996, 28; Hudson 1998, 256). Central to the restorative model is the idea that a flesh-and-blood human being is wronged when a crime is committed, not an abstraction called the state.

From this perspective, far from being at odds with justice, forgiveness is understood as a necessary part of reparation and reconciliation. According to Retzinger and Scheff, even before material reparations to the victim are considered, there must be symbolic reparations in which forgiveness has a role to play: "The ideal outcome, from the point of view of symbolic reparation is constituted by two steps: the offender first clearly expresses genuine shame and remorse for his or her actions. In response, the victim takes at least a first step towards forgiving the offender for the trespass" (Retzinger and Scheff 1996, 316; also Dickey 1998, 107, 118; Dinnen 1997, 255).

Hudson and Galaway reach further and see victims as having a responsibility both to "accept the expressions of remorse made by the offenders and to express a willingness to forgive" (Hudson and Galaway 1996, 2). Finally, Archbishop Tutu has argued that "justice, restorative justice, is being served when efforts are being made to work for healing, for forgiving, and for reconciliation" (Tutu 1999, 55).[6] According to many advocates of restorative justice, forgiveness is an important component to reconciliation (Estrada-Hollenbeck 1996, 311–12).

Without judging the restorative model's critique of current criminal practices or assessing its empirical claims to being able to meet its stated

5. Dickey 1998, 107; Hudson and Galaway 1996, 2; Hudson 1998, 241; McCold 1996, 86–87; McElrea 1996, 72; Messmer and Otto 1992, 2–3; Minor and Morrison 1996, 117; Minow 1998, 81; Van Ness 1989; Wright 1991, 117; Zehr 1997, 68–71.

6. According to Tutu, the spirit behind restorative justice in South Africa is *ubuntu*, which is a concern for "the healing of breaches, the redressing of imbalances, the restoration of relationships" (Tutu 1999, 54–55; see also Battle 1997).

goals, we can ask whether this model does indeed overcome the alleged conflict between justice and forgiveness. The answer, I believe, is that it does not. The central point in support of this conclusion is that restorative justice remains within the conceptual framework of rectificatory justice as set out earlier: it requires offenders to make some attempt to rectify the wrongs they have done. In fact, the critical character of the restorative model derives from the belief that current criminal justice practices view the victim as a passive witness and not as someone who should be made whole. To the extent that the restorative model starts by assuming that the offender owes both symbolic and material reparations to the victim and that it is a good thing for these debts to be paid, this model cannot advocate that victims surrender their claims by forgiving the victim of his or her debt. Indeed, victims who forgave too easily would short-circuit not only the claims of justice but also what some advocates of restorative justice see as the socially useful *reintegrative shaming* of the offender (Braithwaite 1996, 12; Hudson 1998, 249). The point of such shaming is not to stigmatize the offender but to express disapproval of the offense, "while treating the person as essentially good" (Braithwaite 1996, 12). If the victim simply released the offender without the offender admitting guilt or engaging in reparations, the process of restoration would never get off the ground.[7]

Despite the fundamental opposition between the initial requirements of restorative justice and forgiveness, the restorative model does eventu-

---

7. One reason this conflict between forgiveness and justice is not more evident is that the restorative model tends to rely on a sentiment-based view of forgiveness. If we take Braithwaite's statement that restorative justice "aims to *restore harmony based on a feeling that justice has been done*" (Braithwaite 1996, 16), forgiveness seems to entail the elimination of (or willingness to eliminate) certain inharmonious feelings—probably feelings of resentment, anger, or vengefulness against the offender on the part of the victim. Similarly, when John R. Gehm discusses the connection between forgiveness and restorative justice, he sees much of the research focusing "primarily on anger, its healthy resolution, and the role it plays in allowing individuals to get on with their lives less encumbered by the pain and power of the past" (Gehm 1992, 545; see also Dickey 1998, 107). To the degree that forgiveness is primarily a matter of how the victim feels, the conflict between receiving what is due and releasing someone from what is due is hidden. For example, in considering the relationship between forgiveness and justice, Dean E. Peachy concludes that "the task of justice in response to crime is undoing that harm" (Peachy 1992, 552). In addition, he argues that "forgiveness is not something that a victim does for the benefit of the offender. Real forgiveness is the process of the victim letting go of the rage and pain" (556). To the extent that undoing the harm is eliminating that anger, Peachy can also claim that forgiveness is a "way to restore justice" (553). When he talks of forgiveness balancing the scales of justice and canceling the debt, he seems to be seeing rage and pain as a kind of debt. He doesn't see forgiveness as entailing the forgiving of whatever compensation or restitution the offender owes the victim. Consequently, he reconciles forgiveness to a conception of justice that entails peace, harmony, and an absence of ill feeling.

ally incorporate forgiveness. The point at which forgiveness becomes reconciled to justice, however, is when justice is not simply a matter of rectification but of the restoration of harmony and peace among the parties. Nevertheless, I would suggest that this view of justice is distinct from and much broader than one that involves the repayment of debts. The focus on terms such as harmony and peace evokes what Aristotle saw as the general conception of justice, insofar as forgiveness leads to the happiness of the regime as a whole. In other words, the ability of the model to incorporate forgiveness into justice is due to its ultimate subscription to a very broad but distinctive conception of justice. As mentioned above, this should not be surprising, for not all understandings of justice are in conflict with political forgiveness. What must be kept in mind is that the general conception of justice is not the only conception operating in the restorative model. Another way to look at the restorative model is that it does not see forgiveness as appropriate unless some movement toward rectificatory justice has been made, for example, compensation, restitution, an admission of guilt, or an apology. This condition is also a key component of political forgiveness.

Although restorative justice appeared to be a promising way to theorize political forgiveness, the central conflict between victims receiving what is their due (justice) and victims releasing what is their due (forgiveness) remains. Since this model sees restitution or compensation to the victim as key to reconciliation, forgiveness should not short-circuit that process. To state this conclusion more strongly, if offenders could restore their victims fully, then political forgiveness would once again be squeezed out of political theory.[8] This does not mean that other conceptions would play no role, for example, sentiment-based conceptions of forgiveness dependent on the elimination of anger, but that there would be no debt to forgive, which is central for political forgiveness.

The Limits of Justice

The second way to find some theoretical space for forgiveness is to argue that justice is not complete. It is impossible, in other words, to ensure that everyone always receives his or her due; there are limits to justice. The idea that there are such limits is not new. For example, communitarians argue that liberal understandings of justice rule out or

8. It could be argued that even in the instance of full restoration to the particular victim, the degree to which a crime is also a public wrong would remain unaddressed. Political forgiveness would be fully squeezed out of consideration if the victim was also always able to repair that public wrong and if it was always a good thing to demand its repair.

devalue "benevolence, altruism, and communitarian sentiments" (Sandel 1982, 60). Utilitarians, to the extent that they see justice as serving the general welfare, are also open to other values trumping justice if the greater good is served. These kinds of consequentialist positions, which are highly critical of stringent deontological understandings of justice, raise important questions regarding the value of justice vis-à-vis other values and the appropriateness of using the standards of justice to govern private relationships. The possibility that the demands of rectificatory justice could be outweighed by other values and that forgiveness could advance those values opens important space for the plausibility of political forgiveness. (I consider this possibility later in the chapter.)

The limitations of rectificatory justice that I discuss first draw on Judith Shklar's arguments that rules and institutions cannot always give what is fully due. If this is true, then even the best regime cannot live up to our highest expectations regarding justice. Our institutions and our fellow citizens will inevitably disappoint, not merely because they may "do wrong" but also because their responses to the wrongs done may frequently be inadequate. This may lead us to question more closely the utility of our rectificatory institutions and perhaps to entertain more seriously anarchic or antinomian alternatives. Alternatively, it may prompt us to ask whether our social interactions and institutions may require a stance of generosity even during the best of times.

Why is it that justice can be incomplete, particularly when considering the rectification of a wrong? Why is it that when things go wrong, we cannot devise procedures or institutions that can always give what is due? According to Shklar, one reason is that "in actual political life there is no way to avoid a huge gap between the personal sense of injustice and established norms" (Shklar 1990, 107). Very briefly, her argument is that justice is general and injustice is particular. When we are treated unjustly, we experience a certain and tangible injury that gives rise to our own sense of outrage. When we seek redress within civil society, however, we encounter bureaucracies, courts, legislators, officials, clerks, and lawyers who are concerned with institutions, rules, procedures, and generalities. Justice is rule-bound and abstract, whereas injustice is not. Consequently, "courts as agents of the law must remain general and abstract in their decisions, enhancing our sense of injustice occurring in the very act of being just. That is why our sense of injustice is not always appeased by fair decisions" (110).

At a theoretical level, the problem of the intractability of injustice as it relates to rectification can more easily be seen in theories in which the legitimacy of government is supposed to rest on its rectificatory abilities. Theorists such as Thomas Hobbes, John Locke, and Robert Nozick, who begin with the "inconveniences" of a state of nature and then see government as a mechanism to relieve those inconveniences, probably provide the best examples. Of these positions, it may be most useful to consider the case of Locke, who sought to balance limited government with the need for sufficient authority to rectify wrongs. Indeed, for Locke, government is necessary only because the state of nature cannot guarantee rectificatory justice. In the end, however, while a Lockean government may mitigate the "inconveniences" of the state of nature, it does not eliminate them. Even in the minimal state in which government is a simple nightwatchman, problems with rectification remain. If this is true, then the maintenance of government may require not only justice but also understanding its limitations. The limitations of justice, then, provide a possible opening for political forgiveness to pick up the slack.

Locke and the Intractability of Injustice

Locke's story in *The Second Treatise* is a familiar one: although we naturally know how to treat one another in a state of nature, given our access to natural law, this anarchical situation quickly falls into a state of war. Given the problems of the state of nature, we are not able to live peacefully together without government. To improve our situation, we first unanimously agree to abide by whatever the majority decides, and then we agree to abide by whatever government the majority creates. Government exists to remedy the problems of the state of nature, and if government consistently violates the original contract under which it is authorized, then the people have the right to establish a new government, even if that means violent revolution.

What must be added to this thumbnail sketch in order to reveal the intractability of injustice is some elaboration of the inconveniences suffered in the state of nature. The most obvious difficulty is that the state of nature is a system of self-help. If one suffers a wrong, there is no process to rectify it, other than acting on one's own.[9] We do, Locke thought, possess enough of the right kind of reason to direct us to the laws of nature and to identify a violation of those laws, but when a wrong occurs we cannot be assured that justice will be obtained at all or in the right amount. Even if by some chance we catch the miscreant, "it

---

9. For Locke, the wrongs usually involve violations of property, and by property he is broadly referring to our "lives, liberties and estates" (Locke [1690] 1980, 66).

is unreasonable for men to be judges in their own cases, . . . [because] self-love will make men partial to themselves and their friends: and . . . ill nature, passion and revenge will carry them too far in punishing others; and hence nothing but confusion and disorder will follow" (Locke [1690] 1980, 12). Because of bias and the overzealous enforcement of the laws of nature, a state of nature slips into a state of war. In this condition, we lack an impartial judge to decide the facts of a case and a moderate executive to enforce decisions. Later, Locke points to the absence of a legislature that can promulgate laws that are understood to be "the standard of right and wrong." What may be key in legislation are not the standards of right and wrong (for these are discernible through right reason), but the fact that legislation is based on common consent. This is needed, Locke believed, to drive home the point that the law is binding in our particular cases (66), a point that may not be evident in the state of nature.[10] In any case, by punishing too harshly in cases in which we are involved, we create another injustice that calls for rectification. In our pursuit of justice we can become what Shklar calls "actively unjust."

Given the difficulties associated with the state of nature, Locke argues that we must establish a government composed of a legislature, a judiciary, and an executive. Out of these institutions emerges a rule of law that can produce rectificatory justice. My argument, however, is that the inconveniences of the state of nature continue to haunt the institutions designed for their solution. In addition, government itself generates new possibilities for injustice that were unthinkable in the state of nature. Locke's contract may entail the mitigation of some problems of rectification, but the empowering of officials to enforce the law also means that it becomes extraordinarily difficult to respond to the many injustices that government will inevitably commit. Even while the whole point of government is the rectification of wrongs, it seems that injustice is intractable.

The key problems with the state of nature are our tendency toward bias and a difficulty in squaring the punishment with the crime. These same difficulties are not eliminated in the creation of government. The judiciary, for example, is established in order to remedy the problem of biased judgments and the unfair application of the law. Locke's assump-

---

10. How does consent solve this problem? What we consent to, it could be argued, is the proposition that if there is some doubt as to whether the law applies, we will be willing to have the matter settled by the law itself. The legislature, in other words, can establish an indifferent (although Locke cannot say "independent," given his notion of legislative supremacy) judiciary to determine whether and how the law applies. This convenience is not available in the state of nature.

tion is that a third party would be less caught up in the emotions of a particular case. This, of course, is plausible, but Locke does not demonstrate that third parties cannot or will not be driven by passions and emotions beyond the demands of justice. Judges, legislators, and ordinary citizens can all be caught up in the heat of the moment, even though they may not be one of the parties of the dispute.[11] Government may mitigate the problem of active injustice by relegating punishment to a third party, but this by no means eliminates the problem.

The judiciary, however, is not only meant to be indifferent to the passions of the parties but also to mete out just the right amount of justice. Although Locke does not seek to set out the measure of punishment, he does argue that "each transgression may be *punished* to that *degree*, and with so much *severity*, as will suffice to make it an ill bargain to the offender, give him cause to repent, and terrify others from doing the like" (Locke [1690] 1980, 12). In the economy of punishment, the judge must take away whatever gains the transgressor may have accrued through his action and teach the rest of us a lesson. Locke's assumption here is that our passions and interests stand in the way of our ability to fine-tune a set of punishments. The indifference of the indifferent judge permits not only a cooler judgment but also an accurate one.

It is delusional, however, to believe that judges are always on the mark in providing criminals precisely the right amount of punishment. Even if we put aside the problems of measuring exactly what severity of punishment may deter other criminals, the comparatively minor difficulty of discerning what punishment constitutes an "ill bargain" for the criminal but does not go beyond what is deserved is daunting. Strictly speaking, one day of undeserved imprisonment is a grave injustice. (If one doubts that this is so, then spend one day in prison as an innocent individual.) But perhaps what justice demands is fuzzy, and the mark is not precise: any crime demanding punishment would license a range of possibilities and not simply a set number of years in prison or a specific fine. Yet, if it is fuzzy in civil society, it should be just as fuzzy in the state of nature. Assuming a wide mark (but how wide?) available for punishing, individuals driven by their emotions in a state of nature may just as easily hit that mark as judges (potentially driven by the winds of poli-

11. In the case of the United States, it is even possible to supersede the judgment of the judiciary, ignore the particulars of a case, and institute the biases of specific interest groups: automatic sentencing for drug smuggling, three-strikes rules, and the registering of sex offenders may all be examples of the biases of the legislature or the electorate overriding the sense of judges.

tics) do in civil society. The very problem that drives individuals to government is not remedied but only bewigged and robed.

The remedy, a Lockean could say, is not found in the quality of the institutional decisions but in the fact that we've consented to accept the punishments mandated by the legislature or handed down by the judge when we signed the social contract. But Locke is clear: this is not a matter of positive law. The natural standard is "reparation and restraint" (Locke [1690] 1980, 10). Simply because the legislature mandates or a judge issues a sentence does not make it just. Our consent does not transform the standard. Even in Locke's terms, it is not self-evident that government improves the matter.

In the case of executing the law, however, it is clear that government does remedy the tenuous if not dangerous use of self-help that defines the state of nature. With the creation of government, the responsibility for carrying out the law and delivering punishment now falls to a class of officials who are authorized to do so. With a well-armed set of officials, the risks to the executor of imposing punishment are lessened and the probabilities of being successful are increased, at least as compared to a state of nature.

The problem, however, is that in remedying one problem (the risks of self-help), the institution of government generates another. The potential to enforce the law also implies a potential for the official abuse of the law. We have substituted the inconveniences of self-help for the potential inconveniences of tyranny. Whether government can be so constructed as to overcome the latter inconveniences is, for many, the central issue of political philosophy. Whether we talk about a Newtonian model of politics, the role of professionalism, or the importance of civic virtue, none of the proponents of these various schemes and plans advertises the elimination of the potential for the injustice of tyranny. Indeed, some of these schemes admit the entirely contingent and momentary nature of a regime in which the rulers and the ruled do the right thing.

Another example of the multiplication of opportunities for injustice can be found in the institution of the legislature. In the state of nature, we possess a natural ability to discern what is required of us as rational creatures. Locke finds the laws of nature plainer and more easily understood, "as much as reason is easier to be understood, than the fancies and intricate contrivances of men, following contrary and hidden interests put into words; for so truly are a great part of the *municipal laws* of countries, which are only so far right, as they are founded

on the law of nature, by which they are to be regulated and interpreted" (Locke [1690] 1980, 12). Unlike the obvious laws of nature, citizens must now deal with the contrary and hidden interests of legislators who may twist the law to serve their own purposes. In exchange
for the equal understanding of the natural law, we have a positive law
that is potentially obscure and biased. Not only can law be obscure
and biased, but it may also violate the demands of natural law. More
strongly, government cannot guarantee that this violation won't occur,
and if we think the legislature is requiring us to do something that violates the laws of nature, then there is no earthly judge who can settle
the matter. The system itself cannot deal with the difficulty. In passing
laws that violate the natural law, the Lockean legislature creates the
potential for injustices that did not exist in the state of nature. To help
deal with this problem, Locke calls for an infrequently convening legislature so that the chances for unjust laws and the number of obscure,
biased laws are minimized.

Finally, the potential for abuse is compounded by executive prerogative, which permits the executive to act against the law or to secure the
good of the commonwealth when the law is silent (Locke [1690] 1980,
84). As Locke notes, "prerogative is nothing but the power of doing public good without a rule" (87). What will keep the executive focused on
the "preservation of all?" For Locke, there is "no judge on Earth" to settle a dispute as to whether the executive exceeded his or her authority
and so the "people have no other remedy in this, as in all other cases
where they have no judge on earth, but to *appeal to heaven*" (87). In seeking to prevent some injustices we seem to create others.

Where Justice Can Be Supplemented

From this abbreviated account, I draw three implications from the Lockean
position and one historical concern that open theoretical spaces for political forgiveness. Whether political forgiveness can actually fill these spaces
is considered in chapter 5, where the problem of pardoning is raised, in
chapter 7, where the questions of forgiving dirty hands and imperfect procedures are explored, and in chapters 6 and 8, where forgiving past political injuries is considered. From the incompleteness of justice, one cannot
necessarily conclude that forgiveness is a reasonable or appropriate
response. But we need to take the first step before taking the second.

The first implication is that given the biases that flow from our passions, the obscurities that are written into the law, and the difficulties

of calibrating the punishment to the crime, our political institutions will, at best, be imperfectly just. Even though we may know what justice demands (and sometimes we may not know even that), we have no guaranteed path to get there. Although the usual example of imperfect procedural justice is the familiar idea that fair criminal proceedings cannot guarantee that the guilty are punished and the innocent are set free, it is difficult to think of any complex political procedure that is perfectly just. The Lockean system suggests that a set of institutions may be worthy of our respect (perhaps because they emerge from our own will, perhaps because they do frequently yield justice), while still yielding outcomes that are wrong or harmful, such as finding the guilty innocent, and vice versa. In politics as elsewhere, wrong outcomes can come from good procedures. Even the best regimes will be only nearly just.

The second and third points are implied by Locke's discussion of executive prerogative. Locke believes that, on occasion, it may be necessary to act against the law in order to pursue the common good. The rules and restrictions that normally govern and guide the executive may sometimes be too rigid for the circumstances. In these cases, the executive is forced to choose between the legal but harmful and the illegal but helpful course of action. When this power is clearly being used for the crucial good of the people over the long run, the choice is also clear— violate the law. But Locke's discussion suggests, moreover, that at other times the choice may not be so clear-cut. In such circumstances, questions can arise between the executive and the people as to whether the illegal action was the better choice. One way to read this kind of situation is to say that either the people are too dull to understand that breaking the law was really in their best interest, or the executive is overreaching her power and simply evading the law. In these situations, the fault is either one of ignorance or treachery.

An alternative reading is that in a given situation, the executive may be faced with a choice between two courses of action, both equally wrong. This is the situation of a tragic choice or moral dilemma in which the actor must dirty her hands. Within moral philosophy there are significant disputes over whether this problem is a real one.[12] Some argue that moral dilemmas do not exist, and because they do not exist, it is never necessary to do wrong in order to do good. If, however, such situ-

---

12. One of the best collections of essays on this problem is Christopher Gowens's *Moral Dilemmas* (1987).

ations do exist, then the problem of dirty hands raises yet another example of how injustice may be intractable.[13] In general, I believe that although dirty hands is an infrequent problem, its significance when it does arise is enormous, as in the case of nuclear deterrence, and the temptation to portray situations as raising this problem is always great, as in hoary appeals to necessity or national security. On this reading, it is partly because of the existence of a "realm of necessity" that the idea of executive prerogative must be taken seriously.

The third way in which Locke's argument creates space for forgiveness concerns the power to pardon. Locke writes that executive prerogative may be exercised in cases in which someone comes "within reach of the law, which makes no distinction of persons, by an action that may deserve reward and pardon; 'tis fit the ruler should have a power, in many cases, to mitigate the severity of the law, and pardon some offenders: for the *end of government* being *the preservation of all*, as much as may be, even the guilty are to be spared, where it can prove no prejudice to the innocent" (Locke [1690] 1980, 84). Here, it is not entirely clear that Locke is talking about only one class of cases in which pardoning would be justified. First, he discusses using pardon to reward an action that under the strict terms of law should be punished: perhaps someone steals a vehicle in order to rush an accident victim to a doctor. In the second case, someone is found guilty of a crime, but punished much too harshly; in receiving thirty years' imprisonment for stealing a screwdriver, for example, the offender doesn't receive what is due.[14] The final case entails sparing the guilty where it may not burden or harm the innocent, given that the purpose of government is everyone's preservation.

The first two cases can be understood as using the power to pardon to rectify failures of procedure. In both cases, the law is imperfect and doesn't adequately provide what is due. Locke sees the executive's power to par-

---

13. What is also troubling about Locke's position is that he seems to suggest that as long as the majority does not rise up and "appeal to heaven," then the executive could continue to have right on her side: "Nor let any one think, this [appeal to heaven] lays a perpetual foundation for disorder; for this operates not, till the inconveniency is so great, that the majority feel it, and are weary of it, and find a necessity to have it amended" (Locke [1690] 1980, 88). This position would seem to license the executive to sacrifice the rights of minorities and individuals in exercising its prerogative, given the knowledge that it is the majority that "counts" and that most people are docile most of the time. Locke's concern that the mere mention of a right to revolution not inspire disorder hides the degree to which the government can do injustice prior to the point of actually inspiring rebellion.

14. This, of course, was one of the central inconveniences of the state of nature.

don as being able to step in and correct the law to provide precisely what is due. In these cases, rectificatory justice and pardoning are not at odds in the sense that both require delivering what is due. In contrast, political forgiveness entails releasing what is due. These uses of the concept of pardoning seriously question whether my association of pardoning with political forgiveness is a mistake. As is argued in chapter 5, the power to pardon need not be restricted to giving what is due. This is somewhat clearer when we turn to Locke's last example of pardoning, although even it is subject to at least two interpretations. One interpretation of Locke's statement is that he is referring to sparing criminals the death sentence when a pardon would not adversely affect those who have done no wrong. This kind of a gracious action stresses the notion that the government is meant for the preservation of all, even though Locke firmly believed that one could, through one's own actions, forfeit one's right to life (Locke [1690] 1980, 17). Although I think that this form of pardoning is a kind of forgiving, it raises the problem of whether it is an appropriate form of political forgiveness, given its gracious character.

Another interpretation of this last case of pardoning is that Locke is not talking about preserving those on death row but about preserving the regime. This kind of pardon, which can be called a public welfare pardon, does not result from the imperfections of procedures but from the possibility that the common good could occasionally be served by refusing to punish those who may deserve it. For example, as Alexander Hamilton suggested, the well-timed offer of a pardon to those engaged in insurrection may be a useful tool to secure peace. Here the problem is not the intractability of injustice but whether refusing to pursue rectificatory justice is ever justifiable—even if it were possible to obtain it. As the South African thinker Wilhelm Verwoerd noted, "(criminal) justice is not the only social goal, nor always the ultimate value" (Verwoerd 1999, 480). The problem of overriding justice is considered below.

Historical Wrongs

The final claim that I make regarding the intractability of injustice is connected to the vicissitudes of history and the historical durability of past wrongs. No regime is drawn on a blank slate. States and citizens are creatures with pasts that they can never entirely escape. In part, this may be an advantage, insofar as the past can and does validate who we are and what we do. Unfortunately, not all that is past is good. Part of the incompleteness of justice, then, is that actors in the present can never fully escape the injustices of the past. Slavery, Nazism, apartheid, "the disappeared," death squads, collectivization, the Rape of Nanking are all welded to present politics like the chains attached to Marley's ghost. It is not difficult to think of additional recent illustrations. There is something intractable about historical injustices. As the past recedes, historical wrongs become increasingly difficult to repair. This is true for a number of reasons: the original victims or transgressors may be dead; the original victims or transgressors may both be gone, but the descendents of victims and transgressors may continue to suffer from or be benefited by the original wrong in extraordinarily complex ways; the original harm or wrong may become a core part of the identity the victim or transgressor; or, as we rethink the past, we may uncover wrongs that had been buried or marginalized for a very long time. For all these reasons, it may be impossible to ensure that people receive their due for past wrongs. The simple passage of time presents another instance in which injustice may become intractable.

Overriding Rectificatory Justice

There are good reasons for contesting the normal model of justice. Because the demands of justice cannot always be completely satisfied, political forgiveness may be a way to supplement justice even in the nearly just regime. In addition to finding space for a political conception of forgiveness through the intractability of injustice, such space may also exist if rectificatory justice can be overridden by other values. Despite the extraordinary value we attribute to having debts repaid, victims made whole and transgressors punished, other goods may be lost in a relentless pursuit of justice. The demand to be paid to the penny forecloses opportunities for generosity or magnanimity. The attempt to provide victims of a past tyranny with full restitution may put in jeopardy economic stability. The desire to punish the tyrants and their minions may sacrifice the peaceful transition to democracy.[15] In each case, it may be possible to do

15. The practical difficulties of relentlessly pursuing justice vis-à-vis former officials may be staggering. This is particularly true if those officials retain some measure of power and if the new regime has not taken root. In creating a peaceful transition to the new regime, the expectation may have been created that these officials would not be subject to criminal proceedings. In addition, the difficulties of pursuing the trial option may be significant: the financial cost may be enormous, evidence and witnesses may be missing, or unreliable and statutory limitations may have been exceeded. In the case of the South African transition, Desmond Tutu argued that the combination of all of these obstacles made the trial option unfeasible (Tutu 1999, 20–26; see also Minow 1998, 25–51). (The theoretical difficulties associated with forgiving officials of an unjust former regime are considered in chapters 6 and 8.)

the right thing and give what is due but, in so doing, lose other things. Political forgiveness can be a way to release the demands of justice and pursue competing goods.

Four assumptions must be made to support a permission for overriding rectificatory justice through an act of political forgiveness. The first is that not all goods can be placed under and reconciled with the category of rectificatory justice. Receiving one's due is not necessarily the same as establishing peace, stability, or prosperity. Second, these other goods are (on occasion) more important than receiving what is due. Third, those who are creditors or who find themselves as victims of wrongdoing have some discretion over how to press their claims. That is, they may choose not to pursue justice fully. Finally, political forgiveness must somehow advance these other values. This final assumption is unpacked in later chapters, where I discuss whether and when governments and citizens may forgive. The first two assumptions are relatively uncontroversial. Even those who believe in the ultimate harmony of all virtues need not believe that everything resolves to receiving your due. The second assumption would seem to be denied only by those who are strict retributivists or stringent deontologists. In chapter 5, the claim that governments have some discretion in forgiving criminals through the power of pardoning requires rejecting a retributivist conception of pardoning. Under a strict form of retributivism, criminals should receive their due and governments should have no discretion in the matter. Far from releasing convicts of their due, pardons should be used only to ensure that the innocent are not punished or that the guilty are not punished too severely. In contrast, as is implied by Hamilton's use of the power to pardon in cases of insurrection, if other goods may outweigh rectificatory justice, then it is possible to conceive of a notion of pardoning in which forgiveness serves goods other than justice.

The third assumption, that creditors and victims have discretion not to push their demands of justice, also appears unproblematic: as we saw, creditors and victims have a right to enjoy and not a duty to claim what is owed. If they happen to believe that other values can be secured by not pressing for justice and that forgiving advances those values, then what could be objectionable about forgiving? Indeed, the implication of the question is that it may make perfect sense to abandon completely one's claims of justice and forgive, if forgiveness procures more important ends. But should political forgiveness be, by itself, a sufficient response to wrongs and debts? There are certain limits to political forgiveness, some of which are built into the illocutionary character of political forgiveness.

Other limitations, I maintain, are built into what it means to be a citizen of a democratic society. In other words, in certain situations, the discretion to abandon one's claim is not as wide as originally thought and citizens should continue to push their claims of justice because they are citizens (see chapter 7). Some minimal threshold of justice is, however, a necessary condition for political forgiveness, first, because the success of political forgiveness requires meeting many of the same conditions needed for rectificatory justice. Second, forgiveness needs to satisfy the minimal conditions of justice in order to distinguish it from grants of amnesty and help prevent forgiveness from being twisted into an insult. To some extent, justice can be overridden in the pursuit of other values. However, political forgiveness cannot completely displace the pursuit of justice.

Traveling the Road of Justice and the Distinctiveness of Forgiveness

The first argument supporting the claim that some minimal threshold of justice is an indispensable condition for political forgiveness begins with the reminder that political forgiveness must be conveyed from the victim or creditor to the transgressor or debtor in order to be successful. The illocutionary character of political forgiveness requires that the relevant parties understand who is forgiving whom for what. It misfires or fails if victims or creditors don't know who holds the debt or if transgressors or debtors don't realize they've been forgiven. To achieve these conditions, political forgiveness must also meet some of the same conditions that are necessary to fulfill the demands of justice. In other words, the mother of a child who had disappeared, the political activist who was blindfolded and tortured, or the child of a father killed by a lynch mob could not forgive (in this political sense) the perpetrators of these wrongs unless he or she knew who their tormentors were. Similarly, rectificatory justice must also meet these conditions. Such identification is essential in order to help determine if a wrong had occurred. Was it merely an accident? Was the agent coerced? Was the agent competent? Answering these kinds of questions is a requirement of both rectificatory justice and political forgiveness.

Another way to draw the requirements of justice into political forgiveness is, paradoxically, by emphasizing the distinctiveness of the idea of forgiveness. To distinguish forgiveness from ordinary forms of forgetting (or unconditional amnesty) and to prevent forgiveness from being used as an insult, it is necessary that the parties involved share an understanding of the character of the wrong or debt. How precise an understanding depends on the circumstances and the relationship between the parties.

Nevertheless, for a victim to release a wrongdoer from her debts without recalling the extent of responsibility or the true nature of the wrong is to engage in a form of forgetting. Although we may forgive and then forget, forgiving is not the same as forgetting. Forgiving requires recalling and understanding the past, whereas forgetting lets go the past with little attempt to understand it. As the original meaning of the word suggests, amnesty is an official form of forgetting. When it is unconditional, an amnesty requires neither an official investigation of what happened nor the prosecution of wrongdoers. A general grant of amnesty completely shuts down the pursuit of justice.[16] Distinguishing political forgiveness from amnesty rests on an account of what happened and who did what to whom. In other words, it requires that a minimal level of justice be obtained.

Moreover, forgiveness without a shared account of responsibility runs the risk of becoming an insult. To forgive another for something she hasn't done is both to accuse her backhandedly of doing wrong (or having a debt) and to inflate one's own moral standing. Nowhere is this illustrated more clearly than with Charles Dickens's fictional character, Mr. Pecksniff. In *Martin Chuzzlewit*, Pecksniff forgives people for wrongs they haven't committed. In his hands, forgiveness becomes a weapon to insult and degrade others. When his victims try to evade his forgiveness, Pecksniff's reply is that it cannot be done. This potential for abuse can also be seen in the actual practice of pardoning. For example, in his response to the Mexican government's 1994 pardon of the Chiapas rebels, Subcommander Marcos wrote, "For what do we have to ask pardon? For what are they going to pardon us? For not dying of hunger? For not keeping quiet about our misery? For not humbly accepting the enormous historical weight of contempt and abandonment? . . . Who has to ask for pardon and who can give it?" (*EZLN* 1994, 89–90). If one is pardoned or forgiven for wrongs that one didn't do, then the pardon becomes a way to elevate the pardoner at the expense of the pardoned. For Marcos, the government's pardon was an insult. To prevent this kind of abuse, both parties must agree on what is being forgiven. Arriving at this understanding is also a component of rectificatory justice. The arrival of a publicly verifiable account of the wrong or the debt is a necessary condition for understanding what is due. Other understandings of forgiveness,

16. As Alexander Boraine notes, "It is understandable, therefore, that general amnesty is looked upon by human rights organisations and human rights lawyers as a betrayal of those who suffered those violations and is something to be avoided at all costs" (Boraine 1999, 472).

obviously, do not require this condition, but in political forgiveness it helps prevent political forgiveness from becoming an insult.

Finally, in claiming that a shared account of what happened (who did what to whom, who owes what to whom) is a condition for political forgiveness, I also want to claim that this understanding must, in principle, be publicly verifiable. Political forgiveness requires more than an agreement between the victim and transgressor, or the creditor and the debtor. It requires that the account of the debt be based on publicly accessible evidence that can be contested and defended. The implication of this publicity requirement is that political forgiveness is never merely a relationship between a victim and a transgressor, or creditors and debtors. There must be a way publicly to corroborate or verify the story. This does not preclude political forgiveness if only the victim and transgressor were present when the injury was done or a debt created, nor does it necessarily demand living up to more rigorous requirements of legal evidence, although this would generally be true in the case of pardons. But in order for political forgiveness to be political, the transgressor must be publicly identified and the story publicly confirmable. The private confession of a transgressor to his victim is not, on this account, sufficient for political forgiveness.

Is a publicly verifiable account of what happened also necessary for rectificatory justice? The reasoning in support of this proposition is that such a condition helps prevent unequal power relationships between the parties from skewing the common understanding. Having victims or transgressors simply accept their common story as the baseline may actually be harmful if the story that is accepted advances the interest of one party at the expense of the other. In the case of a financial debt, precisely determining the amount that needs to be repaid prevents the kind of loan-sharking in which the amount that is owed is constantly moving. Similarly, it is conceivable that a kind of moral or emotional loan-sharking or blackmail could occur in which victims feel powerless to contest the story of the transgressor (or, perhaps, vice versa). For the parties to truly receive their due, the account of what is due must, in principle, be publicly verifiable.[17]

If we bundle these conditions together, we can say that political forgiveness and justice require that the truth be established and be publicly verifiable. Political forgiveness must travel fairly far along the same road

17. Political forgiveness, however, goes beyond the demands of justice insofar as the historical account must be shared by the parties. In contrast, justice could be done even though one party insisted on his innocence.

as justice. Justice, of course, can demand a great deal more than this, which raises the question of whether more is needed before political forgiveness can be justified. For example, shouldn't political forgiveness also require apologies, promises to change one's ways, or some minimal amount of restitution? Why set the threshold for political forgiveness with establishing a shared truth and not at some higher level? Why not require remorse, sorrow, or contrition on the part of the offender? Political forgiveness does not require that the public account be transformed into what Tavuchis has called an "apologizable" discourse in which the voice of sorrow comes through (Tavuchis 1991, 20, 36). There are three ways to respond to these questions and criticisms. The first is that the connection between political forgiveness and justice set out here is largely conceptual. It is possible to imagine a set of circumstances in which victims of wrongs believe that far more is necessary before they are willing to consider political forgiveness. It is not clear, however, whether those conditions can be generalized at a theoretical level. In claiming that some minimal threshold of justice must be met, this position leaves open how much higher that threshold can be (beyond what is set out above) in order for political forgiveness to be justified.

The second response is that the discussion of political forgiveness is meant to encompass both moral and financial debts. At this level of generality, many of the requirements for rectifying wrongs—apology, imprisonment, public memorials, lustration, criminal prosecution, restitution—have no place in responses to financial debts. If, then, one conceived of responses to wrongs as a subset of this more general theory, would the threshold for justice be raised? The answer to this question may be the response noted above: that a higher threshold may exist but cannot be generalized. The most that we may be able to say in this regard is that establishing who did what to whom, and who owes what, are necessary (albeit not sufficient) for political forgiveness.

Finally, political forgiveness does not require remorse or an authentic display of regret on the part of the offender before it takes place. In part, the justification for this exclusion turns once again on the generality of the theory; regret is not necessary for the forgiveness of financial debts. In addition, this exclusion is connected to a desire to try to theorize about forgiveness assuming an agency-based conception of politics, one that shies away from resting on particular sentiments. Within this theoretical framework, we do not need to look into the hearts of the offenders, and consequently what lies in their hearts should not be a precondition for forgiveness.

At a practical level, an analogous dispute arose over the requirements for the conditional amnesty granted in South Africa to facilitate the transition from an apartheid to a democratic state. One criticism of the South African Promotion of National Unity and Reconciliation Act was that it said nothing about applicants for amnesty having to express remorse for what they had done. Although the amnesty required that their crimes be fully disclosed, be political in nature, have occurred between 1960 and 1994, and satisfy the demands of proportionality, the application did not require that they feel sorry (Tutu 1999, 49–50). Tutu believes that such a condition could have been corrosive to the process:

> If the applicant was effusive in his protestations about being sorry and repentant to satisfy such a requirement for remorse, then he would have been condemned for being totally insincere and just laying it on thick to impress the Amnesty Committee panel. If, on the other hand, he was somewhat abrupt and merely formal, he would have been accused of being callous and uncaring and not really repentant. It would have been a "no-win" situation. As it happens, most applicants have in fact expressed at least remorse and asked for forgiveness from their victims. Whether their requests have stemmed from genuine contrition is obviously a moot point. (50)

The possibility that the genuineness of their contrition could be a moot political point reflects an extraordinarily restrained concept of politics.[18] However demanding this may be as a practical, political matter, it is consistent with the view of politics assumed here.

The Limits of Political Forgiveness

By appealing to the limits of justice, it is possible to discern theoretical space for political forgiveness. But in arguing that some level of justice remains a necessary condition for political forgiveness, the limits of forgiveness are revealed. The argument that political forgiveness is not unconditional implies that when the relevant conditions are not met, it cannot be justified. From one perspective, highlighting these limits further defines and distinguishes political forgiveness from other understandings of forgiveness. From another perspective, these limitations reveal what

18. It should also be noted that even in Tavuchis's analysis of apologies, he argues that the authenticity of collective or corporate apologies does not depend on a sincere expression of regret or remorse. What is important in these forms of apologies is placing what happened in the public record (Tavuchis 1991, 102). This way of understanding institutional apologies is more compatible with an agency-based conception of politics.

could be seen as the impoverished character of political forgiveness insofar as it fails to resolve the most horrendous wrongs of politics.

The first point regarding the connection between justice and forgiveness is that the idea of political forgiveness is deeply entwined with reason-giving. The argument that political forgiveness needs some minimal amount of rectificatory justice points to the importance of being able to give reasons for forgiving in politics. Unlike other conceptions in which forgiveness is seen as a gift, analogous to the grace of God,[19] political forgiveness is somewhat less mysterious. If it were such a mysterious gift, then political forgiveness would be an example of extraordinary generosity: transgressors or debtors could do nothing to "merit" forgiveness and victims and creditors would not need reasons to forgive.[20] In contrast, the linkage between justice and political forgiveness suggests that while generosity may be an element of political forgiveness, it should not overwhelm our sense of justice. Unless a just groundwork has been laid, political forgiveness is an inappropriate response to moral and financial debts.

In the absence of that groundwork, political forgiveness cannot find root. Most obviously, this means that in situations in which it is impossible to know who did what to whom, political forgiveness is ruled out. Not only the actors but also their actions may be forever lost. But if the understanding of who did what to whom must also be publicly shared, then the dead can neither forgive nor be forgiven. They cannot forgive, as chapter 4 shows, because that right belongs to the victim. They cannot be forgiven because they are unable to contest their guilt and responsibility. Forgiving the moral debt of the dead runs the risk of becoming an insult, assuming that we can wrong the dead.

Finally, it is important to consider whether wrongs exist that are so severe that they are absolutely unforgivable. We may call such acts evil. According to George Kateb, evil may be understood as "the obliteration of personhood and hence the deprivation of all the personal and political rights of one, few, some, or many" (Kateb 1992, 201). The problem that evil acts pose is that they fundamentally challenge the capacity of victims to receive their due. The nature of that challenge is simple: after the obliteration of one's personhood, what does justice mean? Those

19. Adams 1991, 288; Lewis 1980, 243; Minow 1998, 21; Morris 1988, 16; Yancey 1993, 26.
20. In other spheres of life, the notion that forgiving needs to be based on reasons may be viewed as wrong-headed and destructive. Forgiveness could very well be understood as an act of grace in our religious, familial, or private associations. Consequently, theorizing political forgiveness is not and cannot be a replacement for these other understandings.

who gave and executed the orders to torture, murder, and make disappear have, in a sense, gone beyond what can be restored or corrected. For the victims of evil, there is no recourse that could make them whole. Or, to put it another way, evil can be defined as that action in which victims push for justice, not because it rectifies the wrong, but because it is, at least, a response.[21] In the face of evil, justice is a second-best solution, where no best option exists. The enormity of evil acts and the impotence of justice would appear to rule out the possibility for a political forgiveness that spins in the orbit of justice.[22] It is from this perspective that Arendt observes: "Men are unable to forgive what they cannot punish and . . . they are unable to punish what has turned out to be unforgivable" (Arendt 1958, 241). Because the notion of justice barely responds to evil, political forgiveness may never appear on the scene. Perhaps evil is politically unforgivable. Those who have committed evil acts cannot expect that those whom they have directly victimized will put the past behind them and initiate a process of restoring respect and trust.

One criticism of this view that sees evil as unconditionally unforgivable is that it fails to distinguish actors from their actions. While certain deeds may be unforgivable, all actors possess the capacity for moral change. To hold that someone is unconditionally and absolutely unforgivable is to "fail to acknowledge the intellectual and moral capacities of persons" (Govier 1999, 70). By employing a secularized version of the Christian distinction between the sin and the sinner and respecting the moral worth of all individuals, no perpetrator is absolutely unforgivable. Evil, therefore, should not be understood as beyond the reach of political forgiveness.

A sharp distinction between doer and deed, however, is less applicable to a conception of political forgiveness in which what is forgiven is a moral or financial debt. Although one need not take the Nietzschean route and collapse doers and deeds, it seems more plausible to say that what is forgiven in political forgiveness is neither the deed nor the doer alone, but both. The debt is owed by an agent to an agent. Consequently,

---

21. On this analysis, doing justice to those who have committed evil is necessarily forward looking. (In contrast, corrective or rectificatory justice is backward looking.) We punish evildoers to dissuade evildoers in the future or for the symbolic purpose of acknowledging our horror for what is done. These claims may very well be true, but they do not save rectificatory justice from the challenge of evil.

22. This displacement holds for the relationship between direct victims and perpetrators of evil. It may not hold for those who are secondary or indirect victims of an evil act. This exception is important in considering whether governments may pardon those who commit evil acts (see chapter 5).

if the act was evil and appalling, it creates an enormous debt to the victim that is borne by the perpetrators. If the act is absolutely unforgivable, then the doer cannot be forgiven for that debt. That human beings possess the wonderful capacity for moral change does not necessarily mean that all their debts can be cleared.[23]

A second criticism of the view that evil acts are unforgivable is that this position demonstrates the difficulty of a conception of political forgiveness that is tied so closely to rectificatory justice. The problem here is with the conceptualization of political forgiveness itself—that it is uninspired and middling. Only by fully breaking out of the orbit of justice can the great traumatic events of history be overcome. Without moving beyond a cramped conception of political forgiveness, human beings will not be able to move beyond past evil acts and arrive at a higher state of peace and reconciliation.

This criticism carries whatever weight it does on the assumption that some larger notion of resolution, reconciliation, or unity is more compelling than rectificatory justice. For forgiveness to play a role within a scheme for universal reconciliation, it would have to be imbued with the ability to recover any past action, even the most heinous. As long as rectificatory justice, however, is seen as an important goal and the hope for an ultimate form of harmonization lies beyond the reach of politics, such recovery may be politically impossible. This debate, however, is connected to the meaning of reconciliation and the kind of reconciliation one can expect from politics in general and from political forgiveness in particular (see chapter 3).

A final critique of the view that evil acts are unforgivable is that this position is incompatible with the connection between justice and political forgiveness set out above. While it may be impossible to deliver fully what is due in the face of evil, that fact does not rule out the possibility of meeting the minimal conditions of justice. What is necessary for political forgiveness is that the parties come to a shared, public account of who did what to whom. Not all evil acts preclude this minimum from being

23. By joining the debt to the debtor in this manner, the relevant question may become not one of moral change but one of change in identity. If Abel is literally no longer the same person as he was when he did some evil act, then he is no longer in debt (assuming such a radical transformation is possible). The issue of identity becomes particularly relevant to the continuity of governments and their responsibility for moral wrongs. However, if such a transformation on the part of the offending state or individual does occur, then there is nothing to forgive because the state or individual that bore the debt no longer exists.

obtained. Once it has been obtained, then it would appear that political forgiveness is permissible.

This criticism is compelling and both supports the notion that evil can be politically forgivable and that on occasion it cannot be. Certain evil acts are of such a nature that the minimal conditions of justice cannot be met. If the victim is dead or has disappeared, then the act is unconditionally unforgivable. In this respect, however, situations in which victims are responding to evil acts may be no different from situations in which the minimal conditions of justice cannot be met. Once those conditions are met, then even perpetrators of evil may be forgiven. Nevertheless, in chapter 7, when discussing whether citizens should forgive governments of their wronging acts, I argue that citizens as citizens should not forgive such acts. This latter argument is not based on the character of evil but on the responsibilities of citizens and the dangers of seeing certain wrongful governmental actions as forgivable.

In conclusion, the relationship between rectificatory justice and forgiveness set out in this chapter is not quite as symmetric as it first appears. Political forgiveness is not simply the release of a just claim. Instead, political forgiveness requires a larger background in which a practice of creating debts and demanding repayment exists. One could conceive of a practice of rectificatory justice without a practice of forgiving, but not vice versa. In addition, the assumption that justice is an important value means that unless there are reasons for overriding it or in some way supplementing it, then political forgiveness may not be justified. The positive note in this analysis is that political forgiveness is not precluded by our theories of justice. Rectificatory justice is not complete in a number of ways, and there may be good reasons for overriding the demands of justice. The final point to emphasize about this relationship is that justice does remain an indispensable condition for political forgiveness. This point comes up again when we consider the role of political forgiveness in mediating the relationship between citizens, and between citizens and their government.

3

Political Forgiveness and Reconciliation

In order for Rwanda to turn its eyes toward the future, toward reconciliation, we have first to assume our responsibilities and acknowledge our mistakes. . . . In the name of my country, I pay tribute to the genocide victims, and in the name of my country, my people, I beg forgiveness.

—BELGIAN PRIME MINISTER Guy Verhofstadt's apology for his country's failures during Rwanda's 1994 genocide (*Los Angeles Times*, April 8, 2000)

WHAT ARE the purposes of political forgiveness? As we saw in chapter 1, the primary purpose or illocutionary point is to release debtors and offenders from their debts. In accomplishing this feat, political forgiveness is also connected to reconciliation. To understand this connection we need to know something about the character of reconciliation and whether the notion of political forgiveness is linked to a utopian, objectionable conception of reconciliation. After briefly considering various meanings of this term, I describe how political forgiveness advances both a reconciliatory process and a particular state of reconciliation. This distinction between process and state provides a useful way to consider the possibility and limitations of political forgiveness as a means for restoring a valued political relationship. In addition, these effects are consonant with an understanding of politics that is pluralistic and agency-based.

Reconciliation

A map of the political uses of the concept of reconciliation would quickly reveal a diverse set of meanings that encompasses a range of aspirations and values. In its more soaring uses, reconciliation suggests that antagonists have been brought into a grander harmony or unity: those who were once enemies are now friends, those who were divided are reunited, and that which was cacophonous is now harmonious. At the other extreme, reconciliation can be used to express acquiescence or submission. One may be reconciled to a political settlement, not because it expresses a greater sense of unity and harmony but because one has no other choice. Reconciliation as submission need not be a good thing, especially when it is akin to surrender or resignation. Somewhere between these uses is a notion of political reconciliation that refers to bringing conflicting parties into a state of peace. They may not be friends, they may not be part of a larger harmonious political system, but they can be said to be reconciled.[1] In such cases, as perhaps suggested by Guy Verhofstadt's apology set out above, national reconciliation may mean no more than that the civil strife has ended, the wrath of the parties has subsided, and a modus vivendi has been established. Finally, there is a sense in which political reconciliation can blend into the notion of correcting a set of injustices: "Reconciliation, in this its rich and meaningful sense, is thus a real closing of the ledger book of the past" (Asmal et al. 1997, 47). Parties may be reconciled when discrepancies or inequalities have been balanced out. Here, the reconciliation of parties has the flavor of settling accounts.[2]

In addition, various qualifications of and conditions for political reconciliation could be mapped out. Cheap, easy, or spurious forms of reconcili-

1. Ralph Martin notes that "at its simplest the verb [to reconcile] denotes 'the action by which peace is made between personal enemies,' as Moses brought together his estranged compatriots (Acts 7:26: the verb here is *synallassein*). It is the work of a mediator whose office is 'to make hostility cease, to lead to peace' " (Martin 1981, 104–5).

2. For alternative, related maps of political reconciliation, see Asmal et al. (1997, 46–47), and Pankhurst (1999, 240). David Crocker sets out three meanings of political reconciliation: (1) "simple coexistence"; (2) "liberal social solidarity"; (3) "forgiveness, mercy (rather than justice), a shared comprehensive vision, mutual healing, or harmony" (Crocker 1999, 60). In contrast, the vision of political forgiveness offered here is more compatible with "liberal social solidarity" than with a thicker notion of healing and harmony. Under Crocker's second conception of reconciliation, "Former enemies may continue to disagree and even to be adversaries, they must not only live together nonviolently but also respect each other as fellow citizens" (60). If this second conception is understood as a state of reconciliation, then political forgiveness can be understood as initiating a process of reconciliation that may lead to its achievement.

ation could be distinguished from actual, true, real forms of reconciliation. Making these kinds of distinctions may give rise to other claims regarding the processes or conditions needed to avoid the former and achieve the latter forms of reconciliation. A description of the concept of political reconciliation would inevitably consider the relationship between reconciliation and other conditions and concepts.

Despite its rich practical, political pedigree, however, the concept of reconciliation is largely ignored in political philosophy. As far as I can tell, the one exception to this can be found in the work of Hegel, for whom reconciliation is essential. Michael Hardimon notes that "Hegel was the first modern thinker explicitly to claim that reconciliation is the proper aim of political philosophy" (Hardimon 1994, 6). Hegel's conception of reconciliation entails overcoming one's alienation and accepting and embracing the world as one's home. It implies that although conflict may still be present, those conflicts exist within a set of basic social structures that are fundamentally acceptable.[3] Once we have established a social world in which humans can actualize themselves as individuals and as members of a community, then reconciliation is at hand. For Hegel, such actualization was indeed at hand in modern politics.

But the concept of reconciliation may also provide a lens for viewing other political thinkers. To the extent that Platonic and Christian thinkers placed a high value on notions of unity and harmony, their projects could be seen as driven by a goal of reconciliation. To the extent that Hobbes saw civil association as the mechanism to avoid a state of war and establish peace, his project was also a project of reconciliation. Finally, to the extent that Locke, Rousseau, Kant, and Rawls have focused on the basic acceptability of political institutions, their projects were also projects of reconciliation (Hardimon 1994, 128–29).[4] Obviously, these traditions and thinkers could be lumped under the concept of reconciliation only if it was understood that they were employing distinctive understandings of that concept.

3. The notion that Hegel's conception of reconciliation does not mean the end of conflict is also supported by J. G. Finlayson: "With regard to Hegel's concept of reconciliation it is a mistake to see it as a state of harmony and absence of conflict. . . . Reconciliation is not a harmonious redemption of suffering" (Finlayson 1999, 502–3; see also Hardimon 1994, 92–93).

4. In *The Law of Peoples*, John Rawls comments, "Political philosophy is realistically utopian when it extends what are ordinarily thought to be the limits of practicable political possibility and, in so doing, reconciles us to our political social condition" (Rawls 1999, 11). Later in the book, Rawls notes that there are important limits to reconciliation. Fundamentalists, presumably, "could not be reconciled to a social world" that Rawls has described (126). These uses of reconciliation seem to match Hegel's understanding as emphasized by Hardimon.

Reconciliation as Process and as State

It is possible, however, not only to distinguish between kinds of reconciliation but also between reconciliation as a process and reconciliation as a state. As Hardimon notes, "The process may be variously described as a process of overcoming conflict, division, enmity, alienation, or estrangement; the result, as the restoration of harmony, unity, peace, friendship, or love" (Hardimon 1994, 85). This general distinction between process and state opens the possibility of talking about a process of reconciliation without being committed to a claim that a state of reconciliation has been or even can be ultimately reached. By seeking to diminish conflict or establish trust-building measures, adversaries may be involved in the activity of reconciliation. This activity can be intelligibly understood even though they have not reached a grander reconciliatory state. Similarly, it may be possible to be in a state of reconciliation without having to talk about a process. This separation would be plausible if the state of reconciliation was a state of resignation or surrender to one's circumstances. While it is certainly possible to talk about becoming reconciled (resigned) to one's situation, it doesn't seem as though a reconciliatory process is necessary in order to reach a state of resignation, although it could be.

The importance of this distinction between process and state for understanding the relationship between political forgiveness and reconciliation is the following: political forgiveness can evoke certain reconciliatory effects. On the one hand, it can be part of a process of reconciliation that involves the restoration of trust and civility. As part of the process, political forgiveness neither guarantees nor secures a resulting state of reconciliation in which civic friendship is created or restored.[5] On the other hand, because of its illocutionary point, political forgiveness is part and parcel of a state of reconciliation. Political forgiveness

5. It may seem that reconciliation is purely a matter of restoration and not creation. To Hardimon, for example, "The concept of reconciliation contains within it something like a story: two parties begin as friends, become estranged, and become friends again. The basic pattern is thus one of unity, division, and reunification" (Hardimon 1994, 85). Similarly, in her account of the South African Truth and Reconciliation Commission, Antjie Krog claims that in South Africa, "There is nothing to go back to, no previous state or relationship one would wish to restore. In these stark circumstances, 'reconciliation' does not even seem like the right word, but rather 'conciliation' " (Krog 1999, 143). In contrast, I am using reconciliation to cover the idea of conciliation both because ordinary usage permits this coverage (e.g., a prior friendly relationship is not necessary for warring parties to be reconciled) and because the first definition of conciliation is "the action of bringing into harmony, harmonizing, reconcilement" (*Oxford English Dictionary*).

ultimately entails a settlement with the past such that its effects should no longer reverberate into the future. This state of reconciliation, of course, is not a grand vision of harmony, unity, and friendship, but a state in which it becomes possible to start again.

It is easy to see that some such distinction between process and state can be found in ordinary applications of the concept of reconciliation. Desmond Tutu (who firmly believes in an ultimate state of reconciliation) noted that South Africa's Truth and Reconciliation Commission "was expected to promote national unity and reconciliation. It is crucial to underscore that it was meant to *promote* not to *achieve* those worthwhile objectives" (Tutu 1999, 165). Similarly, in the discussion of the role of reconciliation in German foreign policy, Lily Gardner Feldman sees reconciliation as an "open-ended process." In addition, "This concept does not infuse peace with a vision of harmony and tension-free coexistence, but rather integrates differences. Productive contention in a shared and cooperative framework for identifying and softening (but not eliminating) divergence is a more realistic goal than perfect peace" (Feldman 1999, 336–37). The difference between a reconciliatory process and a state of reconciliation is useful for sorting out the purposes of political forgiveness.

Forgiveness and the Process of Reconciliation

As an illocutionary act, political forgiveness has certain effects. From chapter 1 we know that the central effect, or what could be called the illocutionary point of forgiveness, is to release debtors and transgressors from their debts. An additional effect is its ability to invite the generation or restoration of trust in the debtor or transgressor.[6] When a victim clears a moral debt with her transgressor, it opens the door to restoring

6. In Stanley Hauerwas's essay on constancy and Trollope, ordinary forgiveness plays an important role in acknowledging the past while sustaining one's relationship: "It is through forgiveness that a gentleman sustains the standard necessary to remain constant in his loyalty to others, and yet at the same time allows him not to remain indifferent to conduct that is clearly immoral" (Hauerwas 1983, 42–43). Aurel Kolnai sees forgiving as an expression of trust in the world: "It is closely tied up with the demotion of our concern about Certitude and Safety in favor of a boldly, venturesomely aspiring and active pursuit of Value" (Kolnai 1977, 223). For other views regarding the restorative character of forgiveness, see Adams (1991, 299), Duquoc (1986, 40–41), Golding (1984–85, 134), Lang (1994, 115), Murphy (1988b, 6), Shriver (1995, 35), and Snow (1993, 78). Although Norvin Richards argues that forgiveness does not necessarily reestablish a relationship as, for example, when one accepts an apology from a stranger (Richards 1988, 79), one could still be seen as trying to restore a relationship of civility, even in this example.

that party's civic position. In this case, the process of reconciliation involves establishing respect or recovering a lost sense of financial trustworthiness. This invitation makes political forgiveness part of the process of reconciliation, even if an ultimate state of reconciliation is never obtained.[7]

The invitation issued by an act of political forgiveness to restore the transgressor or debtor has several important characteristics. The first is that this invitation has effects beyond the immediate parties involved. For it is issued to those for whom knowing the status of an individual as a debtor or as a wrongdoer has made a difference, for the worse, in their treatment of that debtor or wrongdoer. Because the victim or creditor has forgiven the transgressor or debtor, others are invited to reconsider the standing of that individual in their dealings with him or her. For example, when an executive fully pardons a criminal this means not only that the government will no longer hold that crime against the offender but also that the rest of us should consider doing the same, at least in our public actions. The act of forgiveness invites seeing the transgressor as an equal.[8] In financial matters, the extension of this invitation means that other creditors may become willing to extend credit because the debtor is no longer under a crushing debt. Nevertheless, this invitation may be declined (or perhaps even never received). For this reason, the effect of political forgiveness on the process of reconciliation is uncertain and contingent upon the response of others. As a political matter, however, the invitation is part of a process of restoring or creating a sense of civic friendship. Strictly speaking, the failure to obtain such a state of reconciliation does not mean that political forgiveness has itself failed. The debt is relieved even though the process of reconciliation may never be completed.

Is political forgiveness a necessary component to the process of political reconciliation? Some, especially those who subscribe to a conception of restorative justice, argue that forgiveness is an important if not the most significant component to this process. If Tutu is right that there is "no future without forgiveness," then forgiveness would be utterly

7. To use Austin's language, the effect of restoring the transgressor can be seen as a perlocutionary sequel of the act of forgiveness. Unlike a response or a sequel that is conventional, the perlocutionary effects of an illocutionary act need not be conventional. That is, these effects are not regular or solely the result of the act of forgiveness (Austin 1962, 117–18).

8. Nicholas Tavuchis claims that forgiveness entails the "recertification of bona fide membership and unquestioned inclusion within the moral order" (Tavuchis 1991, 27). Although he frames the connection too tightly for this conception of forgiveness, it may be useful to think of political forgiveness as initiating a process in which this "recertification" takes place.

essential. But even from this perspective, it is unlikely that forgiveness is sufficient. Other kinds of acts must usually accompany forgiveness: apologies, remorse, reparations, compensation, and so on. However necessary for the process of political reconciliation it may be, no one appears to believe that it is enough to forgive. As we saw in chapter 2, the explanation for this state of affairs with regard to political forgiveness is that meeting some level of justice is a necessary condition for engaging in political forgiveness.

If political forgiveness is not sufficient for the process of reconciliation, is it necessary? Unfortunately, to the extent that this is an empirical/predictive question regarding how the process of political reconciliation has occurred or must happen, I am not qualified to make a determination. In a series of case studies, Donald Shriver claims that forgiveness has indeed been a key component of the process of renewing political relationships. (Shriver reserves the notion of reconciliation for the endpoint of this process [Shriver 1995, 8–9].) Nevertheless, even Shriver's stories of reconciliation rarely note a public conveyance of forgiveness from one party to the other. Rather, it is just as plausible to think that the process of reconciliation—the restoration or creation of civic friendship—may be the result of increased cultural, economic, and social integration.

But perhaps an argument could be made that a sentiment-based conception of forgiveness is a necessary component to reconciliation. If, for example, one believed that the process of political reconciliation required the diminution and ultimate disappearance of anger and resentment on the part of the injured party, then a version of forgiveness promising just that kind of self-enactment could be essential. Whether forgiveness is in fact essential would rest on the claim that it is the only path to removing anger and resentment. Such a claim is highly unlikely, however. Victims are able to "get over" their anger not only by forgiving but also through forgetting. Moreover, if the removal of resentment and anger were necessary elements of reconciliation, then it is also unlikely that political forgiveness as understood here would be essential.

Although it may neither be necessary nor sufficient for initiating a process of reconciliation, political forgiveness can be a way to start that process. A willingness to engage in a process of reconciliation, however, may require more than relieving one's transgressors of their debts. At the very least, the parties must be committed to sustaining an ongoing political or financial relationship.

Political Forgiveness and the State of Reconciliation

Political forgiveness is also linked to a particular state of reconciliation. The relevant state here is one that lies somewhere between submission or surrender and a settling of accounts. What is surrendered through the act of political forgiveness is the ability to use past wrongs or debts to make future claims. Victims and transgressors, creditors and debtors, are reconciled through forgiveness in the sense that past wrongs and debts remain in the past. In this state of reconciliation, future wrongs and debts are always possible, but the past has been settled and overcome. Political forgiveness is, in part, a promise not to use the past against the future.

The creation of the expectation that the past will not haunt the future follows from the illocutionary character of political forgiveness. By releasing debtors and transgressors from their debts, any claim based on those debts has been rendered null and void. In effect, not only is the past settled but also the expectation is created that the settlement will be durable. For a creditor to forgive a debt and then demand payment is no different from demanding what isn't due—because payment is no longer due to the creditor. Similarly, a victim who has forgiven a transgressor and then turns around and presses for justice takes with one hand what is given by the other.[9] Nevertheless, as with all promise making, it is always possible for someone who has forgiven to fail to live up to this expectation. In other words, the state of reconciliation could be disturbed, but only if one fails to understand or live up to one's act of political forgiveness. When the illocutionary point of political forgiveness is obtained, however, it creates a stable state of reconciliation with the past.

Obviously, forgiveness is not the only way to settle the past. Aside from forgiving what is due, one could receive one's due. Indeed, a primary effect of rectificatory justice is to ensure that the past does not haunt the present or the future. What is done is done, and if the parties have received their due, then they've been reconciled with the past. In light of this conception of a state of reconciliation, completely fulfilling the demands of justice should also settle all accounts. Consequently, political forgiveness could be understood as a different path to the same reconciliatory state.

9. This would seem to suggest that victims of crime who forgave their offenders should not press for punishment or compensation. In an important way, this is correct; if, however, we assume (as in chapter 5) that not only individual victims are wronged by crime but also the larger political association, then a decision on the part of the individual victim to forgive need not affect the decision of the larger association to prosecute the matter. But as a practical matter, if the victim refuses to cooperate, that may make prosecution impossible.

The claim that political forgiveness or justice is a way to put the past behind us may be seen as a particularly rosy, if not Pollyannaish position. It could be argued that even though offenders and debtors have been forgiven, it is still possible to hold the debt against them. Victims or creditors can refuse to trust or respect their debtors and decline to associate with them, even though they have forgiven their debts. Consequently, forgiveness doesn't necessarily bring closure to the past. In response, the reconciliatory state that concerns us here is very specific. It has to do with releasing debtors and offenders from a set of specific debts. The standing of those debts is now such that they cannot serve as the basis for legitimate, public claims in the future. This is different from making a claim that political forgiveness would yield a state of greater harmony and friendship. As I have suggested above, political forgiveness can also be seen as part of a larger process of reconciliation, but this process is very contingent. The invitation to begin to restore trust and respect is issued through an act of forgiveness but may be left unopened.

Could political forgiveness be sufficient for achieving the more limited state of reconciliation? Sufficiency here would mean that the reconciliatory state could be obtained simply by having the victim or creditor release the debtor. Because some minimal threshold of justice must be met in order for political forgiveness to reconcile the past, political forgiveness cannot be sufficient for obtaining a state of reconciliation. One implication from the argument in chapter 2 is that there are instances in which it may be impossible to put the past to rest (in the sense of precluding a future legitimate claim) either through justice or forgiveness.

Political forgiveness is not sufficient for reconciliation. From the discussion above, we also know that it is not necessary for reconciliation because we can arrive at the same end by fully meeting the demands of justice. It could be argued, however, that in situations in which justice can be partially but not fully met, political forgiveness is necessary for reaching closure with the past. Perhaps in cases such as South Africa, to the extent that the Truth and Reconciliation Commission has revealed a shared, public account of who did what to whom, and where some attempt is going to be made for restitution, important elements of justice have been achieved. However, given the amount of restitution, the nature of the crimes, and the absence of punishment, full justice will not be attained. In this kind of a case, could political forgiveness be seen as necessary for reconciliation? Could political forgiveness be the only way to resolve the irresolvable claims of the past where some minimal level of justice can be met?

One response is that reconciliation could just as easily be accomplished through ignoring or forgetting the past. Obviously, in order for forgetting to be plausible, the victims or creditors need to be willing to walk away from what happened. If only the offender or debtor sought to forget the whole affair, it is unlikely that the victim or creditor would be so inclined. However, if victims or creditors do not push their claims and are willing to forget their due, then isn't that good enough for reconciliation, at least when some minimal level of justice has been obtained?

Fairly significant impediments prevent forgetting from becoming a virtue in a political context. One deep problem is whether individuals can choose to forget. For governments, official forgetting takes the form of granting a blanket or unconditional amnesty. At the individual level, however, it gives rise to the problem of whether forgetting is wholly involuntary. If we do not choose to forget, then it makes little sense to suggest it as an option. But the view of forgetting as involuntary may not be attentive to the complexities of this activity. Without wading into the intricacies of philosophical psychology, we can ask whether forgetting is an appropriate response—assuming that such a choice is possible.

Even if victims or creditors can choose to forget, and it is clear that they are willing to do so, or they simply decide to drop the matter, this is not the same as making a promise to keep the past in the past. What has been forgotten or dropped can always be recalled or picked up. Unless one argues that wrongs and financial debts have a temporal limitation or that time heals all wounds, forgotten past claims are merely dormant, and dormancy is not the same as reconciliation. If time itself does not corrode or depreciate the claims of victims, then closure need not come with the simple passage of time. Individuals who continue to benefit from the effects of the past may have no incentive to reflect on or even raise that past. They may wonder why "those people" just can't get over it. But to the extent that "getting over it" requires either having one's just claims addressed or releasing debtors of those claims, it also requires either justice or forgiveness.[10] And if justice is incomplete, political forgiveness may be the only path to this particular reconciliatory state.

10. One needs to be careful about what can be inferred from the fact that victims have not pressed their claims. For a decision on the part of victims not to voice claims may be the result of a belief that justice would not be forthcoming if they did so. Alternatively, such a decision may be based on fear of reprisal, if the offenders still hold power. What may look like forgetting may be symptomatic of a deeper injustice in which the voice of the victim is effectively silenced.

Amnesty and Reconciliation

The disjunction between forgetting and a state of reconciliation raises the important question of whether amnesty is compatible with reconciliation. As an authoritative form of forgetting, amnesty means that the authorities don't want to know who did what to whom. As Kathleen Moore notes, an amnesty is a declaration that one "forget about the whole thing" (Moore 1989, 5), and as J. J. Moore claims, amnesty "wipes out all legal recollection" of the offense (Moore 1991, 734). Strictly speaking, an amnesty implies the absence of investigations, prosecutions, or trials. The central conceptual difference between amnesty and political forgiveness is that in a grant of amnesty there need be no truth telling, no shared account of who did what to whom.

While many amnesties are granted in the name of national reconciliation and in the belief that it is important to "get over" the past, they can take on either an unconditional or a conditional form. In their unconditional form, the state officially forgets whatever was done and may never even attempt to discern who did what to whom. In its conditional form, amnesty may be granted only after offenders come forward and admit to doing wrong or provide some form of restitution. To the extent that a conditional amnesty, such as what was offered in South Africa, requires that a minimal level of justice be met and a public accounting of who did what to whom, it looks more like what I have called political forgiveness. (This use of the notion of political forgiveness is considered in greater detail in the chapter 5 discussion of pardoning.) The closer analogy to forgetting, then, is an unconditional amnesty. Can an official, unconditional form of forgetting generate a state of reconciliation, in the limited sense I have mentioned?

As a practical matter, governments may find amnesty an extraordinarily attractive alternative. Instead of trying to discover who did what to whom, governments may find it more convenient to try to forget about the past. Such pressures are particularly severe if a government is being torn apart by civil strife or is somehow implicated in wrongdoing in its response to rebellion and wants to move onto more stable ground (see Huntington 1995, 69; Huyse 1995; Pion-Berlin 1995). In recent history, such nations as Brazil, Guatemala, El Salvador, Nicaragua, Spain, Uruguay, Chile, and Argentina (briefly) have all at one time taken the path of official forgetting.[11] In adopting this path, these governments

11. Albon 1995, 44–45; Benomar 1995, 33, 37; Moore 1991; Neier 1995, 177; Zalaquett 1995, 22, 25.

saw themselves caught in a realm of necessity. As Aryeh Neier notes, "A painful dilemma arises when the question of accountability poses the risk of overthrowing a civilian government. Permitting the armed forces to make themselves immune to prosecution for dreadful crimes seems intolerable; yet it also seems irrational to insist that an elected civilian government should commit suicide by provoking its armed forces" (Neier 1995, 179). In granting amnesty, the regime is betting that the gain achieved by not prosecuting or investigating wrongdoing will outweigh the loss of respect for and outrage against the government that may be felt by the victims, their families, and friends. To save the regime, it is necessary to sacrifice not only the core value of rectificatory justice but also the memory of those who had already been sacrificed by the previous regime or by the government's opponents. This tragic choice precludes the pursuit of justice as well as political forgiveness. Ultimately, the wager is that peace and stability do not require telling the truth about the past or any movement toward justice.[12]

Even if the wager is successful and there is a modicum of stability, is this a state of reconciliation? If we assume that all crimes have a public and a private character, then an amnesty effectively means that the state, as a wounded party, will not prosecute or investigate possible wrongs to itself. From the perspective of the government, those past actions no longer matter. And, if it truly is an amnesty, then the government is, in effect, promising that it will not use whatever was done in the past as a way to make claims against a set of alleged offenders—that door has now been closed. For the state to grant an amnesty and then, sometime

12. Now, it may be argued that no dilemma exists here. For no new regime is so unstable that it cannot make some minimal gestures at pursuing justice through truth. Such a position, it could be claimed, is as overblown as most appeals to national security. For example, in her study of truth commissions, Patricia B. Hayner notes that "no truth commission to date has caused a situation to become worse" (Hayner 1995, 230). Martha Minow goes even further in arguing that "amnesty is cowardice if it grows out of fear of the continuing power of the wrongdoers, or even of the costs of naming the wrongs" (Minow 1998, 137). It should also be noted that the decision not to prosecute former officials need not be based on fear. Prosecutors in the new government, assuming statutes of limitations have not been exceeded, have to make the same kinds of decisions that are made over any other criminal case regarding the reliability of the evidence and the availability of witnesses. Just as in other criminal proceedings, the decision not to prosecute need not be a failure on the part of the state to respond to wrongs but rather a matter of living up to the demands of procedural justice. The point, however, is that without any authoritative proceedings determining who did what to whom, the possibility for the state to exercise its power legitimately to pardon does not arise. The state cannot, as a conceptual matter, officially forgive a wrong that has not been acknowledged by the relevant parties (see chapter 5).

in the future, decide to prosecute that activity or revoke that amnesty would indicate a failure on the part of state actors to live up to their commitments. Amnesties appear to be official acts of forgetting that do reconcile the state, as a victim, to the past.

Three problems arise, however, with the above argument linking amnesty to a state of reconciliation. The first is that as a promise not to pursue the alleged criminals, an amnesty is usually made only by the party with the authority to investigate and prosecute such matters. Such a promise may make a great deal of sense if, in fact, the state is an injured party. If the state, however, is not the victim but the victimizer, then the official desire to forget the whole thing can look like the government's attempt to cover up its role in whatever wrongful events occurred. As with the case of forgiving without meeting the minimal conditions for justice, amnesty runs the risk of being an evasion of responsibility.

A second problem associating unconditional amnesty with reconciliation is that because a crime wrongs not only the state but also actual human beings, an official act of amnesty that indemnifies the offender from both public prosecution and (potentially from) private suit would not reconcile the individual victims to the past. They may not know how their sons or daughters were murdered or where their husbands or wives are buried, or who was responsible for their torture. Even if the government forgets, even if the government precludes victims from other legal recourse, individual victims are not compelled to forget. They may use their knowledge of the offenders' wrong to justify a refusal to associate with or trust them. But couldn't a government compel private reconciliation—holding victims accountable for their refusal to trust or associate with transgressors? Although unjustly stifled, the moral claim of the victims upon the transgressors remains.

The third problem is that the past may not be completely reconciled even at the official level. Assuming that one purpose of government is to protect the civil interests of the citizenry, including the rights of innocent parties, then the granting of an unconditional amnesty wrongs the victims. By precluding an investigation into what happened and who was responsible, an amnesty denies a minimal level of justice to the victims. If the amnesty extends to a prohibition against punishment or civil action, then it fails to protect the basic interests of innocent parties to receive their due. Vis-à-vis the offender, an amnesty could settle and reconcile the past. Vis-à-vis the individual victim (as opposed to the state), the amnesty creates a new wrong in which that past and how the state has dealt with it becomes a central concern of the victims. In closing one rift with the offenders, the state opens another with the victims and, in its official capacity, disrupts its reconciliation with the past. Given my argument regarding the inadequacies of forgetting, it would seem that whatever practical calculations a government performed, amnesty is a path to reconciliation only when the participants already have a pretty good sense of who did what to whom. If these conditions are met, however, then what is called amnesty looks much like a form of political forgiveness.

Reconciliation and the Duty to Forgive

Political forgiveness is a path to a state of political reconciliation, perhaps the only path available to ensure that past claims do not continue to press against the future. As such, it provides a way to start anew. In addition, political forgiveness can be understood as part of the process of reconciliation in which victims and transgressors, debtors and creditors, can begin to trust and work with one another. Assuming the importance of these understandings of reconciliation to establishing a just or nearly just system of governance, could it ever be the case that victims or creditors have a duty to forgive?

If such a duty exists, it would be qualified by the conditions set out in chapter 2, namely that until the minimal demands of justice are met, one should not engage in political forgiveness. But assume those conditions are met. If there is no other way to advance the process of reconciliation or achieve a reconciliatory state other than through political forgiveness, and if reconciliation is understood as a highly valued state or process, could a duty exist to forgive? To some degree, the question cannot be answered without knowing more about the relationship between the parties that one is seeking to restore, that is, more must be known about why a particular political relationship is so important. If one believes that the relationship is not worthy of consideration, then clearly no duty to forgive could exist. It may be possible that in a given instance of wrongdoing by an individual or institution, the minimal conditions of justice may have been met, but the relationship to the individual or to the institution is not worthy of creating or restoring: perhaps the relationship is or would be fundamentally unjust.[13] Assuming, however, that the relationship is worthy of respect, could a duty exist?

---

13. Whether one should engage in political forgiveness at all in such situations is considered in chapters 7 and 8.

One way to answer this question is to consider whether such a duty would be perfect or imperfect. Although a powerful case can be made against a perfect duty, the notion of an imperfect duty to forgive proves important in considering the relationship between citizens, and between citizens and a nearly just government (see chapters 7 and 8).

Forgiveness Cannot Be What Is Due

If political forgiveness were understood as a perfect duty, then offenders and debtors would have a right to forgiveness. Such a duty, however, would be incoherent. The source of the incoherence is that victims or creditors, in effect, would be doing wrong when they failed to forgive either moral or financial debts. To see the problem, consider first a situation in which someone has been wronged by another agent. Given a perfect duty to forgive, the victim should forgive the wrongdoer, and the victim does wrong if she does not do so. The second step of the argument is to assume that the wrongdoer has a right to be forgiven. In effect, what is due to the offender is forgiveness. The third step is merely a reminder that forgiveness is releasing one from what is owed and that there is a duty to release people from what is owed. The fourth step is that the wrongdoer can be said to have an obligation to release the victim of the duty to forgive him. In other words, what is owed to the victim is that the wrongdoer should release the victim of her duty to forgive the transgressor. The fifth step is that if, once again, there is a duty to forgive what is owed, then the victim should release the transgressor of the duty to release the victim of her duty to forgive him. A system in which it is wrong not to forgive what is owed has the potential to create an infinite regress. The basic difficulty stems from the assumption that political forgiveness is releasing what is due, and justice is receiving what is due. Under a perfect duty to forgive, *receiving what is due* becomes forgiveness, hence the incoherence.

An incoherence also attends a public duty to forgive when talking about financial matters. The expectation would be that debtors have a right against their creditors to be forgiven. The effect of this expectation is that there is little difference between giving a loan and giving a gift. Those who receive loans will expect that what is due to them will be forgiven. At this point, the argument can go in the same direction as above. If debtors are owed the forgiveness of their debts and people should be released of their debts, then they (the debtors) should release their creditors from the obligation to forgive the debt. (In effect, the creditor should be able to demand payment.) However, if creditors are owed this release from their duty to forgive, then the creditors should release the debtors of this obligation to release the creditors. And so on. An alternative account of the incoherence with the forgiveness of financial matters is that if loans become de facto gifts, then there may be little incentive for creditors to extend any credit (aside from those who want to give gifts). With little incentive to extend credit, then, the whole notion of loaning money makes little sense. The practice of loaning money gets absorbed into gift giving.

Assuming that forgiveness entails releasing what is due, the only way to avoid these problems is to make sure that forgiveness cannot be seen as something that is due.[14] Transgressors and debtors cannot have a right to be forgiven. It cannot be something owed to them as a perfect duty. An alternative possibility is for forgiving to be understood as an imperfect duty—something that should be done but does not need to be done on every occasion. From this perspective, asking and receiving one's due is not to commit a wrong, and no one has a right to be forgiven. The analogous situation would be one in which there is an imperfect duty to give to charity. On this view, one should be charitable, but no one has a right to charity. Consequently, although one could not be criticized for failing to give to charity in a particular situation, a person who never gave to charity would be subject to moral disapprobation. Similarly, victims would have discretion over when to forgive politically. Victims who never engaged in political forgiveness, assuming that the minimal demands of justice were met and that the relationship was worthy of being restored, could be subject to moral criticism. The actual defense of this imperfect duty, however, would require a fuller account of the importance of the political relationship in question.

One could also conceive of the duty to forgive financial debts as an imperfect obligation. Such a conception would depend on the existence of relationships in which the demand to be paid to the penny on

14. There is an additional risk to seeing political forgiveness as a perfect obligation. Seeing political forgiveness in this manner would empower others to judge whether that obligation was being fulfilled. In effect, it would mean that victims could suffer not only the original wrong but also the disapprobation and pressures of those who feel that they should forgive the transgressor. Potentially, Japanese Americans, African Americans, or victims of radiation experiments could be blamed for not forgiving soon enough. The danger is that such pressure could either generate a whiplash in the form of an unending demand for justice or a short circuit in the form of forgiving too early. Judging the appropriate moment for political forgiveness may best be left in the hands of the victim.

every occasion was seen as petty or illiberal. It is, however, easier to conceive of such relationships (e.g., personal friendships, familial connections) existing in the private than in the public sphere, although this may simply be a bias of living in a commercial culture where the demand of being paid to the penny is not surprising. An alternative approach is to narrow the scope of the obligation to forgive. Narrowing the scope could entail, for example, establishing a duty to forgive financial debts only when the debt has become crushing. A crushing debt, in turn, could be understood as one in which the debt is so large that the debtor cannot give what is due without causing exorbitant hardship. Within this narrower scope may be situations in which a creditor does have a perfect duty to forgive.[15] But what makes the case of a crushing debt difficult to sort out is that a debtor may be in debt to a number of creditors. The existence of multiple debts makes the responsibilities of the creditors more difficult to discern because any single loan made to the debtor may itself not be crushing. These problems come up again in chapter 4, in the exploration of who has authority to forgive. There, I argue that the problem of how to respond to crushing debts held by multiple parties may more fruitfully be seen through the rubric of losing the right to forgive to a third party as opposed to possessing a duty to forgive.

If there exists a broad duty to engage in political forgiveness, it cannot be a perfect obligation. In addition, such a duty is conditioned both by the general requirements for political forgiveness (i.e., meeting the minimal demands of justice) and by the value attributed to reconciling the parties. In any case, reconciliation can be understood as one of the purposes of political forgiveness. When the minimal conditions for justice have been met, political forgiveness can achieve a state of reconciliation. Indeed, in situations in which justice cannot be fully met, it may be the only way to achieve reconciliation. In these instances, political forgiveness can supplement justice in securing reconciliation. I have also argued, however, that political forgiveness can be seen as an element in the process of reconciliation. In that process, political forgiveness yields an invitation to restore the place of the transgressor or debtor. Political forgiveness, however, cannot guarantee that this invitation will actually initiate a process of reconciliation or that such a process will come to a successful conclusion. Nevertheless, political forgiveness can play an

15. These circumstances include an "impossible" debt held by a single creditor that can be authoritatively certified (see chapter 4).

important role in opening the future and settling the past. In light of these general comments regarding the meaning of political forgiveness and its relationship to the concepts of justice and reconciliation, we turn to the problem of who or what has authority to forgive and under what conditions that authority may be lost or transferred to another.

4

The Authority to Forgive

And do not forgive truly it is not in your power
to forgive in the name of those betrayed at dawn.

—ZBIGNIEW HERBERT, "The Envoy of Mr. Cogito"

I HAVE postulated that political forgiveness requires, among other things, (1) a relationship between at least two parties in which (2) one party owes a debt to another.[1] Although we know that "uptake" and securing an illocutionary effect require more than one party for political forgiveness to be an illocutionary act, we need to consider who has the standing to forgive and who can be forgiven. The problem of who can be forgiven appears unproblematic: in political forgiveness, the party to be forgiven is the party that has transgressed or is in debt. In chapter 5, however, when talking about governments, we see that this question is not so easily answered. Nevertheless, the more difficult question for *both* individuals *and* governments is who can forgive, not who can be forgiven. More specifically, can someone besides the victim or creditor forgive a wrong or a debt? Can transgressors be forgiven if their victims are missing or dead? Or was John Dryden correct to claim, "Forgiveness, to the injured doth belong"? Ordinarily, Dryden seems to be correct, but why is this the case?

1. The first condition rules out the possibility that political forgiveness could be an exercise in self-forgiveness; for articles dealing with the intelligibility and value of this idea, see Holmgren (1998), Mills (1995), Murphy (1998), and Snow (1993).

The First Right to Forgive

In the ongoing philosophical disputes over forgiveness, all parties assume that forgiving is the victim's prerogative, first and foremost. According to Martin Golding, "The general principle [is] that only the injured party is in a position to forgive, which frequently is taken as axiomatic in treatments of forgiveness" (Piers Benn 1996, 376; Golding 1984–85, 122).[2] Must we accept this axiom? First, it should be noted that certain conceptions of forgiveness allow that someone or something besides the creditor or victim can be in a position to forgive. For example, Maimonides recommends that the community can forgive if the victim refuses the entreaties of the transgressor three times (Lang 1996, 43; Newman 1987, 168). In addition, bankruptcy courts can play this role in the case of financial debts. These practices, however, suggest the possibility that although victims or creditors are the ones who should be doing the forgiving, they could lose this authority to other parties.[3] To understand these cases, we need to explore the basic presumption that victims or creditors have what could be considered the first right to forgive.[4]

For those who see forgiveness as bound to eliminating resentment, the rationale is clear for initially lodging the right to forgive a wrong with the victim: because no one else can change one's attitude, forgiveness must be something that is the victim's prerogative. No one other than the vic-

2. See also Card 1972, 204, n. 26; Gingell 1974, 181; Haber 1991, 46–48; Horsbrugh 1974, 275–76.

3. According to Shriver, forgiveness in the first instance belongs to the victim. But if you "accept shared injuries of social life or the shared responsibilities for the confession and cure of injuries," then you must be concerned with collective forgiveness (Shriver 1995, 113). For William Neblett, vicarious forgiveness is possible under a few situations: (1) if several persons are harmed, and one acts as a spokesperson for the others; (2) the injured is indisposed; or (3) through the actions of judges, priests, and petty officials (Neblett 1974, 270). Neblett's first example is taken up under the discussion of collective forgiveness. The second example is considered under vicarious forgiveness and forgiving on behalf of the dead. The last point is considered in my discussion of pardons (chapter 5).

4. Using Wesley N. Hohfeld's distinction between types of legal rights (Flathman 1973, 436–37; Waldron 1984, 6–7), this right to forgive is a right in the sense of being an ability or power to alter a set of (for our purposes) moral/legal relationships. When Jack forgives Jill, it means that Jack can no longer make a legitimate claim against Jill based on the forgiven debt. Forgiving changes the character of their relationship. In fact, after he forgives her, Jack has a duty not to hold these past wrongs or debts against Jill. As with other rights as powers, the right to forgive makes Jill liable to having her moral position changed through Jack's action. If Jill really was in debt or had wronged Jack, then this liability is not such a bad thing. Political forgiveness as a power may be important to a conception of pardoning (see chapter 5). The one wrinkle in this analysis is that if political forgiveness is a right in this sense, it is embedded within a larger imperfect duty to forgive.

tim can forgive because the victim must be the one to have a change of heart; only the victim can engage in the necessary form of self-enactment.

If, however, political forgiveness is an act of self-disclosure, then obviously a change of heart is unnecessary and the argument for initially lodging the first right to forgive with the victim less evident. Given the character of political forgiveness, it is plausible to think that the question of who has the right to forgive could be answered with reference to its illocutionary point. If the only way to release moral and financial debts is by placing the initial authority to forgive in the hands of victims and creditors, then a fairly strong case could be made in defense of Dryden's view. To consider the plausibility of this position, imagine the opposite situation, in which plenary authority to forgive is placed somewhere else, say, in the hands of a Great Forgiver. In such a world, only the Great Forgiver could forgive Smith after he harmed Jones or forgive Jack after he had gotten himself into financial debt. What would be so objectionable about a practice in which forgiveness was the sole prerogative of a Great Forgiver?

In cases of both financial debt and moral wrong, a Great Forgiver could conceivably satisfy the illocutionary point of political forgiveness. It is not impossible to imagine a financial world in which someone other than the creditor had the first and perhaps the only right to forgive. While such an authority could accomplish the clearing of a *financial* debt, it likely would also have enormous effects on how easily credit was extended. For example, while a generous Great Forgiver could make debtors more willing to take on debt, creditors might be discouraged from extending credit. A stingy Great Forgiver, who had plenary authority to forgive, could have the opposite effect. In either case, placing the initial right to forgive in the hands of a Great Forgiver could satisfy the illocutionary point of forgiveness. Whether doing so would be desirable depends on many things,

---

Hohfeld's other understandings of rights do not seem to apply as easily to the notion of political forgiveness. The right to forgive is clearly not an *immunity* to change. The right itself does not render others powerless in the same way that a constitutional right against self-incrimination does. In addition, it is not a right in the sense of being a *liberty* or *privilege*. Although debtors and victims must be free to forgive, Hohfeld's liberty-right requires that the forgiver *has no* duty not to forgive. In contrast, when the minimal conditions of justice are not met, victims *do have* a duty not to forgive. On occasion, others can object to Jack's exercise of political forgiveness. Finally, the right to forgive is not (entirely) a *claim-right*. In a claim-right, others have a duty not to interfere with Jack's decision not to forgive. In financial matters, the right to forgive a debt can be lost to a third party. In moral matters, as long as the minimal conditions of justice are met, others should let the victims forgive or not forgive. There is, then, an element of a claim-right in the power to engage in political forgiveness.

including the importance of extending credit and the predictability of the Great Forgiver.

Could the erasure of a *moral* debt be accomplished through such an entity? In such a system, if Smith was seeking forgiveness after harming Jones, he would beseech the Great Forgiver, who would have the sole right to provide relief. For this system to establish a reconciliatory state and invite the restoration of civility, Jones would have to recognize the actions of the Great Forgiver as a successful performance of forgiveness. With this recognition, it is not impossible to imagine Jones being reconciled to the past and taking up the invitation to act civilly to his tormentor. Of course, it is also plausible to claim that civil behavior is more likely to occur if Jones is given the first right to forgive. But this claim does not render conceptually implausible the idea of a Great Forgiver of moral wrongs. A Great Forgiver could successfully free a transgressor from the burdens of having done wrong and invite the restoration of civility.

Nevertheless, this account of the Great Forgiver of moral wrongs turns on the claim that such an entity could possess the authority to forgive Smith for what he did to Jones. The difficulty here is that this claim seems to require a particularly disturbing conception of moral agency and moral wrong. If the right to forgive was lodged in a Great Forgiver, the assumption would be that wronged individuals either could not or should not be able to release wrongdoers from their debts. In the first case, perhaps one could still say that Jones was owed the debt but that he was morally incompetent and, hence, unable to understand what it means to be wronged. Alternatively, a Great Forgiver of moral wrongs could be based on an understanding of wrongs in which individuals can do, but not suffer, wrongs. Only the Great Forgiver would feel all wrongs. This alternative way of looking at the Great Forgiver is consistent with Dryden's claim that only the injured has a right to forgive, but at the cost of seeing individuals like slaves—blameworthy but incapable of being wronged.

If we assume a basic moral competency among individuals, that is, they know what being wronged means, and we presume that wrongs are individualized, then a Great Forgiver of wrongs would appear to violate the victim's standing as a moral equal. When a wrong is done, the transgressor violates moral rules usually, although not necessarily, in the hope of gaining some advantage. The victim has been taken advantage of, and his or her equal moral status under those rules has been called into question by the transgressor. Investing the victim with the first right to forgive acknowledges his or her standing and worth. Just as the recognition of being morally blameworthy is part of the individuation of action (Smiley 1992, 246), according victims the right to forgive is the other side of the coin. Such a right assumes that the victim can grasp the significance of being wronged and that, potentially, to be wronged is part of what it means to be an individual. The problem with the Great Forgiver is not that it would necessarily prevent the debt from going away or preclude reconciliation but that it would violate the victim's dignity and standing as an equal, independent source of moral claims.

This deontological justification for an individual's authority to forgive creates a moral economy in which the transgressor, first and foremost, owes something to the victim. Ideally, the transgressor should give what is due and rectify the situation, for example, by offering apologies, compensation, or submitting to punishment. In this moral economy, however, the victim not only acquires a debt but also the initial right to forgive it.[5] On this analysis, one particularly troubling aspect of moral wrongs is that they are doubly coercive for the victim. Not only do transgressors take something to which they have no right, but by doing so, they generate a relationship of indebtedness. It's bad enough to be wronged, but to be continually linked to the assailant or betrayer seems to add to the injustice.[6]

---

5. Golding 1984–85, 128; Hampton 1988a, 38; Morris 1968, 478; Twambley 1975–76, 89. Unlike the creation of financial debts, moral wrongs create debts that we do not voluntarily take on. Generally, we try to make these moral debts "go away" by demanding justice.

6. The tricky character of this relationship includes yet another possible layer. If the transgressor is in debt to the victim, this could generate a sense of resentment on the part of the transgressor. Within a sentiment-based conception of forgiveness, it could be intelligible to talk about the transgressor forgiving the victim insofar as forgiveness is synonymous with removing one's anger and contempt. From the perspective of political forgiveness, this is a deeply objectionable (if not Pecksniffian) use of the word *forgive*. Nevertheless, Edmund S. Morgan finds such a use of forgiveness in the work of Benjamin Franklin, who had claimed that "Great Britain has injured us too much ever to forgive us." For Morgan, Franklin had "explained himself more fully in answer to an overture for reconciliation. Even if it were possible, he said, for Americans to forget and forgive what the British had done to them, 'it is not possible for *you* (I mean the British nation) to forgive the People you have so heavily injured; you can never confide again in those as Fellow Subjects, and permit them to enjoy equal Freedom, to whom you know you have given such just Cause of lasting Enmity' " (Morgan 1998, 16). Hobbes expresses a similar view: "To have done more hurt to a man than he [the doer] can, or is willing to, expiate, inclineth the doer to hate the sufferer. For he must expect revenge or forgiveness, both of which are hateful" (Hobbes [1651] 1994, 59). From the perspective of political forgiveness, the victim could not be forgiven unless the victim wronged the transgressor, for being wronged is not the same as doing wrong. Conversely, in Franklin's usage, the offender appears to be blaming the victim—which is simply a self-serving misrepresentation calling for correction and not the authorization to forgive. Although Hobbes does not talk about offenders forgiving victims, he does believe that doers of harm may come to hate the victim. In Hobbes's context, forgiveness is not a release of a burden but one more hateful thing that victims can do.

Understanding political forgiveness in terms of a moral economy is somewhat more complex than simply transgressors owing debts to victims. One of the complexities is that wrongs diminish both victims and transgressors. The transgressor may find himself in a situation in which what was once a wished-for advantage has become a burden that can be removed either by paying back the debt or receiving forgiveness. If the transgressor receives his "just deserts" or is fully forgiven for the wrong, then it may be possible to reestablish his moral status. Wrongdoing violates the equal standing of the individuals. Political forgiveness invites the public restoration of the transgressor. As we saw in chapter 3, by publicly releasing the transgressor from debt, the victim is promising not to use the past as the basis for future claims and is inviting others to restore the transgressor's moral position. The invitation to restore the transgressor is not a sure thing but must be picked up by others.

The potential significance of political forgiveness to victimizers makes the idea of a Great Forgiver somewhat more attractive, particularly if the victim is absent or dead. If the victim has the first right to forgive and is unable or unwilling to forgive, then forgiveness is impossible unless that right could be lost or transferred. These possibilities are explored in the discussion of vicarious forgiveness below. It may be useful, however, to consider the scope of this first right to forgive by asking whether victims always have that right. More specifically, do victims who are dead retain this initial right to forgive? What harm would be done, if the Great Forgiver *could* forgive wrongs done to those who are dead? Given the importance of asserting the moral worth of (live) victims, one could conceive of a rule in which victims have the first right to forgive unless they are dead. Once they have died, a Great Forgiver could meet the necessary conditions for political forgiveness. The advantage of such a rule would be that the power to initiate a process of restoring the transgressor would not die with the victim. Are there any disadvantages to such a rule?

One proviso that needs to be mentioned in connection with this rule is that if the transgressor is responsible for the death of the victim, then, from the discussion in chapter 2, the act is politically unforgivable. This rule would instead apply to situations in which the victim is missing or dead, but not because of the actions of the offender. For example, perhaps sometime in the past, Jack violated Jill's rights by abducting and torturing her, and his fellow citizens came to identify Jack with these actions. Since that time, however, perhaps because there has been a regime change, Jack has made clear his involvement in those affairs, accepted responsibility, and subscribes to a generally accepted history of who did what to whom. In the intervening years, however, Jill has died. As we saw, political forgiveness is not a necessary condition for the process of reconciliation but can initiate that process. Because Jill holds the first right to forgive, initiating the process of reconciliation through an act of political forgiveness has also evaporated. Could a Great Forgiver offer to Jack what Jill can no longer do?

Wronging the Dead

One way to address this question is by considering whether the dead could be wronged at all. If the dead cannot be wronged, then attributing a right to forgive to a Great Forgiver after the victim dies need not be so troublesome. The ability to forgive a victimizer need not disappear with the victim. To address this problem requires making a few assumptions about whether we survive our deaths. Aristotle suggested that "when friends do well, and likewise when they do badly, it appears to contribute something to the dead, but of a character and size that neither makes the happy people not happy nor anything else of this sort" (Aristotle, *Nichomachean Ethics*, 1101b, 5–10).[7] Putting to the side how Aristotle could arrive at this conclusion, his answer points to the central problem facing anyone trying to discover whether the dead have the same (or any) "interests in" or "rights to" matters they have left behind (ignoring the problem of rewards or punishments given in the afterlife). To avoid the complexities of pneumatology, I presume that subjects do not survive their deaths. Accepting this presumption, however, seems to settle the question in favor of those who argue that we cannot be harmed after death. For without a subject, what is to be harmed? Joel Feinberg, however, has argued against this conclusion. Introducing Feinberg's argument here helps address whether the Great Forgiver would wrong the dead by forgiving on their behalf.

For Feinberg, harm entails a setback to interests, and while we usually know and experience those setbacks, we need not personally experience them in order to be harmed. My reputation, for example, may be sullied without my knowledge. Assuming I have an interest in my good name, I can be described as being harmed even though I may not dis-

7. Aristotle's position on this matter seems to split the difference between two popular opinions that he sees as absurd: that "a dead person's condition changed along with the fortunes of his descendants" and that the "condition of descendants did not affect their ancestors at all" (Aristotle, *Nicomachean Ethics*, 1100a, 25–30).

cover it for a long time, or ever. Obviously, the possibility that one need not experience the harm in order to say that one is harmed has ramifications for the dead. For while the dead can never have their interests *satisfied* in the sense of actually experiencing gratification, their interests can remain *unfulfilled*. According to Feinberg, "The *fulfillment* of a want is simply the coming into existence of that which is desired" (Feinberg 1984, 84). If to have an interest unfulfilled can be a kind of setback, and one need not actually experience the unfulfillment, then an unfulfilled interest could also be a harm. The obvious example here is that of a will. Assuming a dead person does not experience frustration, we could still say that his or her wishes are unfulfilled if the will is not properly executed. But is this enough to say that the dead are *harmed* if their interests are unfulfilled?

The ideas that one need not experience harm in order to be harmed and that unfulfillment of an interest can be a setback are important claims, but they are not enough to conclude that the dead can be harmed or wronged. For the problem of *who* exactly is being harmed remains. Even though a living person need not experience the harm in order to be harmed, a subject still exists upon which one could pin the harm. At this point, Feinberg argues that "the subject of the harm in death is the living person antemortem, whose interests are squelched" (Feinberg 1984, 93). Feinberg further argues that it is possible to describe the dead person "as he was at some stage of his life" and not merely as something "mouldering, perhaps, in a grave" (90). The key to his argument is that if we can see as morally relevant the description of the dead as he was at some stage of life, then a postmortem harm can allow us to redescribe the condition of a person before death: "An event occurs after Smith's death that causes something to happen at that time. So far, so good; no paradox. Now, in virtue of the thing that was caused to happen at that time it is true that Smith was in a harmed condition before he died. It does not suddenly 'become true' that the antemortem Smith was harmed. Rather it becomes apparent to us for the first time that it was true all along—that from the time Smith invested enough in his cause to make it one of his interests, he was playing a losing game" (91). Interests that remain unfulfilled after death are doomed interests before death. If, after my death, something or someone violates or destroys that in which I had a stake, it becomes evident that those interests were doomed or harmed when I had them during my life. Because they were destined to remain unfulfilled, I was harmed even though I did not know it. The subject of harm is the antemortem person. So, we feel sorry for the doomed passengers on the *Titanic* because we know that their lives are to be cut short, even though they didn't know it when they boarded the ship.

What does this argument mean for the Great Forgiver's ability to forgive on behalf of the dead? If the first right to forgive belongs to victims and a third party usurps that right, then the victims' interest in being forgivers in the first instance is violated. We would then describe that interest as being doomed while they were alive. Consequently, in the example above, Jill would be wronged not only by Jack but also by a Great Forgiver that forgave what Jack did to Jill. Murder is not only politically unforgivable because the parties cannot share an account of who did what to whom but would also generate another wrong if the Great Forgiver forgave on the victim's behalf. In both cases, the victim's interest in being able to bestow or withhold forgiveness was set back while she was alive, even though she didn't realize it.

Feinberg's analysis accounts for the paradox that death is itself a harm, even though the subject is no longer present. In addition, it explains our sense of a person's being harmed long after her death, if the things she valued and worked for are destroyed or altered. The advantage of his analysis is that it does these things without delving into pneumatology or arguing that harm is possible without a subject. Finally, Feinberg's approach appears superior to a purely rule-utilitarian account of wronging the dead. According to rule utilitarians, we respect the wishes of the dead because it is necessary to keep the present rules alive. In contrast, Feinberg argues that the harm done is not a diffuse public injury, as the rule utilitarians would argue, but an injury done to some victim. Of course, rule utilitarianism also fails to address the standard argument: If a given violation would not bring down the rule, what is to keep us from violating it?

Feinberg's account, however, is not entirely satisfying. Given the contingency of life and the things we value, Feinberg's retrospective analysis has prospective implications. As a passenger boarding the *Titanic*, I don't know that the ship will sink, but I do know that I am mortal. And even though some of my interests will be fulfilled, I also know that any large-scale, long-term value or interest of mine will eventually turn to dust. Nations, institutions, values, relationships, and pretty much anything that we labor or act upon will disappear in time. Although I may not know when they will go, it would seem that it is our lot to live in a state of perpetual harm—if Feinberg's analysis makes sense. If this conclusion follows from his position, then maybe something is misbegotten about his position.

Two responses can be made to this criticism that Feinberg's position is objectionable. The first is that whether we are currently living in a state of harm depends on what we have a right to expect with regard to the future. I may not think of myself as perpetually harmed because I accept that my goals and interests have a limited time frame and so cannot be "unfulfilled" in the distant future; perhaps they simply evaporate. Second, even if Feinberg's position is overdrawn with regard to our large-scale, long-range projects, it doesn't appear overdrawn with regard to our interests that qualify as rights. It is not unreasonable to suppose that most of those interests, for most of us, will remain intact after death, simply because they will be of little concern to anyone else. It is reasonable to expect that others will not usurp our initial right to forgive after our death, and so most of us don't live under conditions of perpetual harm. If such a violation occurs, Feinberg's argument provides a way to see it as a violation.

The argument up to this point is that it makes sense to place an initial right to forgive in the victim's hands and probably in the hands of creditors as well. In financial matters, the institution of a Great Forgiver could have significant and unfavorable effects on the flow of credit. In moral matters, a Great Forgiver would violate the victim's status as a moral equal capable of issuing moral claims against others. In addition, if we presume that this argument extends to the dead, then there are certain moral debts that cannot be forgiven by other human beings. The initial right to forgive may hold into the grave. As in the case of living victims, a Great Forgiver would set back the interest of the dead.

The argument that a Great Forgiver possessing plenary power to forgive would be objectionable, however, does not necessarily mean that victims or creditors should possess plenary power to forgive. In other words, according an initial right to forgive in the hands of the victim does not necessarily mean that the victim alone has an exclusive right to forgive, only that the victim should have the first crack at it. Could an argument be made for what I call vicarious forgiveness? The political significance of vicarious forgiveness for both financial debts and moral wrongs is easy to see: if the initial right of the victim to forgive could be overridden or lost to others, then forgiveness could be granted without the participation of the victim. The possibility for vicarious forgiveness means that the process of reconciliation could be initiated and a reconciliatory state could be achieved even though the victim was unwilling or unable to forgive—circumventing, for example, the argument against forgiving on behalf of the dead. Similarly, if the forgiveness of financial debts is defensible, then a third party could restore a sense of independence and equality that debtors lose when burdened by crushing debts.

The Vicarious Forgiveness of Financial Debts

In a sentiment-based understanding of forgiveness, the victim not only has the first right to forgive, he or she also has an exclusive right. Given the personal character of self-enactment, no one other than the victim could actually diminish the sentiments of resentment or anger. Because no one else can change your heart, vicarious forgiveness is an impossibility. In contrast, once again, a self-disclosive conception of forgiveness does not so easily settle the question of whether only the victim should be able to forgive. This is particularly true of the forgiveness of financial debts, since in many economic systems some third party has the authority to do this. In the United States, for example, a body of uniform federal laws governs the vicarious forgiveness of financial debt. While the specifics of the law are not my main concern, the point of the law is clear: to provide debtors relief from crushing debts and the possibility of a fresh start. The code does this by encouraging arrangements that would allow debtors to pay off creditors from their available assets, and then, if that does not resolve the debt, it empowers the court to erase or forgive the debt. Forgiveness becomes a consideration when the debtor cannot give what is due or cannot give what is due without causing exorbitant hardship. Consequently, if payment was feasible, then a court would be unwilling to forgive a financial debt. In other words, the court is asked to forgive when it appears that the limitations of justice have been met or when the pursuit of justice becomes too costly. Before forgiveness enters the scene, some reasonable attempt should be made to give what is due. Yet, even in this practice of forgiveness, certain debts cannot be discharged by a court, for example, mortgages, child and spousal support, or punitive court awards. The system of vicarious forgiveness of financial debts has its limits, effectively rendering some financial debts unforgivable.

From the perspective of the individual debtor, the justifications for an authoritative vicarious forgiver are obvious: not only are creditors forbidden to push their claims but the debtor may also eventually get to start over again—even with fresh credit. Going through a bankruptcy may permit one to organize one's debts more sensibly and ultimately remove an unbearable burden.

Vicarious forgiveness of financial debt may also have certain advantages for creditors. From a very broad perspective, creditors in general may profit from this practice insofar as it allows debtors to take on more debt. From a more immediate perspective, a bankruptcy court may also advantage creditors by organizing and paying back the debt, to whatever extent possible, in a fair way. In addition, a bankruptcy court is an official way to establish that a debt has become crushing: creditors need not trust the word of the debtor. More important, although a creditor may incur a loss because of a court's decision, there is always the chance that any given creditor would have lost even more without the court's action. This is especially true if the debtor is in debt to a number of creditors. A debtor who pays Paul may not be able to pay anything to Peter. From the perspective of either Peter or Paul, the situation may have been worse without some kind of third-party acknowledgment and settlement of the debt.

Of course, the reasons supporting an authoritative vicarious forgiver must also attend to the authoritative aspects of the law. In the case of bankruptcy court, the court's standing to discharge financial debt is clearly linked to a larger framework of processes, institutions, and documents that sustain its general legitimacy. Creditors may see the actions of the bankruptcy court as legitimate because they view the larger system as legitimate. Although useful, this explanation doesn't account for the seemingly widespread acceptance of bankruptcy in a market economy. We can, however, narrow the question and ask why a court would have a kind of immediate legitimacy to the parties involved (assuming that it does). In the case of the debtor, the benefits are so clear that questions of legitimacy are of little concern; after all, debtors initiate the process. In contrast, why would creditors accept the preemption of their rights to deal with the debt as they see fit? The most compelling answer, I believe, is the one offered above: namely, creditors see vicarious debt forgiveness as legitimate because they too receive benefits. To some degree, they are better off with this kind of practice than without it.

The Vicarious Forgiveness of Moral Wrongs

Can reasoning analogous to the vicarious forgiveness of financial debt apply to moral concerns? Could anyone, other than the victims, have authority to forgive their transgressors? As in the case of the forgiveness of debts, one could argue that the advantages of vicarious forgiveness of wrongs to transgressors would be clear: it would lift the burden of their wrongful actions and invite the process of civic and moral restoration.

Unlike the case of the forgiveness of debts, however, it is unlikely that victims would ever see themselves as better off because a third party forgave on their behalf. In fact, their authority to forgive having been usurped, they could easily be seen as worse off. While creditors may directly benefit from the actions of bankruptcy court, no such benefit could accrue to victims whose rights had been usurped. Perhaps one could say that an authoritative vicarious forgiver could some day work to the victims' advantage when they've done wrong. Although this argument carries some weight, it is not a particularly satisfying response for those who have suffered from a serious moral wrong. Consequently, no strong, analogous argument supports the vicarious forgiveness of moral wrongs. Nevertheless, if victims have a right to forgive, we must also consider whether they could abuse and perhaps lose that right. If the right can be lost, then perhaps another case can be made for vicarious forgiveness.

Forfeiting the Right to Forgive

The victim's right to forgive moral wrongs appears to place a significant obstacle in the path of vicarious forgiveness. But no right is absolute, and many rights can be abridged or lost if they are misused. For example, Martin Hughes has argued that although the discretionary power to forgive should be initially placed in the hands of the victim, that discretion can be abused: "In some circumstances the discretion to forgive granted by the moral system may, under the same system, lapse" (Hughes 1975, 114). But how could the right to forgive a moral wrong be abused? Kantians would argue that if we forgive too easily, we are not according ourselves sufficient self-respect. Those who forgive at the drop of a hat are abusing the practice of forgiving (McGary 1989, 346). But this is not the kind of violation about which Hughes is worried; rather, he is more concerned with situations in which the transgressor has little or no chance for forgiveness. For Hughes, the cause for forfeiture is not generous but stingy forgiving. Here, the problem is not that the injured lacks self-respect but that, at some point, the injured is too unbending.

From Hughes's perspective, when victims become stingy with their forgiveness, someone else should be able to intercede and provide relief for the transgressor; victims can forfeit their right to forgive. For Hughes, "forfeiting" means relinquishing the discretion to forgive to the "best available representatives of the moral system" (Hughes 1975, 114–15). Unfortunately, because humans tend to be either too detached or too invested in a situation to serve as appropriate moral judges, granting this discretion to particular individuals or the social group is fairly dangerous. This leads Hughes to defend the idea of an all-forgiving God. When the victim's discretion to forgive is forfeited, the transgressor can appeal to God.[8]

Maimonides, as mentioned earlier, provides an alternative conception of vicarious forgiveness, one that places greater faith in the moral capacities of a community. He argues that if the victim refuses to forgive and "the wrongdoer repeats his plea for forgiveness three times before witnesses," then the victim has surrendered his right to forgive. Through such a process, Maimonides believed, the transgressor "is forgiven even if the person wronged continues to reject his pleas. At that point, too, the latter is guilty of wrongdoing, of being 'unforgiving.' Here the community assumes the role of agency, granting forgiveness" (Lang 1996, 43).

When the Transgressor Cannot Give What Is Due

Does it make sense to say that the right to forgive can be forfeited to another? Turning to the problem of financial debts first helps sharpen the issue. To begin, we need to distinguish situations in which the debtor or transgressor cannot give what is due from situations in which he or she can give what is due, but the creditor or victim refuses to accept "payment." As in the case of the vicarious forgiveness of financial debt, the debtor who lacks the wherewithal to give what is due petitions a bankruptcy court to step in to reorganize or forgive a debt. Hughes's or Maimonides' systems for forgiving moral wrongs would look much like a bankruptcy court if the transgressor simply could not undo or adequately compensate the victim for what was done, and the victim still refused to forgive.[9] In this situation, the transgressor is asking a third party (God or the community) to forgive because the transgressor did all he could do to make things right but still fell short.

---

8. For Hughes, God serves as the last court of appeals and opens the possibility for vicarious forgiveness. This conception of God is not without its theological critics. John Gingell, for example, finds an all-forgiving God morally repugnant (Gingell 1974, 182). Fortunately, my concerns are not theological but ethical and political.

9. If the failure to compensate is a matter of financial impoverishment, and the transgressor successfully declared bankruptcy, then in some sense a bankruptcy court is involved in the vicarious forgiveness of moral wrongs.

Would it be appropriate to say that a creditor abuses her right to forgive when she withholds it from a debtor who has done all he can do to make the payment?[10] It would not, of course, be surprising for creditors to argue that a refusal to forgive an unpaid debt is not an abuse. Pressing for the payment of a debt may seem overbearing and somewhat oppressive, but that would not be the same as arguing that forgiveness of financial debt is a duty. Such a position presumes that there really are no "impossible" debts. All debts can be temporized. So assuming all individuals have a future earning power, creditors can always receive their due—even if they do not receive it right away. From this perspective, creditors do not have a duty to forgive unpaid debts because most individuals can "work off" the debt.

But there are crushing debts. Individuals (and nations) can find themselves in a situation in which their debts become so great that they are unable to function, plan, or organize their financial commitments. Debtors can accrue impossible debts that significantly reduce their capacities to earn in the future. If the absence of a duty to forgive turned on the possibility of future earning power, would the absence of future earning power yield a duty to forgive impossible debts?

The problem is that what looks like an impossible debt from the debtor's perspective may appear quite different from the creditor's perspective. For one thing, it is necessary to establish whether the debtor has, in fact, done all he or she could do to pay the debt. Are there, for example, other assets that the debtor could use? Is the debtor hiding assets? What assets could be liquidated to pay the debt, and what liquidations would render the debtor so destitute as to prevent further payment? Although creditors may go some distance in discovering the true state of the debtor's financial situation, the advantage of an authoritative proceeding is that it officially establishes whether the debtor has in fact "done all that could be done" in repaying the debt. Just as important, in dealing with financial debts, courts have an uncontroversial mechanism (i.e., monetary payment) to establish what doing more, less, and enough means in paying back a debt.

If a court did no more than authoritatively establish the debtor's situation, could there ever be agreement that a debtor faced an impossi-

10. In practice, the phrase "all he can do to make the payment" would require further specification. For example, was some other property used to secure the debt? Could whatever collateral used to make the purchase be "called in"? The relevant case, however, is one in which the debt remains after all other methods of payment have been exhausted.

ble debt, and hence the creditor had a duty to forgive? Once again, from the individual creditor's perspective, even the revelation that the debtor truly did all he could need not force the conclusion that a debt is impossible. Part of the problem turns on the number of creditors. For example, if the debtor was unable to repay a number of parties, that each party recognized the crushing nature of the total debt would not mean each creditor would see her portion of the debt as impossible. From the individual perspectives of the creditors, their debt may not be crushing. As in any collective action problem, they need not individually acknowledge or even realize the combined effects of their specific claims. In this analysis, an authoritative vicaricus forgiver steps in, not because individual creditors have failed in their duty to forgive but because they don't individually have a duty to forgive.

This explanation, however, only works in the case of multiple creditors whose individual claims taken separately are not impossible. Would a duty exist if one creditor held a crushing debt? Such a duty would indeed exist as long as some authoritative mechanism could certify the difficult nature of the debt. An individual creditor who sincerely wants her money does have an incentive to be cognizant of the debtor's situation. At minimum, such a creditor should be able to recognize the impossibility of immediate repayment. This recognition, however, would lead the creditor to suggest restructuring the debt to facilitate its repayment. But the incentive in this case is to temporize and not to recognize the impossibility of a debt. Given the normal incentives for extending credit—that it is a loan and not a gift—certifying the impossibility of a debt seems to require an authoritative pronouncement. Once that fact has been established, the individual creditor who held the crushing debt would then have a duty to forgive. Presumably, if such an individual did not forgive, he or she would be a legitimate target for our moral disapprobation. Under such circumstances, a bankruptcy court could also be seen as assuming a duty that the creditor did not fulfill.

If a duty to forgive is triggered only by the relationship between the individual creditor and debtor, then collectively crushing debts (that are not individually impossible) need not generate such a duty. If such a duty could be so generated, a creditor's responsibilities would be held hostage by the decision of whether someone else made an additional loan to the debtor. Consequently, the justification for the authoritative vicarious forgiveness of collectively crushing debts rests on the consequences to both debtors and creditors already discussed. In contrast, a duty on the part of creditors to forgive an individually crushing debt can justify the authoritative vicarious forgiveness of debt.

Abusing the Right to Forgive Wrongs

Can one argue analogously that victims could forfeit their right to forgive to a third party? Central to the argument surrounding the forgiveness of financial debt is the understanding that the debtor has done everything possible and the remaining debt renders a normal life impossible. What is interesting about the case of financial debts is that even though all the parties recognize what must be done to pay back the debt, the possibility of abusing the right to forgive requires an authoritative certification that the debtor has paid what he could. For a variety of reasons, none of these conditions appears to be satisfied in the case of moral wrongs.

In reasoning by analogy, the idea that a right to forgive a wrong could be abused seems first to require that the parties are satisfied the transgressor has done everything possible or that doing anything more would be an unbearable burden. Meeting these requirements, of course, requires having a pretty good sense of what "doing everything possible" means. While this phrase may be relatively clear in the financial world, it is less clear in the moral world. Perhaps in the highly integrated community aspired to by Christians and Jews, it is possible to establish definitively whether a transgressor had done all that could be done. The community may have come to recognize that in many cases a simple apology, or a promise never to do such a wrong again, or the performance of some ritual suffices. Alternatively, an authoritative text, individual, or body may exist that could certify everything possible has been done.

In contrast, the more highly we value the individual and the reality of the individual's experience of harm and injury, the more unwilling we are to accept anything other than the victim's understanding of "doing everything possible." Assuming a robust form of individuality will inevitably lead to differences over what constitutes proper atonement. The Maimonidean system works to the extent that there are publicly acknowledged rules that establish what atonement is needed for what injustice. If our sense of injustice is individualized, then what is a severe injury or insult to one individual may be something that can be repaired with a simple apology for another. What Abel sees as "doing everything possible," Baker may see as highly inadequate. Assuming a high value attributed to individuality, it is presumptuous to think that a definitive sense could be given to "doing everything possible."

Of course, it is not surprising that from a communal perspective, the individualized system of discerning harm may be seen as unable to reconcile victim and transgressor and, hence, as a system that can be readily destabilized. From a perspective that values individuality, however, a vicarious system generates its own instabilities to the extent that it does not (and cannot) match our individual senses of injustice. Such a system lacks a moral authority that could certify that a transgressor has done what could be done.

Even if such an authority existed, the case of abusing the right to forgive a financial debt points us to an additional requirement: the debt must be unbearable or crushing. The call to forgive financial debts is, in part, for the sake of the debtor. In a political context, the analogous argument would be that a failure to forgive a wrong renders the normal life of the transgressor impossible. The only political theorist who comes close to making such a claim on behalf of forgiveness is Hannah Arendt. Although her account is problematic, forgiveness holds an important place in her political theory. According to Arendt, "The possible redemption from the predicament of irreversibility—of being unable to undo what one has done though one did not, and could not, have known what he was doing—is the faculty of forgiving" (Arendt 1958, 237). If the activity of promising creates "islands of security" that stabilize political life, forgiving provides us with the wherewithal to act by releasing us from action's unfortunate results. Without the potential for such release, Arendt believed that "our capacity to act would, as it were, be confined to one single deed from which we would never recover; we would remain the victims of its consequences forever, not unlike the sorcerer's apprentice who lacked the magic formula to break the spell" (237).

As in the case of financial forgiveness, Arendt suggests that we forgive for the sake of the transgressor. She thought that forgiveness released the political actor from responsibility for a whole causal chain of unforeseen and unforeseeable consequences. Because of the possibility of forgiveness, an actor need not be paralyzed by the fear of being held constantly accountable for the inevitable transgressions that result from action. Freed from such interminable accounting, we are able to act—in Arendt's special sense of the word—in a public fashion.

As we saw in chapter 1, Arendt believed that forgiveness could not operate in the absence of mutual respect and that the contemporary world seemed to lack such respect. The problem with her claim that forgiveness is essential to politics, however, has less to do with mutual respect than it does with her analysis of the unbearable responsibility for the consequences of action. But the consequences of action are unbearable only if one accepts her Jasperian conception of moral responsibility. There may be good reasons why we want to hold people responsible for things over which they have no control (for example, in order to ensure that they are especially cautious in their activities), but the cases in which this is true are exceptional and tend to stretch the meaning of responsibility and causality in objectionable ways. Arendt assumes that if one were equally responsible for every consequence of an action, action itself would become morally impossible; such a level of responsibility, she believes, would make us see distant effects as morally equivalent to closer effects. Yet, the awareness could go the other way, making us more cavalier about immediate effects. If the effects of what I do now are no worse than some distant ripple, hundreds of generations in the future, then why be concerned with immediate action? Wanting to heighten our sensitivity to future consequences, Arendt may achieve an opposite effect, namely, our feeling that present consequences need trouble us no more than distant consequences. In any case, Arendt's argument that political action has an unbearable character that forgiveness can relieve only makes sense under a very broad and objectionable notion of responsibility.[11]

Nevertheless, one need not subscribe to Arendt's broad conception of responsibility to argue that a transgressor could do all that he could do and still feel that the wrong he did was unbearable. Perhaps the guilt is so great that he cannot go on. And, in the case of politics, "unbearable" may mean anything from "cannot go on living" to "feeling unworthy to participate in the political life of the polity." Can there be a duty to forgive those whose transgressions have become unbearable? In the case of financial forgiveness, of course, an authoritative process validates an unbearable debt. It is difficult to see how, in the case of moral wrongs, there could exist such an authoritative body that did not rest heavily on the say-so of the transgressor. If this were true, then deciding whether the victim was abusing the right to forgive would rest largely on the feelings of the transgressor. There would then be something triply coercive about being wronged. Not only is the victim wronged and then owed something by the transgressor, but the victim also loses the right

11. In addition, despite the importance that she attributes to forgiving (placing it on a par with promising) and her realization that foundings are rarely free of violence and bloodshed, she doesn't claim that there is a call or duty to forgive.

to forgive if the transgressor says he feels bad enough. Without publicly accessible criteria for determining when the guilt is crushing, the victim is hostage to the feelings of the transgressor.

If it were possible to establish the accuracy of the transgressor's plea that the guilt is unbearable, would that then be enough to transfer the right to forgive to a third party? One problem is that it is plausible to argue that, unlike financial debts, some moral debts should be "unbearable." From this perspective, part of doing all that one can do entails understanding the full weight of one's actions. For example, many of the responses in *The Sunflower* that Simon Wiesenthal elicited from his friends and prominent thinkers convey the idea that a dying Nazi soldier who participated in murdering hundreds of Jews felt just what he should have felt, given what he did. As Cynthia Ozick wrote, "Let the SS man die unshriven. Let him go to hell" (Wiesenthal 1976, 190). It could even be argued that understanding the unbearable character of certain wrongs may make us more careful. Consequently, a practice of vicarious forgiveness would have the potentially unfortunate effect of making us more reckless about the consequences of our actions. It would not only usurp the victim's rights but would also make wrongful action more conceivable. A practice of vicarious forgiveness would tell potential wrongdoers that even if the victim is no longer around, their evil could ultimately be forgiven. It lessens the sorrow of transgressors by increasing the ease with which they can transgress.

For a refusal to grant forgiveness to be an "abuse," it must be the case that the unbearable quality of the wrong is more than what is required. But what would this mean vis-à-vis political forgiveness? If one of the purposes of political forgiveness is to invite the restoration of civility, trust, and moral equality, transferring the right to forgive to another would be tantamount to saying that political actors—citizens, political groups, or governments—must restore those who have harmed them because the transgressors find unbearable the absence of civility, trust, and moral equality. While one could argue that it may be appropriate to forgive for these reasons, political forgiveness does not guarantee such restoration, and victims may see no value in extending the invitation to reestablish political connections. The claim that one could abuse one's right to forgive (and have it then forfeited to a third party) fails, because of the problems of defining what it means for transgressors to do everything possible, and also because of the difficulties associated with establishing what it would mean politically for a transgressor's debt to be unbearable.

Vicarious Forgiveness: When the Victim Refuses What Is Due

If we return to the original analogy between forgiveness of financial and moral debts, two cases required consideration: one in which transgressors cannot give what is due and one in which they can. Up to this point, the analysis has dealt with the first situation. While vicarious forgiveness in such a situation makes sense for financial debts, it appears unjustified in the case of moral wrongs. But what if the transgressor or debtor *can* give what is due, but the victim or creditor refuses to consider it to be "payment" in full? In financial matters, if a debtor is willing to repay the debt fully and the creditor refuses to accept payment, there is once again potential for a kind of vicarious forgiveness. Assuming that the mode of payment is legitimate, one could argue that a refusal on the part of the creditor to accept payment is an abuse of the creditor's rights. Say, for example, instead of U.S. dollars for a U.S. debt, the creditor wants gold. If a U.S. note really "is legal tender for all debts, public and private," refusal to accept payment in that currency may be tantamount to forgiving the debt. If this is indeed the case, then there is a social/legal norm vicariously forgiving a debt when a creditor refuses a legitimate mode of payment.

But, as we have seen, when a moral economy lacks an agreed-upon currency for atonement, there is no analogy to the financial world. Assuming a high value to the individual's sense of injustice, moral "payment" will resemble a situation in which creditors can choose what currency to accept. If the victim alone has an adequate sense of what undoing a wrong would entail, transgressors cannot expect that a third party will know more than the victim.[12]

12. There is an additional difference between moral and financial debts: in our private interactions we sometimes forgive someone even after he or she has rectified the wrong. For example, in certain cases, an apology may be enough to make things right, yet we may still forgive after an apology has been made. For Tavuchis, forgiving after an apology is a way to reinstate the wrongdoer in the social order (Tavuchis 1991, 20). From his account, simply accepting the apology is not enough; an act of forgiveness should follow. In contrast, it would be senseless for a bank to forgive a homeowner who had paid off the mortgage. In this case, there is nothing to forgive.

A less charitable interpretation of the practice of forgiving after receiving justice is that it allows victims a moment to lord over transgressors. By accepting full payment for the moral wrong and then forgiving, the victim may be saying, "Even though you've made things right, my victimhood grants to me a moral superiority over you that can be expressed by my forgiveness." If we stick to a form of political forgiveness that emphasizes its self-disclosive character, however, forgiving after a debt has been paid is, at best, senseless and, at worst, an insult.

The difficulty of justifying vicarious forgiveness is intimately con-nected to the extreme discomfort we feel when someone other than the victim tries assume the mantle of an agent of forgiveness. Lacking com-munal standards of atonement, and given the importance of the indi-vidual's sense of harm, the right to forgive rests with the victim. View-ing political forgiveness as a right, however, does open the possibility of transferring that right to another. We may, in other words, authorize another to forgive in our name. Just as it is possible that someone who is acting as an agent may bind us and even make promises for us, it seems feasible that a right to forgive could also be transferred. If such a transfer occurred and the agent did forgive a transgressor, the victim would be bound just as if the victim herself did it. Without such a transfer, how-ever, one cannot forgive vicariously.

Representing Victims

If the only plausible view of the vicarious forgiveness of moral wrongs entails the transference of a right to forgive, we are left with a very nar-row notion of vicariously forgiving wrongs. This is especially true if the authorization to forgive on another's behalf must be explicit. If actual social contracts are rare, this kind of authorization is even rarer. As social contract theorists have long recognized, however, not all autho-rizations need to be explicit in order to count. Theorists have long deployed a variety of mechanisms to keep alive the democratic sources of authority in the absence of explicit consent: tacit consent, hypothetical consent, ideal speech situations, and so on. These kinds of arguments suggest good reasons to support a particular authorization to forgive on behalf of another, even if victims may not explicitly or actually have per-formed the authorization. Perhaps, if there are good reasons, then we should accept an authority that could forgive vicariously.

A variation of the authorization argument appeals to the representa-tive character of the Great Forgiver. If the Great Forgiver is a government that legitimately represents the victims and chooses to forgive offenders, then the notion of representation may justify third-party forgiveness. For this argument to be compelling, the government must be able to take on the mantle of the Great Forgiver, the representative character of the gov-ernment must be firmly established, and the idea that wrongs can be rep-resented needs to be explicated. Whether governments are entities that can forgive is explored in chapter 5. For the moment, we can assume that the government is representative. The central problem with this position is in trying to make sense of the representation of wrongs that doesn't require the explicit transfer of the right to forgive.

In his discussion of the justification of the amnesty process in the transition of South Africa, Desmond Tutu offers a defense of the representation of victims. Although Tutu never associates the amnesty with forgiveness, these grants of amnesty are closer to political forgiveness than to forms of official forgetting, as chapter 5 shows. Consequently, the idea that victims can be represented in such a way that others can speak on their behalf, opens the possibility for vicarious political forgiveness. In the Promotion of National Unity and Reconciliation Act, perpetrators of criminal acts who petitioned and received amnesty could be freed both from criminal and civil liability. Tutu admits that this was a "high price to ask the victims to pay" (Tutu 1999, 55). Nevertheless, he argues that,

> the bulk of the victims of apartheid violations of human rights were well represented by those whom they would be willing to acknowledge to be their authentic representatives, those who would have had a tacit mandate to speak on their behalf and to make decisions that they would generally be ready to accept as in tune with their aspirations or would be the closest approximations to a fulfillment of those aspirations as they would ever have hoped to get, taking into account the prevailing circumstance and the realities that had to be contended with. (55–56)

Later, he argues that *"it would not be unreasonable to assert* that those who had negotiated and who produced the TRC [the Truth and Reconciliation Commission] law did in fact have the credentials to speak on behalf of the victims" (Tutu 1999, 57). It would not be unreasonable to assert this claim, for two reasons. On the one hand, Tutu believes the negotiators could speak for the victims because they were, for the most part , victims themselves. Those representatives had themselves "suffered the humiliations of the iniquitous pass laws and had seen their people uprooted and dumped as if they were rubbish in the massive forced population removal schemes that had traumatized so many from that community" (56). On the other hand, the representatives could be understood to speak on behalf of others because their efforts were "massively endorsed in a landslide election victory" (56). Tutu argues that "had what they did in the act been at variance with the feelings of their constituency, that would have been reflected in their ratings in opinion polls" (57).

In addition to the argument involving the representative character of the process, Tutu argues that the process of granting immunity from civil suit and criminal prosecution was necessary in order to get the truth out and achieve a peaceful transition. In sum, Tutu's defense of the cost incurred by the victims runs along two tracks: it was a legitimate sacrifice because the victims' representatives approved it and it was necessary. The advantage of this strategy is that if the former argument fails, then the claim of necessity may still stand. First, however, we need to assess the arguments in support of being able to represent the victim.

Does Tutu's case supporting the representative character of the process adequately respect the rights of victims? The electoral argument is very difficult to make. Winners in elections love to read their victories as mandates for their policies, but voters may vote for any number of reasons. Perhaps the alternative candidates were far less acceptable. Even if such a mandate could be drawn from the election, Tutu's argument would appear to require that all victims supported it. If some victims abstained or voted against the government, then it is not clear that the amnesty program was representing their views. Finally, even if all of these other conditions held, the strongest conclusion that could be drawn from the election is that it could be nothing more than an ex post facto ratification of the process. Citizens were being asked to accept a process that could not be changed without tremendous cost. To say that consent after the fact is better than no consent at all implies a kind of arrogance on the part of rulers that what they do will eventually be acceptable to the people. The electoral argument does not necessarily ensure that the process represented all victims.

The argument that because the representatives were themselves victims, they could literally speak for the victims, is also troubling. Can victims necessarily speak on behalf of other victims? Strictly speaking, because these individuals were not making present what was literally absent, but rather making the position of the victim present in the negotiations, they were not representatives (Pitkin 1969, 16). Putting aside this conceptual problem, to say that the position of the victim was actually there in the negotiations, one must assume that the experiences of the victims under apartheid South Africa were so widely shared, so commonly understood and felt, that the wrong felt by one was a wrong felt by all. Consequently, all victims would agree that granting a conditional amnesty and surrendering the right to sue was acceptable. The negotiators were giving voice to what all victims already knew, if only implicitly. In contrast, at this point the individualized character of wrong, assumed above, becomes important. This assumption need not deny that victims may share many things. However, it recognizes the separate experiences of victims. Under this assumption, Tutu's justification does not take seriously enough the distinctiveness of persons and the complex, unique ways in which wrongs may be felt and understood. How a wrong is understood by one victim may be shared by another. But it may not be, and it is impossible to make that determination unless one finds out from the victims themselves. The notion that the victims were adequately represented because the negotiators were victims is not compelling unless one rejects the individualized character of being wronged.

Victims can be represented by others, but only if their rights are clearly transferred to the representative. Tutu's arguments do not provide evidence of such transference. This does not mean that such evidence is impossible to obtain, only that appealing to the experieices of the negotiators and the results of elections are not sufficient. In addition, this negative conclusion should not be taken as indicating that the negotiators should not have surrendered the rights of victims. One may still find the argument of necessity compelling. The argument of necessity suggests that the negotiators faced a tragic choice in which they were forced to sacrifice something of value, whichever decision they made. Sacrificing the rights of victims, on this reading, cannot be made right by appealing to the representative character of the process. It was a sacrifice that the government felt was necessary. The general question raised by such tragic choices (see chapter 7) is how citizens should respond to wrongs done to them by their government: Should the victims whose rights have been sacrificed in the name of peace and order ever forgive the government that performed the sacrifice?

Assuming the Transference of a Right to Forgive

Trying to justify vicarious forgiveness through a representative process only works if evidence of transferring the right to forgive can be found. Perhaps, however, we could just assume that such a transference has occurred. Perhaps we could place the discretion to forgive in the hands of the victim but then claim good reasons for also lodging it elsewhere— reasons that may call for respecting the victim's prerogative initially but accepting the possibility of usurping that discretion in certain circumstances. One argument in support of an assumed transference is that forgiveness provides the way out of the cycle of distrust, violence, and revenge that defines the relationships of so many political actors. If the participants cannot step back from their situation and forgive one another, then there should be an authoritative forgiver, someone with the standing to call a halt to seemingly endless and bitter disputes. While it may be true that such an authoritative figure would usurp the rights of victims to forgive, both parties would also be advantaged by peace—just as a bankruptcy court, when it forgives a crushing debt, can advantage all the parties even though it overrides the rights of specific creditors.

This justification for vicarious forgiveness rests on the belief that forgiveness is the only alternative to violence. Without forgiveness, peace and reconciliation is impossible. As we saw in chapter 3, however, political forgiveness may be neither necessary nor sufficient for initiating a process of reconciliation. Political forgiveness, however, may be necessary for achieving a state of reconciliation. But a failure to achieve a state of reconciliation need not be the same as a state of violent conflict. Participants who have not settled the past are not necessarily at each others' throats. Although dropping, repressing, or forgetting the past would not attain a reconciliatory state, these responses are not synonymous with violence. The empirical assumption that the only alternative to violence is forgiveness does not seem to bear up under conceptual or historical analysis. We can find ourselves getting along with one another, even our enemies, for all sorts of reasons.

Second, this justification would have to rest on the belief that forgiveness is the morally superior response. In cases where the minimal conditions of justice cannot be met (such as when the victim has died), however, political forgiveness simply isn't appropriate. I later argue that other responses may be more defensible when, for example, nearly just governments commit wrongs against their citizens or when citizens must decide how to respond to fellow citizens who had collaborated with a former regime that was unjust.

The question of whether forgiveness is the morally superior response, however, raises a third difficulty with this justification for vicarious forgiveness. For an authoritative Great Forgiver to live up to the requirements of political forgiveness, it would first have to address the parties' demands for justice. The belief that precisely those demands (even at a minimal level) cultivate a cycle of violence may lead to the conclusion that political forgiveness is part of the problem and not part of the solution. Alternatively, a settlement in which the pursuit of justice is completely abandoned could always be characterized as unjust and, hence, unworthy of respect. Moreover, if a recognized authority has the capacity to punish and offer compensation, then the need for an authoritative vicarious forgiver becomes a less urgent mechanism for breaking the cycle of revenge. The cycle would have already been broken with the parties' recognition of an authoritative body that could legitimately dispense corrective justice. Once that body has been recognized, the compelling reason to surrender one's right to forgive dissipates.

Clearly, there are strong reasons to favor the authoritative vicarious forgiveness of financial debts. But the case of financial forgiveness pointed to the deficiencies in the general argument supporting third-party forgiveness of moral wrongs, although such forgiveness can occur if there has been the proper authorization. In specifying the second condition of political forgiveness—that there is a debt owed to one party by the other—it is clear that the nature of the debt affects the justifications of the authority to forgive and the ease with which a third party can assume that authority. Nevertheless, both forms of forgiveness (moral and financial), when performed by the appropriate parties for the appropriate reasons under the appropriate conditions, are forms of political forgiveness. The ensuing discussion, however, elucidates the political forgiveness of wrongful actions.

5

Group Forgiveness and Governmental Pardons

It is basically an act of forgiveness.

—Chris Watney, U.S. Justice Department, referring to the presidential power to pardon (*Los Angeles Times*, January 4, 1999)

WE HAVE considered the illocutionary character of political forgiveness, how this conception could address a set of criticisms against bringing forgiveness into political theory, and the authority of creditors and victims to forgive in this manner. The remainder of the book considers the relationship of this idea of forgiveness to our understanding of wrongs done by governments and citizens. Because governments are one of the few kinds of groups that have authority to forgive politically, and because citizenship structures the idea of political forgiveness in important ways, the discussion primarily focuses on these two entities. Political forgiveness may be employed by other groups, such as corporations or international organizations, and in different circumstances, such as between corporations and individuals, but this analysis leaves those matters open. We begin, then, with the broader question of whether political forgiveness can be employed by and, ultimately, applied to groups in general and then consider the idea of pardoning as an instance of governmental forgiveness.

Relationships of Forgiveness

In general, four kinds of relationships could be reconciled through an act of political forgiveness:[1]

1. An individual forgives another individual, or *one to one*.
2. An individual forgives a group, or *one to many*.
3. A group forgives an individual, or *many to one*.
4. A group forgives another group, or *many to many*.

The first relationship, *one to one*, involves individual citizens forgiving other individual citizens within the context of a nearly just regime and in the case of a regime that has moved from an unjust to a more just set of arrangements (see chapter 8). The last relationship (*many to many*) touches on the role of political forgiveness in international relations. I pass over this relationship because political forgiveness requires a minimal threshold of justice, and so ascertaining its place in the international realm would require saying a great deal more about the role of norms in international affairs. Such an account would take the analysis beyond the immediate concerns of this book. Obviously, the possibility for *many to many* forms of forgiveness exists in the domestic realm (between corporations, associations, parties, and so on), but the core theoretical issues raised by this case also emerge in the other relationships. More specifically, to talk about *many to many* forgiveness, the group that forgives must be capable of being wronged (restricting the analysis to moral debts), and the group forgiven must be capable of doing wrong. The former issue arises in the *many to one* form of forgiveness, discussed here. The problem of whether groups can do wrong and be forgiven arises in the discussion of *one to many* forgiveness (the theme of chapters 6 and 7). At least in the domestic case, the central theoretical problems of *many to many* forgiveness can be addressed through the other forms of forgiveness.

Analyzing the third relationship, *many to one*, requires first, consideration of the general problem of whether groups can engage in political forgiveness. With the exception of the discussion of the vicarious forgiveness of financial debt, the analysis in previous chapters centered on the authority to forgive at the individual level. Here, in focusing on the problem of moral wrongs, we need to consider whether groups can be

1. This framework modifies one that Tavuchis uses in his discussion of apologies (Tavuchis 1991, 48).

wronged and whether the nature of the wrong depends on the kind of group involved. To structure the analysis, Peter French's distinction (1984) between random aggregates, nonrandom aggregates, and conglomerates is introduced. To the extent that random and nonrandom aggregates are wronged, the wrong is distributed to the individuals. Given that individuals have the primary right to forgive, these kinds of groups cannot forgive on behalf of the individuals who are wronged, unless those individuals have implicitly or explicitly transferred the right to forgive to some third party (the only form of vicarious forgiveness of wrongs admitted in chapter 4). In the case of governments, which are conglomerates in French's taxonomy, the group is itself wronged even though the wrong need not be distributed to every member of the group. If the conglomerate is wronged, then we may talk of collective forgiveness. If the conglomerate is a government and the wrong is a crime, then the collective forgiveness of an individual takes the form of a pardon.

Random Aggregates

A group might be a group only because it happened to be wronged. In this situation, a set of individuals finds itself in the wrong place at the wrong time and is intentionally or negligently wronged. Because there is nothing uniting these individuals other than a contingent event, this is a random aggregate. The clearest examples of wrongs that create a random aggregate involve cases of negligence. Perhaps a skywalk collapses, not because of the particular conventioneers at a hotel but because it cannot bear the weight that it should. A plane crashes, not because of whom it is carrying but because it does not perform as well as it should in certain weather conditions. Here the victims are a group only because they are victims.

When one turns to intentional wrongs, it becomes more difficult to find pure examples of random aggregates, although victims of terrorism might form such a group, for example, if the only thing that unites the Mothers of the Plaza de Mayo in Argentina is the fact that the government murdered their children. But even terrorism is not aimed at simply anyone. To some extent, terrorists want to send a message, which in turn requires some identification of the potential victims: wives and children of revolutionaries, middle-class supporters of the government, Western businessmen, citizens of the old regime. What unites some victims of a terrorist act, however, does not unite them all. Terrorists may discriminate, but they are not discriminating.

If the victims who define a random aggregate authorize an agent to forgive the negligent or intentional wrongdoer, then we would have an example of group or "collected" forgiveness. The actions of the authorized party would be equivalent to the sum of the individual actions: "the group" could not be said to forgive if any of the victims were unwilling. This kind of "group forgiveness" is, however, closer to the vicarious forgiveness of wrongs discussed in chapter 4 than it is to collective forgiveness. Given these features, this kind of forgiveness would be analogous to a situation in which representatives of negligence victims pressed the responsible party for admissions of guilt and compensation. Instead of pressing their claims for justice, however, the representatives would express forgiveness.[2]

Nonrandom Aggregates

Not all aggregates are random. Sometimes victims are united not by their victimhood but by a feature or identity that they share. Individuals who are grouped by ethnicity, gender, religious affiliation, physical characteristics, and so on are common examples of nonrandom aggregates. Because a collective decision-procedure and statement of purpose do not usually unite these individuals, they are still an aggregate, and because they are united by more than chance, they are nonrandom. Racial slurs, anti-Semitism, sexism, and negative stereotypes are all examples of wrongs or offenses committed against nonrandom aggregates. As these cases suggest, when the wrong focuses on the shared characteristic or identity that defines the aggregate, there is a sense in which the wrong is distributed throughout the group. A wrong against a member of a nonrandom aggregate reverberates to all those who share the ascribed characteristic or identity.

To help illustrate this case, consider the story in Simon Wiesenthal's *The Sunflower* that I mentioned earlier. When Wiesenthal was a prisoner at Mauthausen concentration camp, he was placed on a work detail that

2. I understand that in receiving compensation, it is not unusual for the victims to surrender all further claims against those who have harmed them. Perhaps this is a backhanded admission that whatever compensation is given may not satisfy the victims completely. Such a surrendering of a right looks like a kind of collected forgiveness for whatever uncompensated harms remain. That it is part of a "deal" (i.e., "We offer this compensation in exchange for immunity from further claims") need not make it any less a case of forgiveness. In this exchange, a reconciliatory state with the past may be achieved. Whether such a settlement invites a process of reconciliation and the restoration of trust and civility is another matter.

took him to a local hospital. While at the hospital, he was brought before a dying German soldier named Karl. Swathed in bandages, the young soldier told his story of growing up in a good, Catholic home, joining the Hitler Youth and then the SS, against the wishes of his parents. On the eastern front, Karl's unit murdered 150 to 200 Jewish men, women, and children. Throughout this extraordinary meeting Wiesenthal tried to leave, but Karl insisted on confessing. The soldier concluded by admitting, "I know that what I have told you is terrible. In the long nights while I have been waiting for death, time and time again I have longed to talk about it to a Jew and beg forgiveness from him. Only I didn't know whether there were any Jews left. . . . I know that what I am asking is almost too much for you, but without your answer I cannot die in peace" (Wiesenthal 1976, 57). Wiesenthal left him without saying a word and later found out that Karl had died the next day.

Karl's request raises in a fairly direct manner the question of whether Wiesenthal could forgive on behalf of those murdered women and children. Josek, one of Wiesenthal's fellow prisoners, says after hearing of the SS soldier's confession, "I feared at first, that you had really forgiven him. You would have had no right to do this in the name of the people who had not authorized you to do so" (Wiesenthal 1976, 68). Wiesenthal responds, "But aren't we a single community with the same destiny, and one must answer for the other?" (68). Josek rejects this claim, noting that "you have suffered nothing because of him, and it follows that what he has done to other people you are in no position to forgive" (68). This exchange is important because each position captures something of the conception of political forgiveness that is being carved out here. Josek's claim that Wiesenthal was unauthorized to forgive on behalf of Karl's victims accords with the view of political forgiveness as a prerogative that the injured possesses first, and usually last. In contrast to Josek's position, however, it is a prerogative that may be surrendered to others. Wiesenthal's appeal to community and Josek's point that Karl did not harm Wiesenthal have less to do with vicarious forgiveness and more with group forgiveness.

Karl had grievously and irreparably harmed a set of individuals in what was once a town on the eastern front. Using Trudy Govier's distinction, we can call these the primary victims of Karl's actions (Govier 1999, 60). In so doing, he had also harmed family members and friends who loved, cared for, and had an interest in these individuals. These would constitute the secondary victims. Given the nature of Karl's crime, it inevitably reverberated well beyond the primary victims. But it is also significant that these victims were not selected just because they happened to be nearby when the German army decided to retaliate after the Russians had booby-trapped a town. These people were murdered because they were Jews. As Jews, their religious/ethnic identity formed a nonrandom aggregate. At least initially, we can call this random aggregate a tertiary victim. Does this mean that Karl's actions also harmed Wiesenthal?

One way to argue that Karl's actions did reverberate throughout the Jewish community is to claim that his actions were a threat to all Jews. Karl may have murdered *these* people, but the threat was to anyone identified as Jewish, or as a homosexual, a Gypsy, or mentally disturbed. But this argument does not appear compelling. For—even in the context of the Holocaust—it is a stretch to claim that Karl and his unit threatened or potentially threatened all Jews. The general threat that Karl posed was not distributed evenly. For some Jews, the threat was immediate; for others, it was very small. In a sense, Josek is correct: Karl did not harm or threaten to harm Wiesenthal. Wiesenthal cannot forgive Karl for either the direct or indirect harm that Karl caused.

Yet, this is not to say that Karl did no wrong to Wiesenthal. Not all wrongs involve actual or potential physical harm. Karl's actions represented a threat to *many* Jews but were an offense to *all* Jews; his actions embodied the standard Nazi message about a master race and inferior beings, and their derogatory, insulting, and dangerous character denied the very humanity of a people. The wrong disseminated by the Nazis' message and carried forth in Karl's actions was distributed to every individual in the Jewish community.[3] In this case, the harm done to the tertiary victim or random aggregate distributes itself to the individuals themselves. Karl did owe Wiesenthal (and any Jew) something, and consequently Wiesenthal did have the power to forgive part of what Karl did, assuming the minimal conditions for justice had been met. It was a power that Wiesenthal was free to exercise.

If we understand part of the wrong that Karl did as an offense to the individuals of an aggregate, we have a collected, as opposed to a collective, wrong. But, once again, it is not a wrong that could very easily yield a form of collected forgiveness. In this instance, as in the case of a

---

3. Ralph Ellison eloquently expressed the idea that the wrong done to an individual may actually reverberate to the group. "Normally the individual dies his own death," Ellison remarked, but the man facing a lynch mob "is forced to undergo death for all his group" (cited in Raybon 1996, 59). The distinction between a harm and an offense is one that I am drawing from Feinberg's work (Feinberg 1984, 12–13).

harm to a random aggregate, the only way to empower a group form of forgiveness is if each individual forgave or if some agent was so authorized. Unless some office or individual represented all Jews (clearly, there are Jewish organizations, African-American associations, and women's groups, but do they truly represent all those who would be considered Jewish, African American, or female?), that is, unless the tertiary victim was something more than an aggregate, the notion of collective forgiveness is unavailable even to nonrandom aggregates.

One problem with using the notion of "offense" to capture the wrong that was done to Wiesenthal, however, is that the scope of the wrong becomes virtually limitless. Was the offense only to Jews? Weren't Karl's actions also offensive to any person with a modicum of humanity? If this is so, then didn't the power to forgive Karl for his offense go far beyond the Jewish community?[4] Although this is correct, the nature of Karl's offense to Jews is far more direct and serious. Surely there is a difference between suffering an insult and witnessing insulting behavior. Both may require an apology from the transgressor (at least), but the more important debt is owed to the person who is the object of the insult or derogatory action. Our moral practices are sophisticated enough to discern these distinctions. The central problem with forgiving wrongs done to nonrandom and random groups is that the harms and offenses are so widely distributed that a collected form of forgiveness is practically impossible and itself offends those who do not participate.[5]

4. This claim has its counterpoint in the language of responsibility. In Karl Jaspers's notion of metaphysical guilt, "There exists a solidarity among men as human beings that makes each co-responsible for every wrong and every injustice in the world, especially for crimes committed in his presence with his knowledge" (quoted in May 1993, 147). If everyone is responsible for evil and every evil is a wrong to every right-thinking individual, then self-forgiveness has the potential for wiping the slate clean.

5. The difficulties of actually forgiving at an aggregate level and the deep bitterness it can raise are most evident in the ceremony commemorating VJ-Day at the site of the Kwai prison camp in Thailand—a camp in which the British prisoners of war were treated with extraordinary brutality. Even the appearance that this ceremony could represent a more general form of forgiveness made the Allied governments uncomfortable and inspired the invective of those who claimed to represent survivors of the labor camps. The atonement by Japanese prison camp guards for their treatment of British soldiers was apparently accepted (or seen as such) by those who attended the ceremony. However, as David Lane of Britain's "Jap Labour Camp Survivors' Association" said, "Anybody who attends [the ceremony] will be ostracized by us. We will never shake hands with the former Japanese guards, not if they pay us £50 million each" (Thomas 1995, 8).

Conglomerates

Aside from random and nonrandom aggregates, French's classificatory scheme also includes conglomerates, which is meant to encompass corporations and governments. A conglomerate is defined as a group united by a decision-making process and an identifiable set of purposes. These characteristics bear on the question of whether governments can be held responsible for their actions. Here we are more concerned with whether governments can be acted upon and wronged than whether they can be held responsible for actions committed in their name. If a government can suffer wrong, then perhaps it can also forgive; and if it can forgive, then the idea of a collective form of political forgiveness becomes plausible.

For those who see forgiving as bound up with the notion of resentment, it is absurd to think that governments could forgive. Even if we act as if governments can be held morally culpable for their actions, governments are incapable of any feeling, let alone resentment or anger. For our purposes, a government is a particular arrangement of a set of principles, norms, rules, regulations, procedures, offices, positions, policies, and enactments that are considered authoritative because they are recognized as such.[6] The advantage of the idea of political forgiveness over competing conceptions of forgiveness is that political forgiveness, as an act of self-disclosure, does not require that governments have feelings at all. A conglomerate may arrive at a decision to forgive by whatever authoritative decision-procedure governs the entity. Forgiveness is not a decision to eliminate a particular "group sentiment." Nevertheless, it does require that we make sense of what wronging a government means. If, following Feinberg, we see a wrong as a setback to an especially significant interest, then we need to consider whether governments can have interests, whether any of these interests are important enough to be considered rights, and finally, whether the setback of any of those rights would be considered wrongs. If governments can be wronged, they can also forgive.

Wronging Governments

Clearly, groups, institutions, and governments can have a stake in particular outcomes and states of affairs and, hence, have interests. This

6. Any attempt to identify this concept satisfactorily would require an account of the ways in which "government" differs from and is related to such terms as *state, nation, regime, administration, realm, commonwealth, republic,* and *country.* In addition, understanding the concept of *government* would also require understanding how governments are instituted, lost, transformed, taken over, recognized, and rendered illegitimate. Given the nature of these questions, a full explication of the concept of government is an invitation that is declined here.

makes sense because we say that conglomerates can flourish or languish depending on whether they exist in a favorable or unfavorable context. Nations rise and fall, corporations go bankrupt or return a profit, institutions become corrupt or flourish. It is not far-fetched to talk about national interests or the interests of a company and, when those interests are set back, reasonable to conclude that they are harmed. As Feinberg notes, however, being harmed is not the same as being wronged (Feinberg 1984, 35). For example, the Anasazi, an aboriginal group in the American Southwest, may have disappeared because shifting weather patterns changed flora and fauna in their environment. The destruction of that ancient tribe of people was clearly a harm to a group (and to the individual members) but was not a wrong or an injustice. Assuming that the matter involved misfortune and not injustice, the Anasazi were not wronged, but they were harmed.[7] A defining feature of being wronged is that one's interests are involuntarily invaded and set back by another. Clearly, not all invasions of interests are wrongs, either; the practice of punishment, for example, entails a justifiable, involuntary setback of interests. What must be set back is an interest protected by a valid claim or right. Feinberg contends that "one person *wrongs* another when his indefensible (unjustifiable and inexcusable) conduct violates the other's right, and in all but certain very special cases such conduct will also invade the other's interest and thus be harmful" (34). Do governments have not only interests that can be thwarted but also rights that can be violated?

At the level of the individual, what Feinberg calls welfare interests serve as the basis of rights claims. Feinberg argues that we possess a roughly similar set of welfare interests—interests that are necessary to secure and protect us regardless of the ulterior interests or purposes that we pursue. These include such things as an interest

> in one's own physical health and vigor, the integrity and normal functioning of one's body, the absence of absorbing pain and suffering or grotesque disfigurement, minimal intellectual acuity, emotional stability, the absence of groundless anxieties and resentments, the capacity to engage normally in social intercourse and to enjoy and maintain friendships, at least minimal income and financial security, a tolerable social and physical environment, and a certain amount of freedom from interference and coercion. (Feinberg 1984, 37)

7. The possibility that their "misfortune" was a result of their actions (e.g., depleting the resources of the area) also need not mean they were wronged. If the harm was done voluntarily, then the notion of wrong is also misplaced.

Feinberg believes that these "reasonable interests" can provide "valid claims against others (moral rights) *par excellence*" (Feinberg 1984, 112).[8] Whatever one may think of the adequacy of this list and the assumption that we all share such interests, is there a comparable list applicable to governments that would include either ulterior or welfare interests?

Those who subscribe to an organic conception of the state or to a strong form of communitarianism or structuralism may very well have a list of social-welfare interests. These perspectives, because they are more open to the possibility of seeing communities or states as independent moral agents may also be more open to seeing groups as having free-standing welfare interests. In contrast, the individualistic stance adopted here is skeptical of according collectives or conglomerates a set of interests that are freestanding in the same way as individual interests.[9] Because they are not autonomous sources of moral claims, the whole notion of wronging conglomerates is placed in jeopardy. If they cannot be wronged, then they cannot forgive.

One way to attribute welfare interests to a conglomerate such as a government is to see the government's interests as dependent on securing the welfare interests of its citizens. The advantage of framing the discussion in this way is that governments, by themselves, can possess a right to survive or flourish as long as they are directed toward securing the welfare interests of the citizenry. This view of governmental welfare interests would also be consonant with a view of a just state as one that enables individuals and groups to pursue what they see as valuable or good in life. A central assumption of this conception of general justice is that governments possess moral standing when they live up to the principles of justice and enable those living within their boundaries to pursue what they see as good (Digeser and Miller 1995). Other institutions and groups are just when they live up to the demands and rules of a just government.

Although undefended, this conception of moral standing may convey what it means to wrong a government: a wrong is a harmful action that prevents or interferes with the government's ability to protect its members' pursuit of happiness. The government's interests can be set back if it cannot perform this function. A government has a moral right to pur-

8. Although more extensive, detailed, and controversial, they resemble what John Rawls calls "primary goods."

9. Obviously, adopting an individualistic stance is not the same as defending it. The problem with making this assumption for theorizing political forgiveness is not that it is an assumption (for there are plenty of those throughout this book) but that it raises difficult problems for how governments could be wronged and do wrong.

sue this function because individuals have a moral right to pursue what they see as the good life. In addition, this implies that a just government is wronged when anyone violates the fundamental interests of its members. The government can thus be wronged when individuals are thwarted in pursuing their interests—including their interests in organizing other institutions and groups.

One implication of this argument is that unjust governments, although they have a set of interests and can be harmed, cannot be wronged insofar as they do not protect their citizens and enable their pursuit of the good. This rather simplistic statement quickly runs into enormous difficulties. From the previous discussion of rectificatory justice (chapter 2), we know that even the best regimes are not entirely just. Does this mean they also lack rights? What does "enable and protect" actually mean? What does the lack of moral standing of a state mean for its international standing and the rights to intervention and revolution? Do all pursuits of value constitute a pursuit of the good life? Answering any of these questions would bring us into the huge literature dealing with domestic and international justice. Having said that, we should be clear that the justice of any government is going to be a matter of more or less, and consequently the strength of its claims to protect itself will always depend on its capacity to serve its citizenry. A key presumption here is that governments that run roughshod over the pursuit of the good life of individuals lack moral standing.[10]

A second implication of this analysis is that it may not extend to other conglomerates. This does not mean that businesses, clubs, associations, and corporations cannot be wronged but that unless their moral standing rests on their abilities to protect the welfare interests of their members, they cannot be wronged in the same way as just governments. Moreover, aside from the forgiveness of financial debt, it is difficult to imagine how the nongovernmental conglomerates would undertake political forgiveness.

Governmental Forgiveness

If governments can be wronged, that is, if they can possess moral rights derived from the rights of individuals living within their purview, then forgiveness becomes a possibility. Governments that are nearly just can

10. This may seem to deprive the state of its nobler or higher purposes and, consequently, of its ability to call upon individuals to sacrifice their lives and treasure for its defense. This is not quite true, for on occasion, states do find themselves in the realm of necessity (see chapter 7).

be victims. The harm can come from outside (conquest, war, embargoes, threats) or inside (crime, desertion, civil disturbance, civil war). Here, I consider whether internally generated wrongs open a possibility for political forgiveness. In the case of criminal activity, the answer in part depends on whether the violation of the law is taken as a purely private matter or is instead understood as a wrong against the political association that created the law. If the former, then theft, murder, and assault are wrongs solely against the victim and his or her family and friends. Under this kind of system, whether to prosecute or pursue punishment would belong to those who had been injured. Political institutions would simply provide a forum within which a proceeding against the alleged transgressor could take place. On this view of crime, because the wrong is done to the individual and not to the larger group, there would be nothing for the government to forgive. The exception would be situations in which the government itself was attacked—cases of treason, desertion, or rebellion. In the latter instances, the harms are aimed at the sovereign and the sovereign's representatives.[11]

The more one sees all crime as a public injury, however, the greater the space for political forgiveness. But how could a criminal act be a wrong that extends beyond the specific individuals who suffered the injury? If the justness of a government depends, in part, on its ability to protect and enable its members, then a criminal action against a specific individual sets back this fundamental interest. Crime is an act against the government's fundamental interest in protecting its members. If crime is seen in this way, the decision to prosecute is not left to the victim, his family, or his friends. In addition, if the political association also suffers the wrong, then a guilty verdict means the perpetrator owes a debt to that association. Although payment of this debt may be unsatisfactory to the individual victim, it can satisfy the political association. Crime creates a debt

11. The restorative model of criminal justice comes close to arguing that crime does not wrong the state. Accordingly, this model criticizes criminal justice practices that focus on the injury done to the state and not the injury done to the actual victim. Nevertheless, nothing in the restorative model itself may preclude seeing a political association as capable of being wronged (Couper 1998, 123). In addition, many advocates of restorative justice see "the community" as one of the parties injured and ignored in the current system. Still, in a very broad sense, the notions of wronging the community or wronging the political association are plagued by similar difficulties: How can the community itself be wronged? Who represents the community? Can the community forgive? (Harland 1996, 508; Hudson 1998, 251). Although the restorative justice model privatizes crime to some degree, it does not avoid the problem of group wrong.

to the association. The just payment of that debt may entail punishment, fines, and other elements of the carceral system. However, the government could act to forgive the debt by pardoning the offender. On this view, pardoning is collective forgiving; it does not necessarily erase the debt owed the particular victim. Rather, a pardon implies the erasing of the public debt and an invitation to restore a civil relationship between the transgressor and the political association. A pardon is a form of collective political forgiveness, which calls for the government and invites the citizenry to restore the offender to his or her place in civil society.

The Case against Pardons as Forgiveness

Kathleen Dean Moore offers the most compelling case against seeing pardoning as a form of forgiveness (see also Haber 1991, 61; McGary 1989, 345). In large part, however, Moore bases her argument on the stipulation that forgiveness refers "to an attitude of one who has been injured toward the one who has inflicted the injury. The attitude of forgiveness is characterized by the presence of good will or by the lack of personal resentment for the injury" (Moore 1989, 184). One consequence of this definition, as we saw in chapter 1, is that forgiveness need not possess illocutionary force. The significance of this point is that because forgiveness is not a performative, one can forgive and still punish. This conclusion, in turn, permits Moore to distinguish forgiveness from pardoning. For pardoning is, first and foremost, an activity that releases the transgressor from punishment. In contrast, forgiveness is merely a change in attitude and, consequently, "is primarily a relationship between persons. Institutions, states, systems of justice cannot forgive—except perhaps metaphorically—because although they may be wronged, they do not resent" (187).

Obviously, Moore's definition of forgiveness differs significantly from the understanding of political forgiveness offered here. I am not denying that a resentment- or sentiment-based conception of forgiveness can be a way to understand the concept, and that this kind of forgiveness need not even be a locution. If we are considering what forgiveness would look like in politics, however, then we may want to take our cue from public and not private instances of forgiveness, and as we have seen, pardoning is frequently taken to be a kind of forgiving. More specifically, it is a kind of forgiving with illocutionary effect. If we combine this claim with the understanding of crime as a public wrong, then pardoning is separable from private acts of forgiveness.

In contrast, because Moore believes that forgiveness need not require an action, she is able to conclude that forgiveness and pardon are "logically independent. A person may forgive a wrongdoer and punish her all the same" (Moore 1989, 185; see also O'Shaughnessy 1967, 338), or one may remit punishment (i.e., pardon) and not forgive. Moore provides two examples to support these positions. Each can be used to illustrate the differences between her understanding of forgiveness and the notion of political forgiveness presented here. In the first, a teenager lies and steals from her parents to support her drug habit. The parents catch the child and, after an initial period of anger and resentment, become concerned and sympathetic: "They forgive her, because they love her." Moore argues that although they forgive her, it is completely intelligible for them to have their daughter prosecuted for theft. According to Moore, punishment in this instance is compatible with forgiveness.

Moore's description assumes, however, that the parents are forgiving and that the law is punishing the same wrong. In a legal system that understood a crime as more than a private injury, however, the parents could conclude that they were not the only ones who were wronged. Strictly speaking, by calling in the police they are also acting as citizens and not merely private individuals. In theory, once the courts take over, whether the parents forgive may become of little or no concern to the prosecution. In this instance, it is perfectly possible for the parents to forgive the injury done to them without forgiving the injury done to the law (because they have no standing to do the latter).[12]

Moore's second example is that "a Governor may grant a full pardon to a rapist without forgiving him, primarily because the governor does not have standing to forgive, not having been raped" (Moore 1989, 185). Once again, from the perspective of a political forgiveness, Moore's analysis does possess part of the truth. It is true that the governor cannot forgive on behalf of the victim because he or she has no standing, and as we saw, the notion of vicariously forgiving wrongs can violate the victim's rights. But the governor, as a duly authorized official with the power of pardon, can forgive the wrong done to the political association. When the governor does this, the rapist's debt to the political association has been erased, and a reconciliatory process has been initiated. On this reading of pardons as a form of political forgiveness, the government should not treat a rapist

12. A less harsh reading of the parents' actions is that by calling in the police, they don't want to punish their daughter; they want her to get help. Perhaps they believe that only through this course of action can they get their daughter into a drug rehabilitation center. But if this is the case, they don't see their actions as punishment at all.

with a full pardon any differently than any other citizen. That particular crime cannot be used as a basis for future claims. Whether the rest of us take up the invitation to reconciliation is something else; those who have been harmed by the rapist may refuse to associate with or respect him. The problem with Moore's analysis of forgiveness is that it does not take into account the layers of wrongs that a crime can entail and assumes that forgiveness must be defined as a change of attitude.

Forgiveness and the Remission of Punishment

Nevertheless, Moore's position that forgiveness and pardoning are distinct concepts can receive support from another quarter. Some have argued that forgiveness does not require a change in behavior but does require the existence of "some special kind of personal, intimate, relationship between a forgiver and the person he forgives" (O'Shaughnessy 1967, 338). In making this claim, R. J. O'Shaughnessy admits that it is "difficult to cash," but he seems to be arguing that successful forgiving requires very careful attention to how the victim and transgressor are related and what they understand each other to be doing when they use such terms as forgiveness, mercy, apology, repentance, and so on.

Presumably, because all forgiveness must be "local," it requires a very personal, intimate relationship. It is difficult enough for forgiveness to get off the ground even if that relationship exists. If a personal relationship does not exist, there are too many ways for the act to "go wrong." What is essential to picking up the local, rich, context-bound, idiosyncratic character of forgiving is being attuned to the attitudes conveyed. Even if a particular act of forgiveness involves remission of a punishment, it always "seems to involve something more than, something over-and-above the *mere* letting off" of the person who has been forgiven (O'Shaughnessy 1967, 344). That something more is an expression of a particular attitude. Consequently, forgiveness cannot be defined as simply the remission of punishment or be undertaken by impersonal officials.

O'Shaughnessy's argument that forgiveness necessitates an intimate relationship is linked to two claims. The first is that only in a personal relationship can the participants pick up the requisite *attitudes* conveyed when forgiving, and second, only in that kind of relationship can we pick up the idiosyncrasies of the *terms* that are being used.[13] If, however, political for-

---

13. These features of forgiveness lead O'Shaughnessy to mistrust attempts to establish "a univocal meaning for the various *terms*" that surround the concept (O'Shaughnessy 1967, 341).

giveness swings free of particular forms of self-enactment, then the conveyance of particular attitudes isn't an issue. Instead, the issue concerns whether the terms of forgiveness need to be ambiguous in order for it to take place. But O'Shaughnessy cannot be making *that* argument. Although forgiveness can go wrong in many ways, these do not preclude the possibility for political forgiveness to be rather straightforward and easily understandable. Rather, he seems to be claiming that those who argue that forgiveness must always be straightforward (e.g., that it is just a matter of the remission of punishment) are ignoring the extraordinarily complex uses of the concept. If political forgiveness is a self-disclosive, illocutionary act, and it is not a necessary condition for forgiveness that the victim and transgressor have a personal relationship, then pardoning can be seen as a form of forgiveness.

One could, however, argue that the notion of political forgiveness advanced here is nothing more than the remission of punishment—whereas it is quite clear that forgiveness is used in many ways that have nothing to do with stopping punishment. According to O'Shaughnessy, those who associate forgiveness with the remission of punishment misunderstand the character of forgiveness.

From a very general perspective, the conception of political forgiveness does not conflict with O'Shaughnessy's conclusions regarding the myriad possible uses for the notion of forgiveness. For I do not identify political forgiveness with the remission of punishment. On the one hand, a refusal to punish or retaliate in politics could be due to all sorts of reasons—prosecutorial discretion, cost, unwillingness of witnesses to testify, the realization of the transgressor's innocence—that have nothing to do with pardoning (forgiving). On the other hand, a plausible case can be made that the forgiveness of debts can be a political act. Unless a continued demand for payment was always a form of punishment, financial forgiveness need not entail the remission of punishment at all. Even though pardoning implies the remission of punishment, not all political forgiveness takes the form of pardoning, and not all remissions of punishment are forms of political forgiveness. There is no straightforward identity between political forgiveness and the remission of punishment, and in certain cases of political forgiveness (e.g., financial forgiveness) the notions are logically independent.

Finally, O'Shaughnessy and others point out that pardoning is performed by an official possessing the appropriate authority and occupying the proper office. These characteristics establish who is authorized to speak for the government when it seeks to forgive those who have wronged it. That those with authority to forgive can successfully forgive is true not only of pardons but other forms of political forgiveness as well. As we saw in the discussion of the vicarious forgiveness of wrongs, an unauthorized third party could not politically forgive on behalf of the victim. From this perspective, what is different about pardoning is the degree to which the authority to forgive on behalf of the injured party (the government) must be specified, usually in a constitutional framework.

What is also distinctive about pardons is that they present the possibility for what appears to be self-forgiveness. For example, an executive with the appropriate authority could pardon herself for whatever crimes she has committed. This would appear to contradict the first condition of political forgiveness, namely that a forgiving relationship have two parties. It is possible, however, to make sense of this action and still preserve the first condition of political forgiveness. To do so, we must assume that the ultra vires action of an official is the personal responsibility of the individual and not the responsibility of the government, although a government that condones such action could become responsible. By pardoning herself, the individual is split between her official role and her role as an offender. Although occupying one body, two parties are divided by the responsibility for the wrongdoing. The underlying presumption is that officials are agents of the government who are not personally responsible for their authoritative acts. This presumption comes under closer scrutiny in chapter 6, where the problem of governmental responsibility is considered.

Pardoning and Desert

Does Moore's general account of pardoning present other difficulties if we associate pardoning with a self-disclosive conception of political forgiveness? Operating from within a retributivist framework, Moore argues strenuously against understanding pardon as either a kind of gift of grace from a ruler or as an instrument for public or private welfare. According to Moore, "The only reasons that should regulate the human institution of pardon are those related to what each offender deserves. When the punishment prescribed by law is more severe than the offender deserves on account of his offense or particular circumstances, pardon is justified. Other kinds of reasons do not have the credentials to justify pardons" (Moore 1989, 227). The key claims in Moore's analysis are that the only reasons that should count in giving pardons are those having to do with justice, and that the only relevant reasons of justice involve whether the individual under consideration deserves the punishment.

Moore superbly analyzes the historical development of the practice of pardoning and criticizes many of the ways in which the power to pardon has been abused in the past. The thrust of her argument is that the power to pardon should be used to rectify a judicial process that has punished the innocent or punished the guilty too severely. More specifically, she argues that pardon can be justified only under the following conditions: innocence (e.g., overriding a false conviction, preventing the punishment of someone with reduced abilities, removing the stigma of a conviction from someone who has become a "new person"); excusable crime (e.g., the action was unintentional, the actor was the only victim, the crime repaired an injustice, the crime was coerced); justified crime (e.g., reducing or preventing punishment for crimes of conscience); and, finally, adjustments to sentences (relieving punishment for an offender who has suffered enough or preventing cruel punishment) (Moore 1989, 11). Pardons, in other words, should be used to ensure that people receive what they are due.

By trying to associate pardoning with innocence, Moore must deal with the problem that pardons tend to connote guilt: "It might be objected that it is wrong to pardon innocent people because a pardon usually implies guilt, and so those who accept a pardon implicitly admit that they have done something to be pardoned *for*" (Moore 1989, 135). Moore argues that although the connection between guilt and pardon is strong, we should simply not make this inference. In most cases, if her system was accepted, the justification for a pardon would be based on innocence: "If one were forced to make an inference, it would be safer to infer that the pardoned person is innocent, just as it is safer to infer that a meteorite will fall on water, the earth being three parts water to one part land" (216). In addition, Moore argues that in cases where a pardon is sought posthumously, it is meant to clear the deceased's name and establish her innocence. Thus, she concludes, an inference that the pardoned individual is innocent is not that far out of line with current practice, and it is compatible with retributivist theory.

In detaching pardoning from guilt, Moore's position requires empowering the executive to establish innocence or disproportional punishment after the legal system has established guilt or the legislature has set out its schedule of punishment. In fact, she requires among other things that a pardon not occur unless the offender has been tried, convicted, and sentenced (Moore 1989, 217). In effect, Moore's understanding of pardon is equivalent to the setting aside of a verdict or the veto of a legislative decision.

Even if Moore could successfully detach guilt from pardoning,[14] her position seems to conflict with the separation of powers, and it raises troubling questions of equity. The former is the case if the separation of powers requires us to distinguish between setting aside or reversing a verdict and pardoning an offender. In such a system, only higher courts, not the executive, may set aside or reverse the verdicts of lower courts. Executives, as executives, do not set aside the verdicts of the judicial branch (although they may effectively do this by refusing to enforce them). If executives could reverse verdicts, they would have the authority to establish guilt or innocence. Similarly, for executives to set aside the punishments mandated by statute would be to claim the authority to establish the proper schedule of penalties. Obviously, as a conceptual matter, nothing would prevent the executive from performing these functions—certain kings often did. Nevertheless, investing an executive with this kind of authority not only raises the question of why courts exist, but it also jeopardizes the possibility for equity: if part of the executive's job is to decide whether the innocent are mistakenly being found guilty or whether sentences are too harsh, then equity would seem to demand that all prisoners who believe they were innocent or unfairly treated should have their day before the executive. A basic sense of fairness would seem to be violated if only a few out of many such claims made it to the executive's door. But if an appeal to the executive must be available to all, then all of those appeals should be presented by competent advocates and governed by a set of fair rules. Essentially, the fair application of Moore's solution would simply create another level of court-like appeal. In a system of separation of powers, this means that judicial decisions would lack the power to be enforced as well as the power ultimately to establish matters of fact and law. In this scenario, the final court of appeals in criminal cases could be the executive. Should executives, who are not judges, play this role?[15] And if executives became judges, why would this solution differ from simply adding another layer of appeal to the judicial process?

14. As long as guilt is associated with being pardoned, Moore's retributivist justification runs into trouble. For Moore, the whole idea of granting a pardon is to give what is deserved. In the case of pardoning innocent individuals, however, they are not getting what they deserve by being pardoned—for they still have the stigma of guilt.

15. Moore suggests that we should be able not only to criticize executives' exercise of their pardoning power but also to employ the power of impeachment. The former option,

If Moore's solution of detaching guilt from pardoning raises questions of equity and rearranges the balance of authority, how does a view of pardoning as a form of political forgiveness fare? If we see pardoning as an official form of forgiving, then the connection between pardoning and guilt is inevitable. Forgiveness presupposes the existence of a debt and, in the case of crime, of a wrong that was done. On this view, to pardon is to relieve what is due, not to ensure that what is due is actually handed out. This is perhaps the central distinction between Moore's view of pardoning and one that sees pardoning as a form of public forgiveness. The latter view tightens the link between guilt and pardons.

If pardons are tightly linked to guilt, then it seems appropriate for executives to distinguish clearly a situation in which the guilty are not receiving what is their due (a pardon) from the setting aside of a verdict for the sake of innocence. Yet, this distinction is rarely made in practice. In effect, Moore's position and the position set out here are both plagued by the fact that pardons are given to the guilty and to the innocent. From the perspective set out here, the question is why should pardoning be at all associated with setting the innocent free. Why not use some other word to differentiate it from situations in which the guilty are set free? The answer may not be philosophical but political: according an executive the power to pardon (as opposed to the power to set aside verdicts) acknowledges and respects the judicial authority's ability to establish guilt or innocence, and the legislature's power to set punishments, but then permits the executive to lessen what is officially seen as "due." On this view, pardons are explicitly not meant to set aside the verdicts of courts or the sentences mandated by the legislature; the legitimacy of the system is nodded to but its decisions are not carried out. The innocent individual is set free but not acquitted of the crime, or the criminal's punishment is diminished but the legislature's judgment is not displaced.

This interpretation of pardoning as the power to forgive may look like a shell game that buys the stability of the system at the expense of the reputation of the innocent individual and the unfairly treated prisoner.

I would think, should always be available in an open democracy. The latter option would require, at least in the U.S. Constitution, something more than simply listing high crimes and misdemeanors. If the executive could establish guilt or innocence, how could abuse be demonstrated? By definition, whomever the president pardoned would be innocent. Moore's only example of an executive who was impeached for abusing the pardoning power was Oklahoma governor J. C. Walton (Moore 1989, 202). Walton, however, appears to have been accused of bribery and giving pardons for the ordinary kinds of reasons that would offend retributivists and nonretributivists.

There is something to that appearance. But pardoning as forgiveness does more than preserve the separation of power, for it does not accord the executive an unreviewable and arbitrary authority to set aside the court's verdicts; the executive cannot turn the guilty into the innocent. It can relieve the amount of punishment given to a victim, but by pardoning (insofar as it is seen as forgiving), it cannot establish that the amount given was undeserved.

Nevertheless, it is also true that to *pardon* an innocent individual is an insult and an offense. From the standpoint of the unjustly treated prisoner, a pardon may go some distance in rectifying his or her situation, but the result is not wholly satisfying—for the government need admit no wrong. Similarly, if punishments can be too harsh and hence unjust, then the wrong is committed not by the convict being punished too severely but by the legal system. Not only is the system punishing too severely, but by forgiving the victim (in this case the criminal), it adds an insult. If there is anything in need of forgiveness, it would be those institutions that set up excessive mandatory punishments or generate an unjust outcome. Pardoning the victim is a move that only Charles Dickens's Mr. Pecksniff could appreciate. Forgiving can itself generate an injustice.

One admittedly minor way to respond to the problem of pardoning the innocent is to give the convicted the option of rejecting a pardon. Although Moore notes that this is not the current practice in the United States, she believes it should be (Moore 1989, 221). Moore's defense of such an option stems from her retributivism: she would try to prevent pardons from being used in a utilitarian regime of punishment. However, if pardoning is a form of forgiveness and a pardon is connected to guilt, it is also necessary for the innocent to have the option of establishing their innocence within the system. To force someone to accept a pardon is to force them to accept the public pronouncement of their guilt. Making a pardon depend on the convicted person's acceptance corresponds to the notion that persons should not be forgiven unless they believe that they are guilty. In a small way, this requirement respects innocence. Yet we should be clear about the reality of the choice: an individual is being forced to choose between being free and publicly thought guilty or being imprisoned and privately thought innocent.

As long as pardoning is associated with guilt and pardoning is the mechanism used to deal with the unjust treatment of the innocent or the guilty, the problem remains. Is it appropriate for citizens to forgive a government that has treated them in this manner? It is argued in chapter 7 that if cases of this type fall under the problems of imperfect procedures, then there may be an opening for political forgiveness. Perhaps forgiveness is one way to respond to the wrongs generated by pardoning the innocent. If, however, the notion of pardoning the innocent (as opposed to simply releasing them) is part of a calculation to preserve the system's stability in exchange for the rights of the innocent, then pardoning itself looks not like imperfect procedural justice but like political actors doing something wrong to accomplish some good. This kind of problem is considered under the heading of dirty hands. If pardoning entails dirty hands, then there are strong reasons for citizens not to forgive a government that pardons the innocent.

Pardoning to Relieve What Was Due

In contrast to Moore's position, I am suggesting that the primary purpose of pardoning is to relieve what is due and not to ensure that what is due is given. From chapter 2, however, the argument has been that political forgiveness should not displace the pursuit of justice. As a form of forgiveness, however, pardoning appears to do just that: by pardoning an offender, neither the offender nor the state receives their due. The possibility that pardoning could displace justice is what retributivists, such as Moore, find so disturbing and why they see appeals to innocence or disproportionate punishment as the only acceptable claims for pardoning.

The basis for the retributivist's argument was mentioned in chapter 2: the good of rectificatory justice. Fully receiving what is due, whatever that may mean, appears to be Moore's overriding value. In contrast, pardoning as a form of political forgiveness admits the possibility that the full receipt of what is due may be overridden by other values. Even in the case of pardoning, however, the minimal conditions of justice must be met. Beyond that point, a case may be made for displacing justice. Making this case must ultimately turn on the value of reconciliation, as a state and as a process, or on what reconciliation itself may foster—peace, stability, an opportunity to express gratitude for meritorious service, or generosity. To elucidate these claims, I compare and contrast with Moore's retributivist account the reasons for political forgiveness.

"Bad Reasons" for Pardoning

If pardoning is a form of political forgiveness, then it is also clear that many of the reasons for pardoning defended here are, from Moore's retributivist perspective, bad reasons. Yet there are also points of agreement. For example, pardoning someone just because she is a woman, or

because she comes from a good family, or because the pardon will personally benefit the pardoner (e.g., bribery) are all unacceptable reasons (but
have been employed) for pardoning, whether it is in the name of justice or
for forgiveness' sake. The areas of disagreement between the two positions include pardoning for pity's sake, pardoning as a response for meritorious action, and pardoning to secure the public welfare. For Moore, the
problem with these latter kinds of pardons is that they are not only undeserved but that in some cases they can also be coercive. For example, a
pardon could be used "to deliver an offender into the hands of another
state for a more severe punishment, to facilitate deportation . . . [or] to
override an offender's decision that execution is preferable to life in
prison" (Moore 1989, 200). In these kinds of cases, the pardon has a coercive character to it because the transgressor has no opportunity to refuse
it. As Moore suggests, one could remedy these kinds of abuses by making
the pardon contingent on the consent of the convicted.

Consent, however, may not remedy all possibility for abuse, especially
when pardons are being justified on the basis of public welfare. In the
name of the public good, Moore fears that the power to pardon could be
used to get convicts to volunteer for activities that they might otherwise
eschew. In these cases, pardons resemble something between a threat and
an offer. For example, Moore sees "pardons granted . . . to turn state's
evidence, to rejoin the army, to populate the colonies, to testify regarding
the details of the offender's own crime, to volunteer for a medical experi-
ment" (Moore 1989, 199) as examples of the kinds of abuses that public
welfare pardons can potentially create. But are they all troublesome?
Some of these activities clearly are incompatible with the restoration of
civil equality and reconciliation (e.g., impressment, deportation, becoming a medical guinea pig) and so would be abuses even if pardoning was
understood as a form of political forgiveness. In the cases of turning
state's evidence or testifying about the details of one's own crime, however, the offensive character of a pardon is not as evident. In these
instances, a pardon could serve an important public good.

Pardoning Those Who Suffer

Before turning to problems associated with other kinds of public welfare
pardon, it may be expeditious to consider first two other reasons for pardoning that Moore considers bad but would be acceptable within an
understanding of pardoning as political forgiveness: pardoning for pity's
sake and pardoning for meritorious action. "Suffering," Moore claims,

"is not a good reason to pardon, *as long as the suffering is no more than deserved*" (Moore 1989, 205). Yet, Moore does argue that pardons can be granted when criminals are near death or because of age, or some special vulnerability they suffer. In all of these instances, she believes, a retributivist theory can accommodate the fact that the punishment has become too severe and the transgressor is getting more than he or she deserves.

One difficulty with Moore's analysis is that desert comes to depend upon the transgressor's reaction. What constitutes desert depends upon the response of the guilty. The risk is that desert for the sensitive would not mean the same thing as it does for the thick-skinned. To punish a hermit by placing him in solitary confinement is not the same as isolating the gregarious. To accommodate cases of compassionate pardoning, a retributivist must change the meaning of what is due. Instead of making desert variable, a perspective of political forgiveness offers an alternative description. A pardon as political forgiveness simply forgives the debt. In this respect, pardoning the sick and the elderly becomes much like forgiving financial debts when they become "crushing" or so burdensome that the debtor cannot recover.

One way to illustrate the difference between Moore's analysis and the analysis presented here is to consider the case of pardoning imprisoned convicts in the last stages of a terminal illness. For Moore, when keeping convicts in prison is more than they deserve, justice demands that they be set free. In contrast, if pardoning is seen as forgiveness, what is deserved is set aside to advance some other value. By seeing pardoning as forgiveness, we keep a clear eye on what precisely is deserved. A pardon is necessary because the demands of justice may not be the only thing of value. In contrast, for Moore, the pardon is a demand of justice. Even if the results are the same, the reasons for the pardon are different.

Although Moore's retributivist account of pardoning seems to offer an intelligible way of dealing with the dying convict, it cannot take into account the suffering of others that the punishment may also cause. According to Moore, it is true that a prison sentence may cause hardships for prisoners and their families. But pity itself should not move us to give less than what is deserved, and "society should provide a safety net so that offenders' dependents do not go hungry," for "pardoning the offender is an unjust way to accomplish what could be achieved by means consistent with just deserts" (Moore 1989, 207). Moore argues correctly that pity is insufficient for pardoning, but the fact of our pity should alert us that something is up. It may be that after we investigate a pitiful situation we find that all is as it should be, but pity should not be dismissed as a reason for public action. The relentless pursuit of corrective justice must be balanced against the good of generosity. Assuming a government in which generosity is a virtue, however, does not necessitate it to be generous on every occasion. A government should be generous, but no particular beneficiary has a right to it on any particular occasion. As with the general discussion of political forgiveness, pardoning is, at most, an imperfect duty. Pardoning becomes one way in which a government can express this duty. A nearly just government that never pardoned would be subject to moral disapproval. To this extent, the very act of pardoning could be understood as an imperfect duty that reflects a fundamental conflict of goods and the value of generosity.

In contrast, Moore links the power to pardon so tightly to the demands of justice that it cannot be discretionary (Moore 1989, 214). In her view, discretion, because it would be unjust, threatens to violate the principle of treating similar cases in a similar manner. For Moore, the duty to pardon is perfect and reflects the moral fact that the innocent and those who are punished too severely have a right to relief. Her argument from equity is a powerful criticism of any view of pardoning that admits discretion. In contrast, if pardoning is an expression of the imperfect duty of generosity, then criminals do not have a right to be pardoned. Consequently, if one individual is pardoned and another individual in similar circumstances is not, the latter is not injured. Nevertheless, the notion that the state can exercise such discretion in its power to pardon is troubling. It is not difficult to see how a generous act could foster resentment and a sense of injustice, even though it is not a duty. What must be stressed in considering pardons is their extraordinary character. Too much generosity is a vice in this case, not so much because of what it does to the giver (because they run the risk of prodigality), but because of the sense of injustice it can generate in the rest of us.

Pardoning for Meritorious Action

Moore also argues that we should refuse to pardon as a reward for past actions: "To the extent that these pardons are not connected with what the offender deserves *as a result of his offense,* they cannot be justified by retributivist standards" (Moore 1989, 204). For example, in the case of Dr. Samuel Mudd who was, it seems, unjustly convicted as part of the conspiracy to assassinate President Lincoln (he set John Wilkes Booth's leg after the actor shot the president), the doctor was pardoned not because he was innocent (a justifiable pardon for Moore) but because while in prison, Mudd fought a yellow fever epidemic "with skill, self-lessness, and tireless courage" (197). For Moore, Mudd's case drew on separate and incommensurable moral accounts. One cannot draw on the good done or the harm suffered in one set of circumstances in order to pay the debt incurred under another. Mudd cannot pay his debt to society by acting or suffering in a manner unrelated to his crime.

To a large extent, I think that Moore is correct—that these moral accounts are separate. Eichmann may have suffered greatly if he had been mugged or robbed while on the streets in Argentina, but such suffering cannot be seen as punishment for what he did during the war. But from this fact I believe we can draw a conclusion different from Moore's. We agree that Mudd's action during the yellow fever epidemic did not clear his debt to society. If it did, Mudd would have served his time, and so there would be nothing to forgive. What Mudd did in fighting the epidemic was courageous and worthy of praise, but it cannot automatically remove the debt that he legally owed. The alleged evil on the one hand and a courageous action on the other are not commensurable.

Because a good action in one sphere does not diminish a debt in another, Moore concludes that we cannot pardon for good works or suffering. I agree with this description of the situation but must add that although good works do not diminish a debt, they may be a reason to forgive. Mudd's being found guilty and serving time indicates some movement toward justice. All the same, Mudd's pardon was a way to reward meritorious action. His courageous work during the yellow fever epidemic seemed to be a good reason to forgive, although the decision need not have gone that way. For example, if Mudd had been a mass killer who happened to act courageously, it is unlikely that he would have been pardoned.

Pardoning, Peace, and Stability

Finally, Moore's retributivist theory rejects using the power to pardon to ensure domestic tranquility. She finds objectionable Alexander Hamilton's claim that "in seasons of insurrection or rebellion, there are often critical moments, when a well-timed offer or pardon to the insurgents or rebels may restore the tranquillity of the commonwealth; and which, if suffered to pass unimproved, it may never be possible afterwards to recall" (quoted in Moore 1989, 26). In general, Moore finds these kinds of public welfare pardons undeserved and hence unjustified. However, she is optimistically ambivalent because in cases where pardons are needed to quell revolution or the potential for revolution in a just state, many of those pardons are deserved, that is, are granted to innocent individuals.[16]

Whether there are solid grounds for such optimism in this connection, it is clear that pardoning revolutionaries or potential insurgents under the rubric of political forgiveness permits a consideration of the effects of the pardon that the retributivist position does not. To the extent that a pardon can advance other significant values, then this use of pardoning can be consequentialist and forward-looking in a manner that Moore's position cannot be. In response, however, Moore could argue that the danger with public welfare pardons is that they may displace justice altogether. Although a pure form of public welfare pardons may run this risk, political forgiveness requires that the minimal demands of justice be met. Meeting this condition means that the timing for the pardon should not prevent all movement toward justice. As a form of political forgiveness, a pardon would require some mutually acceptable account of who did what to whom and an acknowledgment of responsibility and guilt on the transgressor's part. Only after meeting these conditions could a government justifiably release individuals from their debt to society.

The Puzzle of Previous Governments

The possibility that the power to pardon can be used to advance the public welfare not only raises the problem of the relationship between justice and forgiveness, but it also raises questions regarding the permissible scope for deploying pardons. What Hamilton said about a well-timed offer of a pardon applies to both those in rebellion as well as to officials of an ancien régime who have committed atrocities while in authority. In the latter case, former officials of an overthrown regime may still retain significant power and support in the new regime. A well-timed offer of a pardon could provide enough tranquillity for the new government to take root. The philosophical problem here is that solely basing this pardoning decision on future effects ignores the question of whether the successor government has any standing to pardon (or prosecute) these former officials. In order to forgive, however, the government must have been wronged. The forward-looking character of pardoning is not unbounded; the authority to forgive wrongs is tightly

16. For Moore, "It is very difficult to tell a government that it is unjust to take the steps necessary to save itself. Would Kant expect a just society to forbear from the one unjust act that would keep an unjust revolution from sweeping the country?" (Moore 1989, 202). This, of course, is the traditional difficulty of retributivism.

linked to the victim. If this is true, then can governments pardon those who have done wrong prior to its establishment? Does the successor government have the standing to make such an offer?

One argument against such standing is that because the successor government did not exist when the wrongs were committed, it could not be harmed by those wrongs.[17] If the successor government is not harmed, then it has no authority to prosecute, pardon, or grant amnesty to former officials, collaborators, or criminals of the previous regime. While the successor government in some way may be able to act on behalf of the injured parties or international norms, it cannot be wronged by the actions of its predecessor.[18] Without being wronged, would it have the authority to engage in political forgiveness?

One possibility for granting a successor government such authority is if the victims surrendered to the successor government their own rights to forgive the wrongdoer. After such a transference, a governmental pardon would be an example of a collected as opposed to a collective form of forgiveness. Although certainly possible, it is not clear why victims would either explicitly or implicitly surrender their right to forgive. In addition, this solution presupposes that a government's predecessor cannot directly wrong its successor. In contrast, I argue that a case can be made for the existence of this kind of wrong. To make it, we must once again turn to Feinberg's analysis of wrongs and draw an analogy between individuals and groups.

In the earlier puzzle regarding whether an individual can be harmed after death, Feinberg suggested that if one could be wronged unknowingly and if one could describe a dead person before death as a living being with doomed interests, then the notion of harming the dead is plausible. The deceased's interests were set back by the actions of others after

17. However, specific individuals who were injured by those officials and their policies may very well have survived into the new regime (see chapter 7).

18. Even if we accept the notion that ex post facto punishment is itself wrong, that acknowledgment does not completely close down the pursuit of justice by the successor government. First, uncovering and telling the truth about the past need not violate the ex post facto rule, but they are important components of pursuing justice that can be undertaken by the successor regime. Second, prosecution of former officials and ordinary criminals may not be "after the fact" if their actions violated the laws of the previous regime. Third, in circumstances where the previous regime's legitimacy is questionable (as in the case of the puppet governments established by the Nazis), the existence of a legitimate government in exile could provide sufficient moral continuity. Finally, the presence of widely shared international norms against certain objectionable internal behavior can also provide a basis for the pursuit of justice.

her death. In the case of a just successor government, its central interest is to secure the conditions in which its members' interests can flourish. In light of that concern, for example, it is plausible to say that because members of the previous regime imprisoned, spied on, denied due process, tortured, discriminated against, and so on, the new government's capacity to establish the conditions under which some of its members will flourish is greatly impaired. And, in cases where the victim has died, the actions of those officials have made it difficult if not impossible for the new regime to do its job. Because of the life chances that some have lost and the mental and physical scars that others bear, they are unable to pursue fully their own interests. Whatever the new regime may be able to do, it cannot bring back the lost time or erase the pain and damage of the past. The argument, then, is that by harming the victims, the officials of the previous regime have also set back the successor state's interests in providing for the flourishing of its members. Is this argument compelling?

It is plausible to suggest that individuals can be harmed by an act that occurred before they existed. Feinberg offers this example:

> Imagine if you can a criminal so wicked that he wishes to blow up a schoolhouse to kill or mutilate pupils. He conceals a powerful bomb in a closet of the kindergarten room and sets a timing device to go off in six years' time. Six years later the bomb explodes, killing or mutilating dozens of five-year-old children. The children obviously have been harmed by the explosion, and equally obviously (it seems to me) it was the evil action of the wicked criminal six years earlier, *before they were even conceived,* that harmed them. (Feinberg 1984, 97)

Accepting his analysis for a moment, what corresponds to the explosion in the successor regime? The previous regime has set back the interests of its victims. The new government comes on the scene with a number of its citizens living in a harmed condition. But can we then conclude that the government itself was harmed? It all depends on how harm is understood and measured. For example, the notion of being harmed could require a reference to one's previous situation. Jill could be said to be harmed because her fundamental interests in her health or way of life have deteriorated because of Jack's actions. Under this conception, harm requires reference to a previous condition, and because a government is new, it does not have a relevant previous condition. We could not say, for example, that the government had been harmed because its ability to protect and cultivate the interests of its members is worse than it was before. The actions of the officials haven't worsened or deteriorated the interests of the successor state.

To make this notion of harm viable, we need something other than a reference to a previous condition. For example, the successor government may be able to appeal to an identifiable "centerline" to which all nearly just governments can lay claim. If new governments could be said to possess a set of "birth rights," then those interests could be hobbled or violated by the actions of others even before they exist. A state may be "born" with a segment of its population severely disadvantaged or permanently disabled through the actions of others. Consequently, the core right of a government to protect and enable its citizens' interests has also been set back by those actions. The harm done to its citizens before its founding becomes a harm to the government after its founding. Because of this harm, the wrongs done in the previous regime can be understood as public wrongs. And, because they can be understood as public wrongs, the possibility exists for governmental forgiveness (as well as prosecution, amnesty, etc.).

To defend this position it would be necessary to establish the basis and content of these governmental "birth rights." For this discussion of political forgiveness, however, it may be sufficient to say that the content of these rights includes protection against violations of human rights. In other words, violations of human rights wrong not only individuals and groups but also future governments. The basis of these birth rights, in contrast, may be ultimately grounded in the rights of individuals to organize themselves in a manner that effectively protects their values and interests. To the extent that the violation of human rights diminishes the ability of future governments to establish the conditions under which meaningful lives may be led, the government has been harmed by those former officials. The basis of the government's right to act, then, is conveyed through the rights of individuals. If this is plausible, then governments may be wronged by human rights violations that occurred prior to their founding.

But if successor governments may suffer these kinds of wrongs prior to their coming into being, then pardoning such wrongs could take place only after an official determination of wrongdoing. Indeed, following the earlier analysis, all parties would have had to come to some shared understanding of who did what to whom. Although theorizing about political forgiveness does not establish the best way to meet the minimal conditions of justice, the alternatives appear to be neither plentiful nor pure. The full pursuit of justice through formal legal mechanisms may result in the punishment of some wrongdoers but ignore the larger social context and encourage other wrongdoers from telling what they know. Truth commissions may, however, yield a greater understanding of who did what to whom, but at the cost of protecting wrongdoers from prosecution.[19] The most attractive alternative, however, for governments in the midst of a transition from an unjust past may be to grant unconditional amnesty to powerful former officials in the hopes of obtaining peace and stability. Of these three alternatives, only the last closes down the possibility for political forgiveness. The unconditional grant of amnesty completely overrides rectificatory justice and precludes the establishment of a state of reconciliation (as discussed in chapter 3).

The Truth and Reconciliation Commission

To illustrate the meaning of political forgiveness in the context of a successor regime dealing with an unjust past, it is useful to consider the case of the South African Truth and Reconciliation Commission (TRC). Discussions of the TRC that raise the notion of forgiveness tend to frame the concept in terms of the response of particular victims to their transgressors (Minow 1998, 17; Tutu 1999, 106). Although this kind of *one to one* forgiveness may prove to be the ultimate legacy of the TRC, it need not be seen as the only relationship of forgiveness that the process created. For the amnesty process itself could be read as a *many to one* form of political forgiveness that resembles the notion of pardoning discussed above.[20] More specifically, the conditional character of the TRC's amnesty process went some distance in satisfying the minimal demands of justice, creating a reconciliatory state between the new government and those offenders, and initiating a wider process of reconciliation. The message conveyed to the recipients of amnesty was not that their crimes were to be forgotten and ignored, as is true of an unconditional amnesty, but that their crimes had to be made public.

As set out in the Promotion of National Unity and Reconciliation Act of 1995, the conditions of the amnesty required that transgressors "make full disclosure of all the relevant facts relating to acts associated with a political objective" (Ash 1997, 34). In cases where the transgressor committed gross violations of human rights ("an abduction, a killing, tor-

---

19. One of the most recent and nuanced discussions of the problems is Minow (1998).

20. For an alternative reading of the relationship between the South African amnesty process and forgiveness, see Govier (1999, 70–71). Govier, however, is employing a sentiment-based conception of forgiveness.

ture, or severe ill treatment"), then the application required a public hearing, "unless such a hearing was likely to lead to a miscarriage of justice, as in cases where witnesses were too intimidated to testify in open session" (Tutu 1999, 51). According to Tutu, the process required that the offenders take responsibility for their actions, although (as we have seen) not necessarily express sorrow or contrition:

> Amnesty is granted only to those who plead guilty, who accept responsibility, for what they have done. Amnesty is not given to innocent people or to those who claim to be innocent. It was on precisely this point that amnesty was refused to the police officers who applied for amnesty for their part in the death of Steve Biko. They denied in effect that they had committed a crime, claiming that they had assaulted him only in retaliation for his inexplicable conduct in attacking them. (54)

The South African process, however, was not one-sided. Victims also had their say. They could oppose an application by showing that the specific conditions for granting amnesty were not met (Tutu 1999, 50). Although victims could not veto an application, they could tell their story and agree or disagree with the statements of the transgressors. In addition, the Committee on Human Rights Violations established by the act set up a forum in which victims could tell their side of the story. The immediate purpose of the committee was to certify the eligibility of victims for reparations (Ash 1997, 34). It also provided a venue for publicly establishing who did what to whom.

To the extent that the process of granting conditional amnesty met the minimal demands of justice, it looks much like political forgiveness. A few points need to be raised, however, with regard to this illustration. The first is that the South African amnesty was an official act and, consequently, can be distinguished from decisions on the part of individual victims to forgive. From within the framework set out above, what was politically forgiven were wrongs done to the successor government's interest in securing the welfare interests of its citizens. In operating like a pardon, the conditional grant of amnesty should not be understood as an act of forgiveness on behalf of the actual victims; it did not represent forgiveness on their part, if it was offered at all. One significant difficulty with the amnesty was that the South African law also protected transgressors from civil suit. However necessary this concession may have been, it could not be justified by the claim that it represented all victims.

A second point is that South African amnesties were granted for gross violations of civil rights. In the case of murder, this would appear to violate the condition that certain acts are politically unforgivable (for the reasons set out in chapter 2). There are, however, strict and loose interpretations of this condition. The strict interpretation is that by claiming an act such as murder is unforgivable, it is unforgivable for the direct or primary victims and for all those who have been touched by evil (nonprimary victims). The victim of torture should not forgive her torturer, and the family of the victim should not forgive the torturer. Secondary victims have also suffered through the actions of the torturer, although they have not been tortured (or, perhaps, tortured in the same way). The act is unforgivable, and whoever has been touched by that act (all nonprimary victims) should not forgive.

A loose interpretation of the condition is that a significant moral difference exists between being tortured and suffering because a loved one has been tortured. As in the strict interpretation, the direct victim should not forgive. In addition, under both interpretations, a family member could not politically forgive on behalf of the victim. What is different in the loose interpretation is that the family member could forgive the torturer for his or her secondary suffering. The aim of the torture, let us suppose, was not to obliterate the personality of the family member but the personality of the direct victim. Family members could forgive what the torturer had done to them if the minimal conditions of justice were met. On this reading, Simon Wiesenthal could have forgiven the Nazi, Karl, for the offense that he committed against Wiesenthal. He could not forgive on behalf of the Jews that Karl murdered.

One objection to this kind of forgiveness on the part of nonprimary victims, particularly in the case of murder, is that it restores normal relations with the murderer and seems "to allow the crime to stand and the victim to count as nothing." Piers Benn argues that forgiveness entails forswearing "the indignation and outrage I experience on behalf of the murdered person. And to do this seems to involve no longer seeing her death as something to be opposed: it means reconciling myself to its occurrence" (Benn 1996, 377). Forgiveness by nonprimary victims (or what he calls "quasi-forgiveness") is morally problematic because it violates one's personal loyalty to the dead. Loyalty, for Benn, affirms the "eternal value of its object," in this case the victim (380). The claims of loyalty, however, can be met if the transgressor repents and thereby reaffirms the value of the primary victim. Once such repentance occurs, then quasi-forgiveness is justified.

The logic of Benn's argument may apply not only to secondary victims who are close to the direct victim but also to a government that could be called a tertiary victim.[21] For a state to pardon a murderer would be inappropriate because it could also entail "no longer seeing [the victim's] death as something to be opposed." Although one would probably not say that by pardoning, the government violated its loyalty to the victim, one could talk about the government betraying the memory of the victim (see also Govier 1999, 61). As a tertiary victim, the government betrays the primary victim when it pardons the offender. Although it is not the kind of betrayal that would be involved if the government tried to forgive on behalf of the victim (vicarious forgiveness), it is a betrayal nonetheless.

In response, political forgiveness does not require forswearing indignation and outrage, only forswearing acting on those emotions. But this response may not evade the charge that political forgiveness on the part of nonprimary victims still violates a claim of loyalty or constitutes a kind of betrayal. Benn's argument, however, is strongest when considering a blanket amnesty. In an unconditional amnesty, it does appear that the crime is allowed to stand and the victim counts for very little. But this is not the case if the minimal demands of justice are an indispensable condition for political forgiveness. In meeting those demands, the crime must be acknowledged and the parties must share a public understanding of who did what to whom. Although this may not mean the same thing as repentance (in terms of requiring the offender to publicly express sorrow or remorse), it does require that nonprimary victims not forgive unless the crime has been acknowledged and the wrongful treatment of the victim understood by the transgressor.

If we assume the loose interpretation of the prohibition against forgiving certain acts and that the preconditions of political forgiveness meet Benn's objection, then the South African government can politically forgive what was done to it, even though the wrong against the primary victims involved murder. It is possible for the state to pardon murderers precisely because the state is not the direct victim and because the conditions for political forgiveness had been met. The implication of the loose interpretation is that the process of reconciliation initiated by the government's conditional amnesty cannot be extended to certain direct victims of evil acts—

21. If a criminal act simultaneously wrongs the state when the primary victim is wronged, then the state may look more like a secondary victim. If one believes in the intelligibility of so-called victimless crimes (pornography, illegal gambling), then it may be possible for the state to be a primary victim.

those who are dead or missing. In the cases of torture or abduction, however, it could extend to direct victims, but whether they should accept that invitation depends on whether they share the story that came out of the amnesty process. Even if that account is mutually acceptable and meets the minimal demands of justice, those individual victims still have discretion over whether to forgive and reconcile with their former oppressors.

A third point that deserves mentioning is the extent to which truth emerged under the TRC process. For Martha Minow, "Perhaps the greatest practical problem lies here: if journalists, historians, and philosophers endlessly debate what is truth and whether facts can ever be separate from interpretation, it is unlikely that drafters of truth commission reports can resolve such issues, especially in the politically charged contexts of societies emerging from collective violence" (Minow 1998, 85). But Minow may be setting the threshold too high. It is one thing to say that the practical problem of trying to figure out who did what to whom may be a very complicated process—one in which fragmentary evidence and contradictory testimony point to different possible accounts. It is another thing to argue that before any of these practical problems can be resolved, we must first resolve deeper philosophical disputes over the nature of truth. For example, is a correspondence theory of truth less compelling than a coherence theory of truth? Without appealing to yet another theory, it would seem that the former problems could be addressed apart from the latter questions. To give an analogy, it is philosophically very difficult to give an account of time. Nevertheless, and in the face of our philosophical ignorance, we are quite able to "tell time," "make time," give "time off," "spend time," and so on, in our everyday interactions. In practice, we may dispute whether someone was late, but the settlement of that dispute does not require settling the philosophical controversy over the nature of time. As Minow herself notes, "One need not descend into enduring debates over the existence of truth or its accessibility to humans to sense the difficulties in writing a truth commission report" (85). The above suggestion is that what concerns writers of truth commissions will, one may hope, be more prosaic than these enduring debates.

In the South African case, not all of the testimony was evasive or the evidence cloudy. While the difficulties of getting to the truth of who did what to whom can be significant and overwhelming, they are not necessarily insurmountable. Nevertheless, even without the philosophical baggage, the job of getting enough truth for political forgiveness may be exceedingly difficult. For example, Minow distinguishes "forensic truth—based on medical and testimonial evidence about what happened, where, and to whom—from explanatory truth—encompassing explanations, emerging from dialogue, and connecting with larger social and economic contexts of both past and future" (Minow 1998, 85–86). In contrast, Daniel Crocker makes a distinction between "forensic truth" and "emotional truth." The former concerns "information about whose moral legal rights were violated, by whom, how, when, and where," whereas the latter concerns "the psychological and physical impact on victims and their loved ones from rights abuses and the threat of such abuses" (Crocker 1999, 49). The theoretical usefulness of these kinds of distinctions is that they point to the difficulty of firmly establishing how much truth is enough for political forgiveness. By saying that the parties must share an account of who did what to whom, it would appear that Crocker's conception of forensic truth meets the threshold. But the requirement that the account be shared and be based on publicly verifiable information implies more than an authoritative announcement of "forensic truth." How much more than the forensic truth is needed cannot be settled by theory because the political forgiveness of moral wrongs ultimately lies in the hands of the victims.

During one of the more extraordinary exchanges at a Truth Commission hearing, the problem of how much truth is enough became a central concern. In investigating the activities of Winnie Madikizela-Mandela's "football club," the commission heard testimony that linked Madikizela-Mandela to the kidnapping and murder of Stompie Seipei, a fourteen-year-old activist, and the murder of Abubaker Asvat, the doctor who treated Stompie. At the hearing, Madikizela-Mandela was initially intransigent, calling the testimony "ridiculous" and "ludicrous." Eventually, Tutu pleaded for more cooperation:

> I speak to you as someone who loves you very deeply . . . I want you to stand up and say: "There are things that went wrong . . ." If you were able to bring yourself to be able to say: "Something went wrong . . ." I beg you, I beg you . . . I beg you, please . . . You are a great person. And you don't know how your greatness would be enhanced if you were to say "I'm sorry . . . things went wrong. Forgive me." (Krog 1999, 338; also Tutu 1999, 174).

Madikizela-Mandela's response was:

> I will take this opportunity to say to the family of Dr. [Abubaker] Asvat, how deeply sorry I am, to Stompie's mother, how deeply sorry I am—I have said so to her before a few years back, when the heat was very hot. I am saying it

is true, things went horribly wrong. I fully agree with that and for that part of those painful years when things went horribly wrong and we were aware . . . that there were factors that led to that . . . I am deeply sorry. (Tutu 1999, 174; also Krog 1999, 339)

Despite the apology, the passive and evasive character of Madikizela-Mandela's response makes it difficult to pin down for what she was apologizing. In her case, a grant of amnesty looks less like a form of political forgiveness and more like a refusal to face what happened—more like an act of forgetting. On the other hand, something important was revealed in the above exchange with Tutu: it does contain an element of taking responsibility. In addition, a willingness to show humility or embarrassment is not a necessary condition for political forgiveness. From the state's perspective, Madikizela-Mandela's statement met the minimal threshold of justice. Whether the family and friends of Stompie Seipei and Abubaker Asvat came to share and accept that account is a different matter.

In many respects, the South African process did resemble the form of political forgiveness involved in pardoning. As in pardoning, the conditional amnesty sought to uncover what really happened to the victims and provided a mechanism for the relevant parties to tell their side of the story. Moreover, as in the case of a public welfare pardon, the government had made the decision not to give that which is due to those who received amnesty. For the TRC, the hope was that other values would be served through the sacrifice of rectificatory justice. In contrast, the presumption of retributivism is that justice must not only always be met but that it also necessarily trumps all other values. Even if all of the actions of the TRC did not fit precisely into the case of political forgiveness, the South African case does illustrate how reconciliation may be advanced without pushing the claims of justice.

Pardoning, seen as a form of authoritative forgiveness, cannot be done in the name of (rectificatory) justice but in the name of ideas and ideals that may stand outside the orbit of retribution: public welfare, the suffering of the prisoner, or the generosity of the government. This view of pardoning is quite different from a retributivist view. It brings to light the troublesome practice of pardoning innocent or unfairly treated prisoners and widens the scope of pardoning to include reasons that Moore unequivocally sees as "bad." The larger claim here, however, is that governments can forgive. As a *many to one* form of political forgiveness, pardoning can be an appropriate response to wrongs suffered by conglomerates.

6

Governmental Blameworthiness and Its Scope

_____

When the government does wrong, we have a moral responsibility to admit it. The duty we owe to one another to tell the truth and to protect our fellow citizens from excesses like these is one we can never walk away from. Our government failed in that duty, and it offers an apology to the survivors and their families and to all the American people who must—who must be able to rely upon the United States to keep its word, to tell the truth, and to do the right thing.

—Remarks by President Clinton in Acceptance of the
Human Radiation Final Report, October 3, 1996

IN PREVIOUS chapters it was simply assumed that individuals could be held responsible for the debts they had accrued and for the wrongs they had done; no mention was made of the enduring philosophical disputes over the character and justification for moral responsibility.[1] Because of the largely undisputed belief that individuals are responsible for their actions, and in order to keep the discussion focused

_____

1. All theoretical engagements must take certain things as given in order to say other things. These "givens" are not immune from questioning and have only a provisional quality. For example, the discussion of forgiving individuals rests on the assumption that individuals are blameworthy. The question of why individuals are morally responsible for their actions, and whether Kantian, utilitarian, or pragmatic approaches (see, e.g., Smiley

on forgiveness, individual responsibility was taken as given. In comparison to individuals, however, what we mean by governmental "action" is less clear, and it is less evident that governments as such are blameworthy. Consequently, in this chapter the focus moves from forgiveness to a rough account of governmental responsibility. In offering this account, I make a number of assertions regarding the connection between moral responsibility and agency. The discussion begins, however, with Peter French's claim that groups such as corporations and governments are moral beings (and hence blameworthy). The difficulties associated with his position lead me to suggest that we can treat a nearly just government *as if* it were a moral agent in order to provide a degree of moral cover for those who act in its name. The rest of the chapter fills out the significance of this position for the scope of moral responsibility both for citizens and across time.

Governmental Blameworthiness

The idea of governmental blameworthiness raises significant problems regarding the nature of moral agency, responsibility, and historical continuity.[2] For those who argue that individuals are the sole moral agents, saying that governments are blameworthy is a peculiar way of speaking. Institutions, corporations, or procedures cannot be blamed for wrongdoing, because they are incapable of action. Properly speaking, only individuals act. From this individualistic perspective, if we want to talk

[1992] for a defense of the latter perspective and a useful bibliography) provide the most coherent account of responsibility, would inevitably emerge in this discussion. Addressing these issues, however, would divert us even further from the discussion of political forgiveness, and the theorization of responsibility would inevitably give rise to a different set of assumptions that would have to be held in place in order to say anything about individual responsibility.

2. Iris Marion Young and others have made a distinction between blaming and holding responsible (Young 1990, 151). Blaming focuses on the intentional wrongs people commit that can be legitimately punished. In contrast, one can be held responsible for one's unintentional behavior that may harm others. Holding someone responsible is meant to be forward looking in the sense that "from here on out," the responsible party should work to change those objectionable habits and behaviors. Although I use these two terms (*blaming* and *holding responsible*) interchangeably, I am primarily referring to actions that Young would see as blameworthy. Political forgiveness, however, could have a role in responding to unintentional harms, but only if the wrongdoer came to see those habits or actions as harmful (i.e., came to share the story with the offended party). For example, the teller of an unintentionally offensive joke should not be forgiven unless the teller understood the offensive character of the joke. Without a shared understanding of what happened, political forgiveness cannot achieve its illocutionary point and initiate a process of reconciliation.

about forgiving a government, then we must restrict ourselves to forgiving individuals for specific actions for which they are culpable.

There is much to recommend this position. It accords with a commonsensical notion of individuals as moral actors and avoids the mire of positing a kind of super-individual to explain how groups can be held morally responsible. At a practical level, the assertion that only individuals are morally blameworthy denies the existence of a corporate or institutional veil that could insulate individuals from their responsibilities. It pins responsibility on flesh and blood, not paper and ink. In so doing, it forces individuals to act more carefully when they are acting in groups.

But the belief that only individual agents are blameworthy fails to accord with a variety of moral practices that do bestow a degree of moral agency on institutions and corporate bodies. As President Clinton's remarks at the beginning of this chapter suggest, we frequently do blame institutions, corporations, and governments for outcomes, policies, and events. Part of the reason for this practice is that the authority to act in a political or legal office stems not from the individual but from the rules and procedures that establish an office. Without the office, the individual presumably would have no authority to act.

The possibility of holding governments responsible, however, is necessary for clarity and also removes an obstacle from the path of those who wish to engage in public service. Protecting individuals from liability for their official actions may allow them to serve in public office more easily. Similarly, by setting up a private corporation, individuals can more freely take on risky financial ventures without fear of personal loss. Without such legal and moral protections, people may be less willing to serve in public office or be entrepreneurial. And while we cannot throw General Motors, the U. S. government, or the highway code into jail, we do believe that fines, institutional reforms, and revolutions can have some effect on outcomes. Sometimes, simply changing the personnel does not have much effect.

In practice, moral responsibility for official political action is usually distributed between the office and the individual. After all, an executive may act fully within his or her capacity as an executive and still be held personally responsible for those actions by being voted out of office. The important claim here is that in practice we are willing to see the political institution as a kind of moral agent and, hence, blameworthy, even if it is not the only moral agent involved.

The theoretical case for holding governments blameworthy is difficult, particularly if we assume that moral blame turns on action and action requires agency.[3] While some have taken positions that corporate entities are no different from other moral agents,[4] it is difficult to see how the rules, procedures, and institutions that compose a government are the same as the intelligent choosers who are normally said to possess agency. Nevertheless, one finds plausible arguments to the effect that corporate entities, such as states and governments, *are* moral beings, possessing the requisite characteristics of agency. One recent expression of this view is found in the work of Peter French. According to French, governments and corporations are conglomerates to the extent that a decision-procedure and an identifiable set of purposes unite them. In addition, conglomerates are moral persons possessing "whatever privileges, rights and duties as are, in the normal course of affairs, accorded to all members of the moral community" (French 1984, 32).

French presumes that an entity can be called an agent only if it "can be properly described as having done something . . . for a reason" (French 1984, 46). Very roughly, his argument is that conglomerates are capable of acting on reasons because they possess an internal organization and decision structure that stands independent of the individuals associated with that entity. The internal decision structure of a corporation, for example, not only establishes how to arrive at decisions (i.e., what offices must approve what in order for the corporation to act), but also the basic policies and goals of the institution. If a corporation's actions are consistent with its interests and goals, then they are being taken for corporate reasons with corporate intentions. French admits that the personal intentions of the officers may be quite different from the corporate intentions, but as long as those actions can be described as consistent with the corporate policies and goals, they are also corporate actions. That corporations need real human beings occupying places in the organizational chart in order to make decisions "should not . . . rule out the

3. Action, of course, is not necessary for all forms of blameworthiness: I may blame the nail for my flat tire, but the nail did not "act." Action (ignoring the problem of omissions), however, will be assumed to be a key component for the attribution of moral responsibility, as opposed to pure forms of causal responsibility.

4. Jean-Jacques Rousseau, for example, suggests such a position by claiming that "the body politic, taken individually, can be considered as an organized, living body and similar to that of a man. . . . The body politic is, therefore, also a moral being which has a will, and this general will, which always tends toward the conservation and welfare of the whole and of each part, and which is the source of the laws, is, for all the members of the state, in their relations to one another and to the state, the rule of what is just and unjust" (Rousseau 1988, 61).

possibility of their [the corporations] having metaphysical status, as being intentional actors in their own right, and thereby full-fledged moral persons" (47).

One of French's central arguments about moral responsibility and conglomerates is that if a conglomerate is morally responsible for an action, that responsibility is not necessarily distributed to the members of the group. Unlike an aggregate, a conglomerate can itself act without all of the members acting. It can itself bear moral responsibility. Governments, on this view, can themselves be blamed for an action without necessarily blaming all those who work within or are represented by the government. As a conglomerate, the government is an authoritative institution and not an individual nor simply a collection of individuals. In light of this understanding, French's position faces two significant difficulties. Both difficulties draw on an association of moral responsibility with the concept of action and argue that governments fall short of being moral actors. The first problem is that the intelligibility of agency requires being able to distinguish action from behavior. The second difficulty is that governments may be held responsible even though they are not responsive to reasons. Both of these hurdles suggest that we need to look elsewhere for an account of governmental blameworthiness.

Action versus Behavior

In the case of individuals, ascribing moral responsibility requires the ability to distinguish self-activated movements, or action, for which one is responsible from unintentional movements and compulsions, or behavior, for which one is not responsible. For example, we see Abel bump into Baker. It is certainly possible for us to ascribe a goal to this movement, such as a desire to start a fight or push him down, but we need to know whether this movement was intentional in order to attribute a goal and judge Abel responsible. After all, Abel may have accidentally slipped into Baker. The distinction between action and behavior is based on the belief that not all movement (or even all movement for which one could attribute reasons) is the same as action. Or, to put it another way, action requires intentionality, and intentionality requires that the actor possess a particular kind of self-activation. Movement can only be described as action if it originates from the choices or decisions of the agent. In contrast, movement that results from internal forces, impulses, instinctual reactions, or reflexes is mere behavior. To the extent that a set of internal forces prevents self-activation, we are able to differentiate an intentional act from a compulsory behavior, a voluntary motion from a seizure, a chosen gesture from a twitch, and so on. If it were the case that self-activation was completely overwhelmed by internal forces, as is the case for catatonics or those suffering a grand mal seizure, then the agent would not be morally responsible for whatever movements (or lack of movements) that were performed.[5]

It is difficult to see how the distinction between action and behavior could be applied to conglomerates. Although French talks about corporate intentionality, it is unlikely that he also believes there are corporate disorders or inner compulsions that would allow for the distinction. The basic problem is that the form of self-activation (and failures to such activation) found in human beings simply does not occur in institutions, corporations, or governments. While we talk of the whimsical behavior of a majority, or the impulsive reactions of governments, or institutional gridlock, these descriptions do not permit us to differentiate autarchic corporate action from behaviors that are inner-impelled or heterarchic (Benn 1975–76, 113–16). Without the ability to apply these contrasting terms to corporations, the whole notion of action, reason giving, and decision making becomes attenuated when applied directly to institutions. Apart from the individuals who compose them, it seems impossible to tell whether the group is merely acting or behaving. Governments may be self-activated in the sense that what they are doing is not being controlled by other institutions or foreign governments, but they cannot be self-activated in the sense that they are free from being impelled by inner psychological or organic forces.[6]

Even if we assume that the distinction between action and behavior was unnecessary to establish moral responsibility, French's position would still require that we make sense of the notion of how a government

5. Of course, knowing that one is susceptible on a regular basis to such uncontrollable movements could be enough to attribute responsibility if one placed oneself in a situation in which such movements could cause harm. For example, a person who knowingly suffers from frequent, severe seizures decides to drive, has a seizure, loses control of the car, and causes harm.

6. One may argue that linking agency to an inner life and self-activation is merely an anthropocentric bias. Could we simply stipulate that in order to talk about governmental action, we do not need to distinguish between action and behavior, nor do we need to be able to refer to an inner life? The effect of such a stipulation would be to say that despite the absence of an inner life, governments always act; they never merely behave. Whereas human beings can plead lack of intention or accident, there are no governmental accidents or failures of intention, strictly speaking. Governments are agents for whom all of their acts are intended, insofar as they result from the appropriate decision procedure.

could be said to act for a reason.[7] As John Gray notes, this can be a fairly weak requirement. He argues that "what such a requirement [i.e., being able to give a reason] disqualifies as rational conduct is only . . . behavior . . . where no goal or end may be imputed . . . which renders intelligible what he does" (Gray 1980, 520). As long as some goal or end can be imputed to the doer that renders his or her actions intelligible, then we can say the actions were done for a reason. For some, this account is too weak—acting for a reason requires judging the rationality of the goals being pursued. Action requires much more than imputing a reason to a set of movements; it requires that the purposes of those movements meet a thicker conception of rationality. This position, however, is too demanding. It would imply that one could not act on and hence be responsible for mistakes or foolish pursuits. John Martin Fischer and Mark Ravizza suggest a somewhat less demanding position. They argue that in addition to being able to impute a reason for an action, one must also know whether the actor is appropriately responding to reasons that are the actor's own. If, for example, we imputed a reason to an agent's movement that he did not recognize as a reason for movement or on which he did not act (perhaps he even had no reason), then the imputation would be false. Indeed, we may even call into question whether the movement qualified as an action for which the agent should be held responsible.

The claim that agency, acting for a reason, and moral responsibility are linked together, however, poses a special problem for governments, espe-

---

It appears that some such stipulation must attend French's argument regarding the moral responsibility of corporations: they are agents, but not in the way we are agents. The major difficulty with such a stipulation may not be its ad hoc character but its effect on the conception of responsibility itself. If governments are not agents in the same way, is the notion of moral responsibility also different? Does governmental responsibility necessarily become an all-or-nothing affair without any of the shades of gray that accompany a concern with state of mind? Does the scope of responsibility necessarily expand to what would normally be considered "unintended" consequences, if those consequences could reasonably be imputed to render action intelligible? Does this conception of responsibility also sweep into its purview things done by complexly programmed machines that behave according to set of heuristics or algorithms? I raise these questions to point out that a stipulated definition may have ramifications for other understandings that would need to be considered in judging the value of the stipulation. The question explored here is whether any other moves are open to us that do not rest on this stipulation.

7. Using Oakeshott's distinction between intentions and motives mentioned in chapter 1 (fn. 8), acting for a reason need not be understood as acting on the basis of a motive. In this use of the term, a motive turns on the sentiment in which an action is performed, and a reason can be seen as an intentional action that refers to the goal or wished-for end that is being pursued.

cially if acting for a reason means responding to a reason that is the agent's own. Can governments be responsive to reasons in the same way as individuals? Fischer and Ravizza's theory of moral responsibility has some utility here because it comprehensively accounts for what it means for an agent to respond to reasons that are the actor's own. Although they suggest that their position may be relevant to evaluating the moral responsibility of groups (Fischer and Ravizza 1998, 10, n. 13), I nevertheless argue that it is not easily transferable to governments. Holding governments blameworthy is less a matter of seeing them as agents capable of responding to reasons and more a matter of treating them *as if* they were principals in a principal/agent relationship.

Reasons-Responsiveness

Fischer and Ravizza distinguish strong, weak, and moderate versions of the idea of reasons-responsiveness. Strong reasons-responsiveness requires that if someone had decided on a particular course of action but recognized that there were sufficient reasons to do otherwise, she would "choose to do otherwise and do otherwise" (Fischer and Ravizza 1998, 41). Weak reasons-responsiveness requires merely that an agent "who acts against good reasons can be responsive to some reasons" (45). Strong reasons-responsiveness is too strong a requirement for moral responsibility. This is because we clearly hold people responsible who really know that what they are doing is wrong or harmful (such knowledge being sufficient reason for not acting) and still do it (but not because of some disorder that abridges their agency). Weak reasons-responsiveness is too weak, according to the authors, because it would attribute responsibility to individuals who respond to reasons in incoherent or unusual ways (e.g., a serial murderer whose only reason to stop is his neighbor's smoking a particular pipe). In other words, in some cases agents may be weak reasons-responsive, but we would not hold them responsible. Consequently, Fischer and Ravizza carve out and defend what they call moderate reasons-responsiveness. This solution has two components. The first requires that an individual be able to recognize reasons for action and the way in which those reasons play off one another and fit together in patterns. They call this attribute regular reasons-receptivity (70–71). In addition, moderate reasons-responsiveness requires an ability to react to reasons. That is, individuals must have at least a weak capacity to translate those reasons into choices and then into action (73–76). The problem with government is that it may not even be weakly responsive to reasons. If this is true, then the claim that governments are blameworthy must have some other basis.

The possibility of and the degree to which governments can be reasons-responsive would seem to vary greatly, depending on the ethos of the institution, the number of decision makers, and the nature of the decision-making process. It would seem that Fischer and Ravizza's account becomes more plausible the more closely a government is associated with a single individual. Just as an individual could be reasons-responsive, so perhaps could an individual as monarch. In light of the understanding offered earlier, however, a government is something different from the actual individual who occupies the position of authority. Even when sovereignty is vested in the hands of one individual, the monarchy itself is still a government composed of a set of authoritatively accepted rules and institutions that could survive the death of the monarch. But can an institution actually be receptive and react to reasons?

What does it mean to say that a government is receptive to reasons? To say that a government understands what it means when foreign troops are massing on its border, or that the rate of unemployment is high, or that certain segments of the population are being treated unfairly, is merely to say that the agents or representatives of the government understand reasons for action. Without attributing some kind of inner life to institutions, it is difficult to see how they could recognize something in any way other than metaphorically. But this position would appear to preclude the possibility that governments are responsible (other than metaphorically responsible). One possible way around this objection is to claim that if flesh-and-blood individuals are agents, then the government is a principal who bears responsibility. This, I believe, is a plausible solution to how governments are blameworthy; it requires, however, that we further clarify whether conglomerates are not only receptive but also reactive to reasons. In addition, it requires some account of how governments can themselves be principals in a principal/agent relationship.

Governments are receptive to reasons because their agents are receptive. The other half of Fischer and Ravizza's requirements for reasons-responsiveness is that the government must also be reactive to reasons. That is to say, the bureaucrats, legislators, judges, executives, and other officials must not only be able to recognize reasons, they must also be able to translate those reasons into choices and actions. Obviously, governments do act in the sense that their officials issue and carry out orders, commands, laws, regulations, rules, and so on. But despite the ability of officials to recognize reasons for actions, in their official capacities they are not always able to react to those reasons. In fact, depending on the number of actors, the issue, the rules of procedure, and the ethos of the institution, action on the part of a government may be a very cumbersome process. This is particularly true in deliberative bodies or when governmental action requires the coordination of different departments. In addition, the resulting actions need not even be done for the reasons that initiated the decision-making process. An enduring feature of government is that it frequently fails to be reactive to reasons, yet it would still make sense to hold government responsible for its acts and omissions. For example, deliberative bodies are commonly blamed for gridlock, stalemate, and irrational decisions—situations that make the institution unable to translate reasons into choices and then into action. To state the obvious: what one faction in a deliberative body sees as a reason for action (e.g., a rising rate of inflation, decreasing unemployment, or increases in trade surpluses are frequently used as reasons for adjusting the rate of interest, enacting certain fiscal policies, or passing a trade policy), another faction may see as a reason for avoiding action or acting in the opposite way. If both sides are powerful enough, the result may be no action. The recognition of reasons for action is no guarantee that the body will react to those reasons. More important, that inability to act also does not preclude holding government responsible for what is done or not done.

The disconnection between reasons-responsiveness and responsibility is evident as well in situations in which a deliberative body has at least three factions equally divided over three alternatives. Such a situation may set the scene for a voting cycle that has a majority preferring option A to B, a majority preferring option B to C, and a majority preferring option C to A. In effect, at the collective level, a basic notion of transitivity may not hold: that A is preferred to B, and B is preferred to C, does not mean that A is preferred to C. The significance here, however, is that in a process involving the pairwise comparison of alternatives, any of the alternatives could come out on top. In a voting cycle, the outcome depends on the order of presentation or who frames the agenda. In a sense, the problem isn't a lack of reason-reactivity but of potential for any change in the agenda to change the outcome. It is a reactivity not merely to reasons but also to whim, manipulation, or the fortuitous setting of the agenda. Yet despite the problems of reactivity, responsibility for the decision would still fall to the government. In short, making collective, irrational decisions (*irrational* defined here as not living up to the requirement of transitivity) does not free the government of responsibility for such decisions.

The blameworthiness of a government, then, does not turn on its ability to be moderately reactive to reasons. In this respect, Fischer and Ravizza's discussion of reasons-responsiveness is not directly translatable to governments (or probably other conglomerates).[8] If the irrationality of governmental decisions does not release a government from moral responsibility, then the moderate version of reasons-responsiveness is also too strong a requirement. In addition, if we see government officials as existing in a principal/agent relationship, then the government as principal is morally responsible for the actions of its agents. As in the legal relationship between agents and principals, that which the agent does binds the principal. In contrast to the criterion of reasons-responsiveness, one could say that the government is responsible for what its agents do, to the extent that they act within the parameters of their authority. The authority of the agents, in turn, is established by the rules, procedures, norms, and so on that are themselves recognized as authoritative.

Does this account, in which the government is responsible for the agents' actions, mean that French is wrong to require that an agent's actions be attributed to a reason? The notion that an entity can be called an agent only if it can properly be described as having done something for a reason may still hold in the case of a governmental agent, but the reason may simply refer to the authorization given for the act. This can be a fairly thin understanding of imputing a reason. To put this in Fischer and Ravizza's terms, governmental responsibility may only require that governmental agents are weakly responsive to reason. The more important requirement is that they are acting within their authority.

8. Fischer and Ravizza's theory of moral responsibility requires more than reasons-responsiveness. More specifically, they argue that the kind of control that is necessary and sufficient for moral responsibility is *guidance control*. An agent exhibits this kind of control "to the extent that the action issues from his own, reasons-responsive mechanism. Thus, there are two important components of this account: the mechanism's being the *agent's own* and its being appropriately responsive to reasons" (Fischer and Ravizza 1998, 170). What is important about guidance control is the character of the internal processes that occur in order to act. What matters in moral responsibility is not whether one has any real alternatives (this requires what they call *regulative control*), but whether one's actions are properly reasons-responsive to a mechanism that is one's own. The authors argue that even though an agent may lack the freedom to do anything other than what she does (i.e., she is, in a sense, determined), she can still be held morally responsible for her actions if she could exercise guidance control. As this summary suggests, much of their argument is directed toward defending a position that renders moral responsibility compatible with determinism.

In building on French's theory of the moral responsibility of conglomerates, I have not discussed whether Fischer and Ravizza's notion of a reason being the *agent's own* can be translated to governments. I think that there are difficulties with translating this notion to conglomerates but also that the problems associated with reasons-responsiveness are sufficient to show that the moral responsibility of governments is a good deal looser than that of individuals.

Relying on the agent/principal relationship as a way to account for the moral responsibility of governments, however, leaves open the general problem of how governments can serve as principals. More specifically, does establishing the agent/principal relationship itself require that the government have agency in the philosophical sense? In the strictly legal conception of the relationship, this would appear to be the case, insofar as both the agent and the principal must consent to the relationship (Franscona 1964, 11). But how is it possible to talk about a set of rules and procedures (i.e., a government) "consenting"? While the agent/principal approach helps with assigning moral responsibility for particular actions, it appears to lead to an impasse regarding the establishment of the relationship.

A way around this problem is suggested by Fischer and Ravizza's account of what it means to become a moral agent. In laying out a rough outline of the psychology of individual moral development, they argue that "even before children are fully responsible for their actions, we often find ourselves taking certain attitudes toward them that are in many respects similar to the full-blown attitudes of indignation and resentment (which are, of course, only appropriately applicable to morally responsible agents)" (Fischer and Ravizza 1998, 208). We do this, the authors argue, in beginning the process of training children so that they learn to see themselves as sources of changes in the world for which they will be held accountable. We treat them *as if* they were moral agents in the hopes that the education ultimately takes and they come to see themselves in the same way. At the start of this training, however, they do not have a sense of themselves as moral agents, even though we treat them as such.

In the story that Fischer and Ravizza tell, we would not be likely to treat children as if they were moral agents unless we believed that they could be induced to adopt a particular view of themselves. That, after all, is the point of the training. Nevertheless, this case is important because it illustrates the intelligibility of treating individuals like moral agents, even though they are not. Yet one may see this is as intelligible only because those children will eventually take responsibility for themselves. In a general sense, this is correct. The problem, however, is that not all children whom we treat in this fashion actually develop the conception of themselves as agents. What we may find out later in a child's moral development may lead us to conclude that the child shouldn't be held morally accountable. But this reassessment won't erase the fact that at some earlier point, despite knowing that moral agency was absent, we acted as if the child had agency.

How is it possible to see governments as principals with the moral capacity to take on responsibility for the actions of their agents? Following the discussion above, one solution is to act *as if* they possess it. More specifically, a government can be assumed to possess enough moral agency to author the actions of its agents or to serve as a principal. This assumption solves the problem of the absence of an internal life and self-activation. Because the agents of a government possess agency, they sustain the notion of choice. They make the decisions, but the responsibility is lodged with the principal.

The Point of Governmental Responsibility

Governments are blameworthy because they can be understood as if they were the authors of their agents' actions. But why understand government in this way? What purposes are served by acting as if the government were a principal? To answer these questions, two assumptions must be made. First, most governmental actions disadvantage the interests of some. Only a few, perhaps symbolic, actions will not harm or offend any segment of the population. Second, despite the first assumption, just governments act to advance the greater good. That is, just governments attempt to preserve, protect, and advance the cause of justice. Both assumptions are necessary to justify acting as if the government were a principal in a principal/agent relationship. For the central result of seeing the government as a principal is that it provides governmental agents with a significant degree of moral/legal cover. Citizens are willing to provide officials with sufficient moral protection to allow them to make the difficult choices necessary to do the right thing. In so doing, this means that citizens of a just regime also provide moral cover to agents when their official actions are ambiguous and perhaps even wrong. This moral cover makes sense only to the extent that the two assumptions above hold. If citizens believed that governmental action need never be problematic (in the sense, say, that the only interests that individuals should have are embodied in a general will), or that the government was no longer concerned with advancing the cause of justice, then moral indemnity for official action would also evaporate.

This justification for acting as if a just government were a moral actor suggests at least two limitations. The first occurs when governmental agents operate outside of their authority. In acting ultra vires, their moral cover slips because the principal is responsible only for those actions it has authorized. Officials who are not acting in the name of the government, but are using its instruments and powers, are individually responsible for their actions. To the extent that the government condones or permits the unauthorized actions of its agents, it too may share in the responsibility. The primary responsibility for ultra vires action, however, falls on the individual who did the deed.

The second limitation implied by this analysis is that if the government is unjust, then it should not be treated as if it were a principal. In such cases, moral responsibility does not evaporate but falls squarely on the shoulders of those who perform the actions. As suggested above, in an unjust government, the institutions, rules, and procedures of government support the individual interests of those who hold power and their cronies. In such a situation, the government is no longer serving the cause of justice.

To the extent that the government is not responsible for the actions of its officials, then it cannot be forgiven. In cases of pure ultra vires actions (pure in the sense that the government is not an accessory) or when the government is unjust, political forgiveness cannot be applied to the government. In these instances, the question is not whether to forgive governments but whether to forgive the individuals who have performed the actions. In the case of ultra vires action, the problem of forgiveness will most likely arise as an issue of pardoning corrupt officials, which I mentioned in chapter 5. Whether to forgive officials of an unjust regime for their wrongful action is considered in chapter 8.

The Responsibility of Citizens for Governmental Wrongs

Although this theory of governmental responsibility opens more questions than it answers, it is important to consider what the theory implies about the scope of moral responsibility. By scope, I am concerned with the degree to which citizens themselves are morally responsible for their government's actions. The idea of scope also involves a historical question: Are governments responsible for what their agents have done in the distant past? Such a question helps us assess the synchronic and diachronic limitations to this understanding of moral responsibility.

To what degree does governmental responsibility for wrongs spill over to ordinary citizens? According to Arendt, the responsibility for official wrongful acts extends quite far: "For politics is not like a nursery; in politics obedience and support are the same" (Arendt 1963, 279).[9] An alterna-

9. Karl Jaspers voiced a similar sentiment in discussing what he calls political guilt: "This, involving the deeds of statesmen and of the citizenry of a state, results in my having

tive way to arrive at this extreme position is suggested by Thomas Hobbes, for whom citizens are the true authors of official action. From this perspective, the sovereign is not the principal but an agent of the people. Consequently, while we may blame the sovereign for doing a better or worse job, ultimate responsibility for official action lies with those who have authorized the sovereign. For Hobbes, the sovereign cannot, in effect, wrong the people, because their authorization is complete and absolute.

At the other extreme would be a view in which the government indemnified citizens by serving as a moral buffer. The view that the buck does indeed stop with the government is implied by those who see ordinary citizens as unable to judge authoritative action. For some, this incapacity is a function of differences in knowledge and power that should be resisted and overthrown. Ordinary citizens are not responsible because those interests, classes, or groups that really hold power run their lives. For others, this inability is a natural and, hence, unavoidable difference between elites and the masses. Those in authority may have power, but they also have a responsibility to govern, given most individuals' lack of interest or capacity to govern themselves. In either case, citizens can be excused of moral responsibility to the extent that they lack the knowledge and power to affect the course of government and the execution of its laws and policies.

It is plausible, however, to appeal to the criteria of knowledge and power in discerning the responsibilities of citizens without arguing that this is a form of blanket protection. Michael Walzer, for example, suggests that the degree of responsibility for official actions may vary depending on the degree of freedom and the amount of information that an individual possesses (Walzer 1977, 298). If we assume such a rule, the scope of responsibility not only varies from regime to regime but within regimes as well. Ordinary citizens, living in a regime in which they have very little say in the laws that govern them, may also bear little responsibility for those laws. In representative democracies, neither citizens nor state actors

to bear the consequences of the deeds of the state whose power governs me and under whose order I live. Everybody is co-responsible for the way he is governed" (Jaspers 1995, 159). As a practical matter, this sentiment was repeatedly expressed regarding the degree of collaboration necessary to keep the communist regimes of Eastern Europe afloat. For example, Václav Havel argued that "we have all become used to the totalitarian system and accepted it as an immutable fact, thus helping to perpetuate it. In other words, we are all—though naturally to various degrees—responsible for the creation of the totalitarian machinery. None of us is just its victim; we are all responsible for it" (cited in Huntington 1995, 69).

may be let off the hook for governmental wrongs, but not all citizens may be equally responsible. For Walzer, the sharpest hook is reserved for those with the greatest information and control over the situation. The difficulty with positions such as Arendt's and Hobbes's is that not all obedience is necessarily done with full knowledge and full freedom of action, even in the most open regimes. The effect of Walzer's rough rule of thumb pushes the question of responsibility beyond governments to those who have the capacity to resist or object to wrongful governmental actions.

Blameworthiness and Historical Wrongs

The second problem raised by the scope of moral responsibility for governmental wrongs concerns the extent to which a government is responsible for the past. Of all the issues raised in connection with the problem of forgiveness and politics, none of them has a higher profile than the problem of how to deal with past wrongs. In the United States, the question of slavery, the treatment of Native Americans, radiation experiments, Mississippi's Sovereignty Commission, and the Tuskegee experiments are examples of wrongs done in the recent or more distant past that have become a present concern. The problem of past wrongs has also arisen for newly democratic regimes that have emerged from totalitarian or authoritarian systems. Questions of transitional justice surround the problem of how to deal with former officials, collaborators, secret police files, the "disappeared," and compensation to victims. These issues vex such nations as Argentina, Chile, Uruguay, South Africa, and the states of Eastern Europe, as they had a generation earlier for Germany, Japan, France, Belgium, and the Netherlands at the end of the Second World War.

The problems of diachronic justice raise troubling issues of whether and to what extent present institutions and governmental actors are responsible for the past. For example, even if it was clear what was due the victims in the immediate aftermath of the wrong, the passage of time may make those demands increasingly difficult to sort out and fulfill. One reason is that either (or both) the original perpetrators or victims of the wrongs may no longer be around, although their absence does not dissolve all claims of wrongdoing. In addition, a wrong that initially affected the life chances of two individuals may ultimately affect the life chances of many more after a few generations have passed. Intertwined in these issues is the philosophical puzzle of the extent to which a government is the same and, hence, responsible for actions taken in the past.

The practice of responsibility generally rests on and is circumscribed by the existence of a discrete, enduring identity that authored the act. Consequently, children are not responsible for the sins of their parents (although parents may be responsible for the actions of their children), and individuals are not responsible for what other members of their family, class, tribe, or group have done just because they share that identity. In a secular context, we generally find holding individuals responsible for what others have done to be either a gross injustice or blatant stereotyping.[10] To a great extent, this is the way we think about political responsibility. The British government is not responsible for the actions of the German government; the Mongolian government is not responsible for what the Polish government does, and so on. Nevertheless, the practice here is somewhat mixed. For there is a sense that the present Japanese government is responsible in some way for the actions of General Tojo's war government, and the present German government is still held to some extent responsible for the evils of the Holocaust. Whether the character of governmental responsibility can account for this variation in moral practice is considered below.

Given the above analysis, however, one thing is clear: if just governments are responsible for the conduct of their agents, then the time horizon of responsibility expands. In contrast to unjust governments, where the responsible party dies when the actual agent dies (the individual governmental actor or official), the time horizon for responsibility for nearly just governments can last as long as the government lasts. This position naturally raises the question of identifying whether a government at time one is the same as the government at time two. Is the current government of the United States responsible for the treatment accorded African- and Native Americans in the nineteenth century? For the purpose of assigning responsibility, when does one government end and another begin? At the level of the individual, the problem of identity over time is somewhat unsettled in both moral and legal practice. For example, it is difficult to establish whether a person can change so significantly (through drugs, illness, psychological transformation, religious conversion, maturation, and so on) that he or she is not the same person who did whatever was done.[11] The same problem haunts political entities.

10. There are exceptions—strict liability, for example.

11. To some extent, however, even this fuzzy area involving diachronic identity reinforces the prevailing practice of tightly linking responsibility to identity, for it also assumes that responsibility must be connected to discrete identities.

Peter French's position suggests one way to understand the limitations of responsibility over time.[12] As we saw in the beginning of this chapter, he argues that the moral agency of a corporate body (or what he calls a conglomerate) rests, in part, on the internal decision structures and basic principles of the group. In a government, these attributes are usually expressed in a constitution. The advantage of using the constitution to mark the continuity of a government's moral identity is that it does account for the boundaries of official responsibility (when officials act ultra vires), and it doesn't let a government off the hook for a past wrong simply because a law or a policy has changed. One implication of this position is that a change in the constitution can present a moral firebreak. If this is true, then the present German government is not responsible for the actions of the Third Reich, not only because the officials of the Nazi regime bore responsibility for what they did but also because the constitutional structure is different.

Hooking the identity of governments to the constitution, however, also presents two challenges. The first is whether the constitution presents a sufficient criterion for moral identity. The second is that, if it is sufficient, when is a constitution a new constitution and, consequently, when is a government a new government? However broadly we may consider a constitution, say, to include both written and unwritten authoritatively recognized principles, rules, and procedures, constitutions remain assemblages of authoritative ideas and concepts. Clearly, this ideational component is a necessary feature of government, particularly a government that is understood to entail the rule of law and prin-

---

12. Another solution to the puzzle of the diachronic limitations of governmental responsibility connects the moral identity of government to some more enduring entity that it represents; for example, the people, the nation, the folk, and the culture are all alternative candidates for bearing the stain of official wrong. Even if the Nazi government is gone, perhaps something called the German state (or *Volk*, nation, culture, society, or even capitalist class) is ultimately responsible for the government. In addition, just as we treat government *as if* it were a moral actor capable of taking on the role of principal, so perhaps we could treat any of these other entities *as if* they were responsible beings.

As we saw earlier, however, the plausibility of treating governments as moral agents does not merely require an "as if" form of reasoning. It also requires an account of how that entity can act. In the case of governments, there is a notion of an agent/principal relationship that makes the account somewhat more plausible. While some may believe that they act on behalf of the *volk*, or that they speak for the culture, these claims are usually utterances of vainglorious self-assessment, for it is impossible to see how one could be authorized to occupy such a position vis-à-vis these larger social groupings. As I have suggested, it is difficult enough to make a plausible case for governmental responsibility. These other forms of groupings simply do not have the capacity to "act."

ciple as opposed to personality or violence. Nevertheless, in order to exist, a government must govern something. Constitutions frequently refer to place or geographic location and are held to be binding on some places on earth and not on others. Yet governments not only survive from one generation to the next but may also survive extraordinary expansions and contractions in territory, even while the constitution remains unaltered.[13] Nevertheless, a government that governed no one and no place could not exist. The moral continuity of government rests on the continuity of certain ideational elements (primarily embodied in the constitution) plus maintaining a minimal connection of actually governing a territory and citizenry. Neither element is sufficient. Consequently, a significantly different constitution in the same land with (roughly) the same population is not the same government (as in Eastern European states pre- and post-communism). Similarly, the same constitution without a citizenry would fail as being the same government (a "government" in permanent exile). Although the constitutional features of government are key, they are not sufficient to maintain the moral identity of a government.

Given that governments may remain the same despite enormous changes in population and territory, something must be said about the possible latitude for change that constitutions can admit. One approach to this problem is to look for some core identity within the constitution—some set of necessary and sufficient conditions that would make the identity of a constitution an all or nothing affair. For example, if a set of principles, procedures, or institutions existed that defined a particular constitution, then altering or eliminating those conditions would transform the government. In the U. S. Constitution the separation of powers, or due process, or the Bill of Rights may all serve as candidates for such entities. The problem, of course, is that even these entities are not all or nothing affairs. While eliminating Congress and investing plenary legislative power in the president would certainly be a fundamental constitutional change, shifts in the balance of power between the branches may be a great deal more subtle over time and effectively, through salami-like tactics, lead to the same result. Despite enormous

13. Governments may even survive in exile and hence be deprived of both territory and people, but they cannot remain in that condition indefinitely without eventually becoming governments in name only. Enormous changes can occur to population and territory without a correspondingly dramatic change in government. Theoretically, there are no necessary limitations on changes in territory; it is even conceivable for governments to be detached from any particular place on earth and still govern.

shifts in power from the Senate to one man, not many Romans at the time would have seen the rise of Caesar as the death of the republic. Nevertheless, drastic and far-reaching constitutional changes can signal a new regime in an obvious way. But not all constitutional changes take this form. Instead of seeing the identity of a constitution as an all or nothing affair, it may be more useful to see it as a bundle of characteristics (principles, procedures, and institutions) that, through amendment and use, can also be altered bit by bit. A regime is the same regime when enough of these elements remain the same. What constitutes "enough," of course, is a difficult problem and is not simply a matter of number but also significance. For example, repealing the First Amendment to the Constitution is more significant than changing age requirements for office. The point here is not to define what a significant change would be but to suggest that identifying a government's transformation may be a great deal more tricky than only looking for the grand sea change.

The implication of seeing the identity of a constitution as a matter of degree, as Locke noted in his discussion of personal identity, is that government A at time one may be the same as B at time two, and B may be identified as the same as C at time three, but C and A are not necessarily the same. If identity is a matter of degree, then it is not transitive.[14] If it is not transitive, then the changes in a regime over time may be so significant that moral responsibility for previous action becomes attenuated. Today, the U. S. government possesses a great number of elements that it possessed in the early nineteenth century. But significant and fundamental shifts in power between the states and the federal government, basic changes in the notion of due process, elemental transformations in the economic role and size of the federal government, and crucial redefinitions of personhood and citizen have all occurred in the past two hundred years. Is this the same government? The question, I am suggesting,

14. I am appealing to Derek Parfit's (contested) reductionist vision of personal identity to make sense of constitutional identity. Parfit argues that the identity of persons is not a transitive relation but rather depends on what he calls "relation R." Relation R is a composition of the memories, goals, projects, and ideals that compose an individual's identity. As an individual lives her life, new memories, desires, and projects are acquired, and old memories, desires, and projects are lost. If "enough" of the strands are maintained, the person A at time one is the same as person B at time two. However, because identity is a matter of degree, it is not transitive. A may be the same as B, and B may be the same as C over time, but A and C could be said to be two different individuals. This vision of identity may more adequately describe institutions than individuals (although I still believe that it has some power in describing individual identity as well) (Parfit 1984, 199–347).

is a difficult one, and upon it hinges the problem of moral responsibility over time.

The possibility that the identity of regimes is tied to ideational and physical components implies that, over time, moral firebreaks do exist when those changes are significant. This is not particularly good news for the victims of official wrongs or their descendents. While they may still suffer, the perpetrator may have disappeared. Nevertheless, it is not unusual to hold new governments responsible for the crimes of their predecessors. The most obvious of these involve war and crimes against humanity. The present German government continues to pay reparations for the Holocaust, and the Japanese government did apologize for the Tojo government's actions in Korea. Perhaps in international relations, the sins of the predecessors are passed to the descendants.

Given a set of assumptions about the nature of responsibility and governmental identity, certain attempts to hold past governments responsible for their actions does not make sense in theory. Nevertheless, it is possible to give two accounts of how new governments become responsible for what their predecessors have done while still holding on to those assumptions. One way is if the new regime prevents victims of the previous regime from having their story told, if it tries to cover up or deny what its predecessor had done, or if it protects individuals implicated in war crimes and other wrongs. A new regime may become entangled in the actions of its predecessor and become an accessory after the fact. Although the difference between murdering and covering up a murder is significant, the latter crime pulls one back toward the former. New regimes with new constitutions may start with a clean moral slate, but they can very easily stain it with the past.

New regimes, however, can become responsible in a different way. Here, the concept of responsibility is meant as a virtue. A responsible person, in this usage, is someone who comes across a mess that is not of his or her making and cleans it up. Obviously, when taken to an excess, there can be something viciously self-destructive about this kind of action. Yet, if we can use the notion of responsibility in this way, then a responsible government is one that cleans up a mess not of its own making. A new regime that wants to see itself as "responsible" in this sense may try to repair the injuries of its predecessor and take on reparations. The new German government was acting, on this view, as a responsible government when it took on reparations for the Holocaust. Correspondingly, although after the war the East German government had no obligations to pay reparations, it was not acting "responsibly" when it ignored them.[15] Obviously, this conception of being responsible is not a duty to clean up the mess. Rather, it would seem to be part of the virtue of generosity (a virtue that was raised in the discussion of pardons).

Just governments are not only responsible for their agents' actions, they may also be responsible for what their agents did—as agents—in the distant past. Considering the extent to which a government's organizing principles have changed also tells us something about the extent to which a government is responsible for "its" previous acts and omissions. If the effects of a governmental harm can ripple over a number of generations, then it would seem that both victims and transgressors might endure for quite a long time. But even if we assume that governments are blameworthy, that is not enough to conclude that their actions are also forgivable. In raising this issue, we move back to the problem of political forgiveness—this time, from the perspective of citizens forgiving their government.

15. If there is an obligation to be responsible in this sense, it is an imperfect obligation.

7
Forgiving the Government

STRICTLY SPEAKING, political forgiveness of a government cannot arise in cases where the government is either fully just or unjust. In the former situation the wronged parties could always receive what is due, and in the latter situation the individual actors, not the government, are responsible for the wrongdoing. Thus, the circumstances of political forgiveness vis-à-vis governments range only over cases of nearly just governments. The difficulty of imagining a situation in which people always received their due suggests the importance of thinking about forgiveness (or other responses to the intractability of injustice) in politics. As for what kinds of governmental wrongs are forgivable by citizens, I claim that it is necessary, although not sufficient, for the wrongs to have a resistant or intractable character. To illustrate intractability, I focus on the cases of imperfect procedures and tragic choices. Although a conditional argument can be made for citizens forgiving wrongs that result from imperfect procedures, such a conclusion is more difficult to support in the case of tragic choices. Nevertheless, in light of a particular understanding of what it means to be a citizen and of what the intractability of injustice involves, political forgiveness can play a role in supplementing justice in a nearly just regime.

Nearly Just and Fully Unjust Governments

A nearly just government can be understood as one in which basic rights and liberties are protected and individuals are free to pursue their conceptions of the good. In a nearly just government, economic and social inequalities are arranged such that they are to the advantage of the least advantaged of society. In short, this kind of government is an expression of John Rawls's principles of justice (Rawls 1971). In addition, it also has a responsibility to secure domestic tranquillity by punishing criminal conduct, protecting innocent people, and providing a common defense. What makes such a government "nearly" just are the unavoidable presence of historical wrongs, procedural imperfections, and tragic choices. In other words, nearly just governments are not immune from commiting wrongs. Responsiblity for those wrongs, however, extends to acts and omissions committed by those acting in an official capacity. Nearly just governments are not responsible for the unofficial or ultra vires actions of their officers. They can become responsible if they somehow condone or permit such action, but at least initially, the individual actor and not the government is responsible in such cases (see chapter 6).

An unjust government is one in which a core feature, persistent quality, or key institution of the government fails to live up to the rough standards of justice mentioned above. Using a set of distinctions developed by George Kateb, one could say that a government is unjust if its policies are evil, if it engages in oppression, or if the injustices it commits violate the central purposes of good government (Kateb 1992, 201). Doing evil entails the obliteration of personhood and, hence, can preclude the possibility for political forgiveness if the minimal conditions of justice cannot be met (see chapter 2). Not only does responsibility for evil fall to the individuals who do it, but in cases where the victim is dead or missing, it is also politically unforgivable.[1]

Similarly, a government may be unjust if it is deemed oppressive. One way to see oppression is as "the denial of many or most personal and political rights" (Kateb 1992, 201). In an oppressive regime, the pursuit of justice is marginalized or entirely closed down. As long as the oppression continues and the demands for justice are snuffed out, then political

---

1. Is it possible for a just government to do evil? Kateb suggests that the existence of the death penalty in a nearly just regime would be such an example. In addition, in some instances of supreme emergency, a nearly just government may dirty its hands by doing evil. Given the analysis presented above and assuming the evil character of such actions, would a nearly just government that employed this penalty provide moral cover for official actions that are evil but more or less isolated? I argue that because the government is just or nearly so, it is responsible for what is done in its name. The officials who perform the action would seem to have some relief from moral culpability because of the character of the government. Because the action is evil (and, hence, ultra vires), an official cannot entirely escape responsibility. Although not a particularly clean solution, responsibility in this case would seem to be shared between the government and the individuals who performed the actions.

forgiveness is largely irrelevant. Remedying oppression, then, requires not forgiveness but the replacement of the regime. As in the case of an evil, unjust government, an oppressive government does not carry the responsibility for the unjust actions; the individual "official" actors do. Assuming the minimal conditions of justice are met, acts of oppression are not inherently unforgivable. However, meeting those conditions requires replacing the government. Whether officials and individuals that participated in the oppressive acts of a former regime can be forgiven is considered in chapter 8.

Finally, a government can be unjust if it commits significant injustices. In contrast to oppression and evil, injustice can be seen as "the denial of one or a few personal or political rights" (Kateb 1992, 201). The systematic violation of particularly important rights, for example, the right to vote, to assemble, or to speak freely may be sufficient to categorize the whole government as unjust. Once again, when the government is unjust, then the wrongs committed are the responsibility of the actual actor and not an abstract entity called a government. It is possible to conceive of what John Rawls has called decent, nonliberal societies in which basic rights and the demands of justice are met but which are organized in a manner that does not recognize all individuals as free and equal (Rawls 1999, 59–60). They may, for example, be organized around a particular religious doctrine but still respect other religious beliefs and core international norms. In addition, a government may commit injustices and still remain just if the injustices are unsystematic and real avenues for repairing the wrongs exist. A just regime (whether liberal or decent) can sustain its character when it commits injustices largely because the avenues for the pursuit of justice are open.

The focus of this discussion of political forgiveness is restricted to cases where the government is nearly just but has committed injustices that are sporadic or not core to a conception of a just government. A nearly just government (and ordinary citizens), however, can also commit an additional kind of wrong. This category of lesser offenses includes insults, affronts, indignities, and misrepresentations that are not part of depriving individuals of their personal or political rights but appear in ordinary political and bureaucratic interactions. For the most part, these kinds of wrongs are citizen to citizen, but governments are not above such actions in their official pronouncements and enforcement of rules and regulations. As in the case of injustices, this category of lesser harms creates moral debts that can usually be addressed. To the extent that these wrongs are committed by political actors in a political context (and are not private insults or misrepresentations), the possibilities for political forgiveness and reconciliation also exist.

Should nearly just governments that have committed injustices or lesser harms be forgiven by those they have wronged? While governments can clearly wrong groups, other governments, and individuals who are not citizens, this chapter assumes that the wronged parties are citizens. I do not deny that the question of forgiveness can arise for other relevant political entities (e.g., international actors, nongovernmental organizations, and social groups, foreign nationals); rather, the elements of political forgiveness may be illuminated more clearly by focusing on political individuals called citizens. Given the purposes of political forgiveness, focusing on the citizen/government relationship, and not just on any individual's relationship to an offending government, may pose the best chance for justifying the forgiving of governments by individuals. The connection of political forgiveness to reconciliation and the possibility that citizens should sustain and support a nearly just government support the possibility of using forgiveness to repair that relationship. Restricting the discussion to wronged *citizens*, however, requires a brief excursion into the meaning of citizenship, because the way in which citizenship is understood affects the analysis of whether such citizens can or should forgive their government.

Citizens and Governments

Using Richard Flathman's distinction between "high," "low," and "chastened" forms of citizenship, I adopt the conception of a chastened citizenship that can occasionally and legitimately move into the more withdrawalist mode of citizenship (Flathman 1989, 65–108). Very roughly, "high" citizenship, as understood and advocated by such writers as Jean-Jacques Rousseau, Carol Pateman, and Benjamin Barber, presents an ideal in which participation in politics is a high (if not the highest) ideal. Through participation, authority and citizenship can be reconciled to each other, in the sense of being fully compatible. Our capacities as citizens are only fully realized in the exercise of authority, and through the exercise of authority, we gain a form of political freedom and common good that is unavailable in other engagements or activities.

In contrast, a chastened view of citizenship is skeptical of the possibilities for such a harmonious state of reconciliation between authority and citizen. This stance requires that citizens keep an eye on their government and jealously protect their liberties and rights against official infringements. This view of citizenship requires that citizens are deeply suspicious of the political authority's ability to resolve all conflicts, reconcile all positions, and generate a Rousseauvian general will. In contrast to high citizenship, where the realization of both citizenship and authority occurs when these two roles collapse, this view holds that such aspirations can be realized only at a great cost to individuality and the legitimate differences that distinguish us from one another. An imperfect instrument, at best, for realizing our common and individual conceptions of the good, government must be empowered to act and perpetually restrained in its actions.

Flathman's conception of "low" citizenship, as suggested by Thomas Hobbes and advanced by Michael Oakeshott, argues that the role of citizen entails obedience to a set of rules and offices that are held to be authoritative. Authority itself, not participation, is the basis of our obligations. Political authority is a necessary evil, and consequently little intrinsic value is attributed to the role of being a citizen. Because what is really valuable to individuals is found in their private interactions, low citizenship implies a form of political withdrawal. In general, this vision of citizenship is certainly skeptical of the grander claims of political harmony but is also generally opposed to the capacity of ordinary citizens to judge, interpret, or assess authoritative commands and laws. Flathman finds most troubling this last attribute of low citizenship. He argues that "this position is incoherent because citizens and subjects who do not understand the reasons for a law *cannot* discharge their obligation to obey it; they cannot do so because knowing what counts as obeying a rule, knowing *what* the rule demands or forbids, requires understanding the reasons for it" (Flathman 1989, 106). For Flathman, a chastened conception of citizenship is more plausible. For even though this view remains skeptical of the higher aspirations of "high" citizenship, the "low" conception's notion of citizens surrendering their judgment is incoherent.

The focus on citizens and, more specifically, this chastened conception of citizenship reflects the understanding of and relationship between rectificatory justice and political forgiveness that chapter 2 discussed: namely, that in order for the question of political forgiveness to arise, the demands of rectificatory justice must be addressed, at least to some extent. If individuals are considered to be less than citizens (e.g., slaves, children, or oppressed subjects), then the question of political forgiveness does not arise until a kind of government is established that is consistent with a conception of free and equal citizens. That is, political forgiveness on the part of citizens presupposes a nearly just government.

But this conception of citizenship also structures the justification for political forgiveness of governmental wrongs.

Whether political forgiveness can apply to governments comes down to whether nearly just governments can be forgiven for the sporadic injustices they commit against their citizens. It is entirely possible that in many injustices the victims can fully receive their due (assuming the avenues for pursuing the good of justice are open and accessible to those who have been wronged). This possibility, of course, narrows the focus somewhat further. Political forgiveness of a nearly just government arises only when something is problematic about the relentless pursuit of justice or when justice is intractable.

The Intractability of Injustice

The intractability of injustice can make its appearance in cases involving historical wrongs, tragic choices, and imperfect procedures. Governmental responsibility for historical wrongs depends not only on whether the government authorized or condoned the past injury but also whether the present government is the same as the responsible government. When a previous, unjust government committed the wrong, the responsibility for it falls to the individuals who committed the wrong. The relationship between these kinds of wrongdoers and victims is explored further in chapter 8 (and is framed as a matter of *one to one* forgiveness). In cases in which the offending government is similar enough to its past manifestation, then the victim continues to have a claim against the present government.

The intractability of historical wrongs is connected to the problem of discerning what is due to whom and whether what is due can be given without seriously violating the expectations and rights of others. This book has passed over the problem of defining "what is due" and has assumed that this marker for the idea of justice makes some amount of intuitive sense. The passage of time, however, does give rise to expectations and claims in which the rectification of wrongs cannot be accomplished without setting back the fundamental interests of others. Past wrongs that have entailed the acquisition of territory through conquest, the violation of treaties, the forced movement of peoples, or the arbitrary establishment of international boundaries can, over the course of generations, create a set of expectations and rights claims that would have to be disrupted in order to give the victims (or their descendants) their due. The thorny theoretical questions raised by historical wrongs primarily revolve around issues of identity (and responsibility) over time, clearly establishing the nature of what is due, and the possibility of tragic choices in which state actors must choose between two wrongful actions (although not all historical injuries need raise tragic choices). The first problem was briefly discussed in chapter 6. The second raises the larger question of the nature of justice, which is not considered here, and the final problem is discussed below, under the rubric of dirty hands.

Here the focus is mainly on tragic choices and imperfect procedures. The former situation, illustrated by the problem of dirty hands, points to another limitation in seeking reconciliation through forgiveness. In contrast, the problem of imperfect procedures illustrates how justice can be supplemented through forgiveness. While it may be appropriate to forgive just institutions that have produced unjust outcomes, citizens should be extremely suspicious of and unforgiving toward politicians and institutions that claim that wrongdoing was necessary for doing good.

An important assumption of this chapter is that dirty hands and imperfect procedures are real, moral difficulties and that governments cannot rule out their occurrence. In other words, in both situations, the actions of the government cannot be excused or justified.[2] Within moral philosophy and jurisprudence, there are significant disputes over whether the tragic choices or moral dilemmas implied by dirty hands are real problems. Nevertheless, we have encountered situations in which state actors are forced to choose between preserving core values of the regime. In some cases, the attempt to rectify historical wrongs may have this character. Perhaps the most tragic of choices, however, occurs when state actors must choose between preserving core values of the regime and risking the preservation of that which is meant to preserve those values. For example, transitional regimes faced with a powerful class of members of the ancien régime have protected those individuals from the just claims of their victims by granting unconditional amnesty or protecting them from civil suit. The decision of the new South African government to indemnify from civil suit those who have been granted a conditional amnesty is an example of the latter situation. One can think of other cases in which state actors have seen themselves as being forced to choose between fundamental values. For example, President Lincoln's unconstitutional suspension of the writ of habeas corpus during the

2. The appendix to chapter 7 explores the possibility of excusing or justifying state actors who have dirtied their hands or governmental procedures that have yielded wrong outcomes.

American Civil War was claimed to be necessary for prosecuting the war despite the sacrifice of liberty to innocent individuals imprisoned under Lincoln's directive. Finally, one can understand nuclear deterrence as a form of dirty hands in which a nearly just state may threaten the lives of millions of innocent individuals to protect its security. In all of these situations, the government is seeking to protect that which is thought to guarantee core values of society by violating core values of the citizenry. Because of the alleged inescapability of the choice, the problem of dirty hands generally arises in what is called a realm of necessity. Once again, the assumption here (explored in the appendix to this chapter) is that the existence of necessity does not fully excuse or justify the state actions.

An example of imperfect procedures is much easier to conceive, and the case of a criminal proceeding should suffice. As suggested earlier, it may be impossible to conceive of a set of rules or procedures that can guarantee the innocent are set free and the guilty are punished. One could, of course, select pretty much any respectable complex bureaucratic, legislative, or judicial procedure and imagine how it could yield an unjust outcome.

Dirty Hands

Who is responsible when a political actor dirties her hands? When an official faces a tragic choice, she is torn between two official duties or fundamental values that cannot both be satisfied. In Lincoln's case, he was obligated to defend the union and protect the rights of citizens. From one perspective, the argument could be made that in dirtying his hands, Lincoln fulfilled a duty to secure a fundamental value (protecting the union). Consequently, the weight of responsibility should fall not on Lincoln's shoulders but on the nearly just government for which he is an agent. From another perspective, Lincoln violated his duty to uphold the constitution and protect innocent individuals from being imprisoned, a view implying that he and not the government should be held responsible for the action. It would not be implausible, however, to presume that in cases of dirty hands, both the individual acting as an agent and the government share responsibility.

As in all of these situations, justice in the case of dirty hands requires that the wrongdoers publicly acknowledge their role and convey that information to those who were wronged. In general, if the official who dirtied her hands is still in office, it may be possible for the official to perform this function herself. In addition, assuming that the avenues for the pursuit of justice are open, as they should be in a nearly just government, then those who have suffered from the government's policies may also pursue other symbolic and material forms of rectification. But in terms of making things right, what is the responsibility of the government vis-à-vis those officials who dirtied their hands? What does justice require of them?

Political actors who have dirtied their hands have done wrong in order to do good. Given the two-sided character of the act, we are tempted to say that they should either be punished or honored. But to adopt one of these responses is to commit an injustice—not to give what is due.[3] To circumvent this problem, Michael Walzer has suggested the obvious solution. In the case of dirty hands, "We would simply honor the man who did bad in order to do good, and at the same time we would punish him. We would honor him for the good he has done, and we would punish him for the bad that he has done" (Walzer 1979, 81).[4] The attraction of Walzer's solution is that it seems to meet the requirements of justice. As a practical matter, however, Walzer is skeptical about this solution, since "there seems to be no way to establish or enforce the punishment. Short of the priest and the confessional, there are no authorities to whom we might entrust the task" (81). Actually, the more difficult problem is whether we can simultaneously punish and honor. Perhaps one could subtract the amount of honor due from the amount of punishment owed. If they zero out, then nothing is owed. If there is more punishment owed, then punish, and so on. This solution would make sense if the punishment and the honor were in the same medium (e.g., a financial reward to honor and a fine to punish), or if there was a way to translate between honors and punishments. Yet if

3. For example, even though the wrong done was to noncitizens and although Walzer argues that it is not quite a case of dirty hands, his example of Arthur Harris, the man who directed the British bombing campaign during World War II, may illustrate this problem. Churchill and others believed that Harris's terror bombing of German cities was necessary, but "there seems to have been a conscious decision not to celebrate the exploits of Bomber Command or to honor its leader" when the war was over (Walzer 1977, 324). If this truly was a case of dirty hands, it was also a failure to give Harris what was due. It was a failure to honor him. Yet, if the British had honored him instead of snubbing him, it would still have been a failure to give what was due.

4. In the case of Harris, "it would have been better," Walzer argues, if Churchill "had praised the courage and endurance of the fliers of Bomber Command even while insisting that it was not possible to take pride in what they had done (an impossibility that many of them must have felt)" (Walzer 1977, 325).

they can cancel each other out, then the message of simultaneous punishment and reward could very easily be lost. Depending on what remained, the ultimate signal conveyed could look like indifference, approval, disapproval, or forgetfulness. In addition, these kinds of solutions suggest that the deeds done (the right and the wrong) are, in a sense, fungible. This doesn't seem quite right, because the nature of a tragic choice is that the injustice remains intact. Finally, even if Walzer's practical objection could be surmounted and we could simultaneously punish and honor, punishing may have future effects that are unacceptable. To punish political actors who find themselves making tragic choices may render other actors less willing to make such difficult choices. To the extent that punishment sends a message—that this kind of activity will not be tolerated—the message is probably false (because the activity is generally tolerated) and potentially dangerous (because sometimes politicians must make choices in tragic situations). It is not evident, then, that Walzer's solution to the problem of dirty hands is ultimately desirable.

If the pursuit of justice in the case of dirty hands brings us to an impasse, it is one that Max Weber believed political actors had either to endure with their eyes open or risk slipping into a relentless and dangerous pursuit of justice. For Weber, this meant adopting what he called an ethic of responsibility. For a political actor who does evil in order to do good, this ethic should lead him or her to conclude, "Here I stand; I can do no other" (Weber 1946, 127). Perhaps understanding the bind that their leaders are in, citizens who suffer as a result of such decisions can adopt a version of this ethic as well. The corresponding ethic for citizens who are victims would admonish them to take it on the chin: simply accept that this is how the world works (sometimes we must do wrong, and sometimes we must suffer it), and get on as best as we can.

As we see below, a form of this argument can be found in the notion of forgetting. At this point, however, we need only mention that if the ethic of responsibility implies a take-it-on-the-chin ethic for citizens, it both fails to acknowledge the extent to which justice can be done (e.g., forcing the government to admit what it has done and demanding some form of compensation) and implies a kind of passive acceptance of such state injustices. The danger in citizens adopting an ethic of responsibility is that it is all too easy for politicians to portray the normal as extraordinary and to claim the necessity of doing wrong in situations in which it is not true. As we also see below, this approach proves incompatible with a chastened conception of citizenship.

Weber's alternative to an ethic of responsibility, however, is troubling as well. This ethic requires that one always intend to do what is good. Paradoxically, Weber believed that this focus could either result in driving people away from worldly involvement or toward a kind of revolutionary millenarianism (Weber 1946, 121–22). In the latter case, one concludes that if wrongs must be done to do good, then let us perform a last unjust act to obtain what is ultimately best: one last war to end all wars, one final revolution to overcome this unjust world, one last sacrifice to end all sacrifices. If politicians must dirty their hands, make sure that it is in the name of ending all tragic choices. There is a path that leads from the dismal character of politics and the difficulties of arriving at justice to a hope in a new Jerusalem.

This path, however, depends on a belief that we can surpass a world in which good can come out of injustice. If one denies this possibility (as I am supposing), then one should reject the argument that a final burst of violence will end all wrongdoing. This kind of immunity, however, would not prevent an ethic of ultimate ends from being driven to its otherworldly extreme—the wholesale rejection of politics. From the realization that the world is such that being a political actor can involve doing injustice, one may conclude that it is better to forgo politics entirely. For citizens who have been wronged by their government and refuse to run the risk of doing more injustice, the relevant principle becomes inaction: better to suffer wrong than to do wrong.

Assuming the path to millenarianism has been rejected, then the counsel of inaction on the part of political victims would make sense only if any response to injustice could violate the principle not to do wrong.[5] But the expectation on which this withdrawal from politics is based is unreasonable. In nearly just societies, victims can frequently push their cause quite far without generating further injustices. On this terrain, an ethic of ultimate ends need not yield withdrawal. In a situation such as dirty hands, however, where the hard tradeoffs of politics emerge, the ethic of ultimate ends may become twisted and dangerous. This may be why Weber believed that an ethic of responsibility is needed to supplement an ethic of ultimate ends (Weber 1946, 127). Once

5. Of course, there may be something wrong by refusing to act, or in not standing up for one's rights, in which case the victim cannot avoid being implicated in injustice.

it becomes necessary to do wrong, an individual with a true calling to politics will know when to stop a relentless pursuit of justice and simply do what must be done. For citizens who have to deal with politicians who have dirtied their hands, this brings us back to a take-it-on-the-chin attitude. Perhaps victims of dirty hands should walk away from and forget the harms caused by such tragic choices.

Forgetting the Wrong

To drop or forget the whole injury or wrong is to preempt completely the pursuit of justice. To condone forgetting injuries is to say that whatever happened to you is not worth dwelling on: whatever you lost or suffered because of the injury is less valuable to you than the time and effort you spend reflecting on the loss. In a sense, forgetting implies that one does not acknowledge the injury as an injury. What lies behind this implication can be inherently ambiguous. On the one hand, forgetting may suggest that the wrongdoer as wrongdoer is not worth one's time. From this perspective, forgetting may provoke and inflate a sense of self-worth and forestall (as Nietzsche thought) the production of resentment in personal interaction. On the other hand, forgetting may reflect a diminished sense of self-worth. One may simply forget the injury because one comes to believe that one is not even worthy of being seen as injured. In any case, the complete forgetting of a governmental-caused injury would seem to be too passive for a chastened conception of citizenship. A citizenry too willing to forget its injuries is not independent enough for the name. To the extent that forgetting implies such depreciation, it is an unjustified response.

The question of forgetting need not be understood as forgetting the whole injury. It could be reframed in a way that is consistent with meeting the minimal demands of justice. For example, even though nothing may have been done to those officials who dirtied their hands, why not simply be satisfied with whatever elements of justice (e.g., public commissions, compensation, or formal apologies) are offered? The counsel to forget that dirty-handed politicians may go unpunished and to get on with one's life does have an appeal—particularly for ensuring the stability of basically just institutions. Assuming that the demands of justice have been met to some degree and that the relentless pursuit of justice would lead to further difficulties, why shouldn't a wronged citizen simply call it quits and forget?

Consequentialist Arguments

One argument against forgetting what I call the remainders of dirty hands (i.e., the authoritative wrongdoers are probably not going to be punished) is that the appeals to necessity generated by this problem are extraordinarily dangerous and have been often misused. Such appeals are all too frequently used in the attempt to excuse injuries and abridge rights. Such depressingly familiar events in recent American history as the internment of Japanese Americans and Cold War radiation and drug experiments on innocent individuals are part of a larger list of pleas of necessity. In light of the difficulties for citizens to discern whether a problem of dirty hands has actually arisen, and given the propensity of politicians to deploy this line of reasoning, forgetting the remainders simply lets the government evade responsibility. In other words, citizens should not forget because the consequences for doing so are unacceptable.

The consequentialist argument against individual acts of forgetting, however, has the obvious defect that it makes little difference whether any particular citizen remembers or forgets that governmental wrongs have gone unpunished. From the individual citizen's perspective, it is unlikely that forgetting such things will have the consequence of encouraging officials to act with impunity in the future. One individual's unwillingness to remember what had happened will probably not affect whether and how future politicians decide to deploy the claims of necessity. This is not meant to disparage the immediate consequence of forgetting, namely, letting the victim get on with his or her life. The problem is that the consequentialist argument can be more complicated than looking at the effects of individual actions.

Rule utilitarians, obviously, would see the matter somewhat differently. They would argue that the relevant calculation is not the goodness or badness of a particular individual act of forgetting, but whether a rule that permitted forgetting would produce more or less utility. If a rule forbidding forgetting produced more utility than one that permitted it, then the former should govern our interactions. From the individual rule-follower's perspective, however, the standard difficulty with rule utilitarianism is that the principle of utility does not apply to specific acts but to rules. Consequently, whether utility is served in any given instance of forgetting would be irrelevant as long as the rule that it is inappropriate to forget yields more utility than a rule making these actions appropriate. The difficulty is that the rule would have to be followed, even if in any given instance, violating the rule derives more utility. In effect, rule utilitarianism becomes a formalistic fetish, a kind of "rule worship." To the extent that rule utilitarians try to write exceptions into the rules to accommodate the myriad possibilities in which more is gained by violating the rule, then rule utilitarianism looks more and more like act utilitarianism (Smart and Williams 1973, 9–12). As we saw above, if we turn to actions, it may very well be the case that forgetting advances the happiness of a particular citizen.

It may be possible to judge the value (to use a more general term than *utility*) of a rule or practice in terms of its consequences, however, without being forced into a strict form of act utilitarianism. One way to do so is to ask what expectations a rule to forget would create in the minds of those who deploy pleas of necessity. If state actors knew their troubles were to be forgotten by those they serve, it is plausible to think that they may be more cavalier with claims of necessity. The knowledge that their actions wronging others would eventually be hidden and lost to history might encourage officials to appeal to the extreme case in order to justify the abridgment of rights or the sacrifice of core values. If this line of argument is plausible, then it is also plausible to argue that a similar expectation would be created if dirty-handed officials knew they could always be forgiven. Because of the extraordinary power of claims to necessity and the extraordinary danger they present to citizens, not to mention the rest of the world, politicians should not expect political amnesia or even forgiveness. If politicians acted in the realm of necessity with the knowledge that what they did was forgivable, or would be forgotten, then the claims of necessity would be abused with more frequency. Wrongs that issue from appeals to necessity should be politically unforgivable and not forgotten.

From the individual's perspective, whether or not to abide by the rule requires understanding whether and why the rule prohibiting forgetting or forgiving is good. The most important element of this understanding is that citizens understand the point of the rule. That is, citizens must be convinced that because the rule renders those actors more cautious with the deployment of claims of necessity, it is good to create and sustain the expectation that what they do will not be forgotten or forgiven. Understanding this, presumably, would be a good reason for a citizen neither to forgive nor forget. That the rule is good because it has good consequences, however, does not ensure that in any given instance there may be other, more compelling reasons for individual citizens to forget or forgive. But as long as these reasons remain exceptional, they may not be strong enough to erode the rule that citizens should not forgive or forget the remainders of dirty hands. This may be the strongest consequentialist argument for adopting a rule to forgo forgetting or forgiving the moral remainders of dirty hands.

Arguments from the Role of Citizens

Aside from consequentialist arguments, it is also useful to consider whether the role of citizen, as such, can tell us anything about how we should respond to political actors who have dirtied their hands. Embedded within a chastened view of citizenship is a set of norms outlining appropriate behavior for citizens whose government has wronged them. Such citizens are not only skeptical of authority but are also watchful of how authority is exercised and are protective of their rights. When wronged, such citizens would be expected to push for justice. All else being equal, a failure to push for justice would be incompatible with what it means to be a citizen.

Does this role of citizen also provide some direction for responding to dirty hands? When it becomes clear that the perpetrators of wrongs will not receive what is due to them (because they acted in the realm of necessity), perhaps a refusal to forget the remainders would make one a better citizen, since it would confirm one's tempered or subdued approach to authority. In this case, not forgetting fortifies one's stance that authority is a dangerous, difficult practice that needs to be monitored and controlled. But saying that remembering the remainders can confirm one's skeptical stance is not the same as arguing that this role of the chastened citizen requires that one not forget. Should good, skeptical citizens not forget the remainders? The strongest case that they should not forget is that forgetting is incompatible with their self-respect as citizens. As citizens, their fundamental sense of equality has been violated through the transgression and remains unrepaired as long as the transgressors are unpunished. More specifically, innocent but wronged citizens are subject to the law, while guilty, dirty-handed authorities are set free. Obviously, simply remembering the wrong doesn't rectify the inequality, but forgetting the wrong lets slide the central value that both rulers and the ruled should have equal moral standing.

Does this chastened role of citizen also preclude forgiveness? I think it does, if we assume a number of things: that true tragic choices are rare, that politicians have a tendency to portray difficult cases in tragic terms, that when these claims are successful they frequently entail the violation of basic values and rights, and finally, that it is very difficult for citizens to judge the accuracy of these kinds of claims (both at the time and in their aftermath). In the context of these assumptions, the role of a chastened citizen is not to forgive those who remain unpunished. The basis for this claim is not the need to send a signal to future transgressors, as is the case in the consequentialist argument against forgiving, but an expression of legitimate distrust of the authoritative story. More forcefully, it is a distrust that good citizens will maintain in the face of any claim to necessity (given the assumptions above). Of course, what has been portrayed as a tragic choice may eventually turn out to have been an unnecessary exercise of power. Assuming the difficulty of definitively judging whether a given situation was truly a case of dirty hands, citizens should withhold their forgiveness of those who have made such appeals.

A consequentialist could argue that this unforgiving attitude would render null and void the appeal to necessity. The distrust of those who must carry out the orders would make it all but impossible to execute the necessary commands when a state really does find itself in a national emergency. Perhaps—but rarely are those who suffer under such orders the same as those who must execute them. Necessity, national security, and the sense of doing what needs to be done "regardless of the cost" will always feel different to those who don't have to pay for the effects of the policy. More directly, the claim that these dirty-handed actors should not be forgiven because they may have intentionally or unintentionally misjudged the circumstances is not the same as giving those who are following their commands a license to disobey. Such doubt would be only one element (among many) in a subordinate's decision to obey authoritative commands that ultimately violate the rights of the subordinate's fellow citizens.

But if we assume that tragic choices are not rare, or that politicians aren't tempted to portray their decisions in tragic terms, or that appeals to necessity no longer entailed serious violations of values and rights, or that it was relatively easy to know when one was really in the realm of necessity, then it might be appropriate for citizens to adopt a more forgiving stance. Unfortunately, there is always the possibility that Lincoln's suspension of habeas corpus or the present policy of mutually assured destruction will look less like a tragic choice and more like the internment of Japanese Americans or Cold War radiation experiments. A chastened conception of citizenship combined with a set of assumptions regarding dirty hands supports the conclusion that forgiveness of unpunished political actors is inappropriate.

The hope that forgiveness could serve as a supplement to justice is not realized when political actors act unjustly in order to do good. As we have seen in other cases, political forgiveness is not always justified. Here, the argument is that citizens as citizens should not forgive or forget certain things. In addition, this position reinforces the notion that political forgiveness should be granted for good reasons. Assuming the plausibility of the consequentialist argument or the attractiveness of a chastened view of citizenship, I have argued that these reasons are absent in the case of dirty hands. Even under a nearly just government, some acts may yield an indelible moral stain. Neither the moral actors nor the institutions for which they act can ever right the situation. Dirty hands entail a tragic choice that is never fully reparable.

Imperfect Procedures

In contrast to the problem of dirty hands, doing justice in the case of imperfect institutions would seem to be straightforward: change the procedures or reform the institution such that *these* unjust outcomes are no longer a possibility. Indeed, imperfect institutions have been improved through reform. We can make procedures and rules less imperfect; eliminating gender, racial, and property restrictions for the franchise decreased the chances that various individuals and groups would be treated unjustly through democratic procedures. Even if we may not obtain a perfect union, we may aim for a less imperfect one. But here, the pursuit of justice begins to encounter difficulties. First, we cannot know with certainty that we have devised the least imperfect procedure or institution. We do not know this because we cannot predict all of the effects of rules for any given situation. This problem does not preclude meaningful reform but does rule out ultimate reform. Second, to the extent that reform relies on imperfect procedures, there is no guarantee that the outcome of reform will be just. We tinker with imperfect rules by using procedures that are themselves imperfect. Third, if in heeding our sense of justice, we should reform institutions to make sure that a particular set of outcomes is less likely, then we run the risk of particularizing institutions and procedures. Our impulse to do justice may lead to the creation of rules to remedy *this* suffering in *these* circumstances. The problem, however, is that the more one attempts to accommodate the particular character of a wrong, the more particularized the rules and procedures become. The more particularized these things become, the more they are seen as ad hoc and unpredictable. A system of rules that is ad hoc and erratic is unlikely to be seen as a system of rules at all. We cannot fully accommodate the particular wrong without undermining the generality of procedures. It is unlikely that the relentless pursuit of justice in the case of imperfect procedures leads to closure.

If the relentless pursuit of justice is problematic, does forgetting, forgiving, or adopting an angle of repose fare any better? As with the case of dirty hands, it is useful to consider how consequentialist and role-based ethical theories deal with each of these options. As in the case of dirty hands, the consequences of an individual act of forgetting primarily involve freeing the citizen from the weight of the past. Unlike the case of dirty hands, however, it is plausible to assume that wrongs resulting from imperfect procedures are somewhat more frequent occurrences for citizens living in large, rule-governed regimes.[8] Given this frequency, one could argue that those imperfections could yield benefits just as easily as harms. Because imperfect institutions yield a mistaken decision does not mean that they always yield harmful decisions. From this perspective, citizens living under imperfect rules should not worry too much about relentlessly pursuing justice by perfecting those rules because, in the long run, the benefits and harms cancel each other out. In the end, it may be better simply to forget the remainders of the imperfections of procedures.

For this last argument to be plausible, it is necessary to assume that procedural imperfections randomly distribute harms and benefits to individuals and that these distributions are frequent enough and of such magnitude that the rewards and harms, at least, balance each other out. However, it is not clear whether procedural mistakes do or should randomly distribute benefits and harms. For example, in a criminal proceeding, the assumption that one is innocent until proven guilty presumably has the effect of freeing more guilty individuals than imprisoning innocents. Alternatively, the assumption that one is guilty until proven innocent may have the opposite effect. It would seem nec-

8. How frequent they are may be impossible to determine. We may assume, however, that wrong decisions are more frequent than tragic situations but less frequent than the ability of procedures to arrive at appropriate decisions. An imperfect criminal procedure that yielded the wrong decision (finding the guilty innocent and vice versa) more frequently than the right one would be worse than a random form of determining guilt and innocence. In order to command respect, our imperfect procedures would have to be significantly better at determining guilt and innocence than no procedure at all (or a random procedure). It is, however, impossible to determine how perfect our procedures can become, which is why the relentless pursuit of perfection is so attractive and so troubling.

essary, given the adversarial character of criminal proceedings, to make some such assumption one way or the other. But whatever assumption one makes will bias the character of the mistakes. Similarly, in the case of mandatory sentencing, the assumption is that it is better for those whose crimes involved extenuating circumstances to go to prison than for those without such reasons not to serve time. The kinds of mistakes that are made can be built into the procedure itself. In some cases, the biases are justifiable and unavoidable. In other cases, the biases indicate that citizens are not being treated with equal respect. In either case, it is unreasonable to assume that procedural wrongs should be forgotten because the wheel of fortune eventually equalizes everything. This does not mean that one shouldn't forget the remainders of imperfect procedures but that one shouldn't forget for this reason.

In the case of dirty hands, I argued that the consequentialist arguments ultimately turned on how forgetting, forgiving, or adopting an angle of repose affected the expectations of those who could deploy claims of necessity. Given their dangerous character, I suggested that forgetting or forgiving were problematic responses if they encouraged governments to make those claims more frequently. However, to the extent that adopting an angle of repose would discourage the abuse of those claims, it was a more appropriate response to dirty hands. In the case of imperfect institutions, assuming the good of a nearly just government and the greater chance for procedurally incorrect results, forgetting or forgiving would seem to be more appropriate than adopting an angle of repose. Forgetting or forgiving may reinforce the status quo: procedures simply would not change as readily. Unlike the case of dirty hands, here it is difficult to see how the government could capitalize on its citizenry's willingness to forgive or forget the remainders of imperfect institutions. Such institutions would not become more imperfect because citizens are willing to forgive or forget, but a citizenry that was willing to do so could reinforce the stability of nearly just institutions. In contrast, adopting an angle of repose may have the effect of engendering a widespread disillusionment and cynicism about political and legal institutions. Assuming the good of nearly just institutions, this kind of effect would not be welcome. The consequences of forgetting or forgiving could be much more salutary than those that result from adopting an angle of repose.

In addition to consequentialist arguments, by using the kinds of norms embedded in a chastened conception of citizenship, we can also look at the problem of how to respond to procedural imperfections. Would forgetting the remainders of imperfect institutions erode a skeptical stance toward authority? Probably not. Forgetting the fact that the institution's imperfections were not cured, even after some movement toward justice had been made, would probably not blind one to procedural imperfections or to the realization that there are many other, more direct ways for those in authority to cause harm. Even if one forgot such remainders, one would not necessarily forget that at times the guilty will be set free or that democratic procedures may be riven by paradoxes or that bureaucratic rules may not be able to accommodate the unique. It is not clear that a chastened conception of citizenship requires that we remember the specific failures of procedure, although these cases will reinforce one's skepticism.

Do the norms embedded in the chastened role of citizen rule out the cynicism of an angle of repose? Once again, assuming that wrong, unjust outcomes from basically just institutions probably occur with greater frequency than tragic choices, adopting an angle of repose could devolve into a jaded attitude. Indeed, seeing the adoption of an angle of repose as an appropriate response may mean that it is next to impossible to maintain one's skepticism. If the imperfection of rules shows itself frequently enough, an angle of repose would simply displace a chastened conception of citizenship. While this idea of citizenship can encompass cynicism in the case of dirty hands (because of its relative infrequency), it may not be able to accommodate such cynicism as a response to imperfect procedures in a world where procedurally perfect institutions are impossible.

A Defense of Political Forgiveness

In contrast to adopting an angle of repose to imperfect procedures, forgiving appears to offer a greater chance for maintaining one's balance as a chastened citizen. It forces one to bear in mind and work through the nature and the depth of the problem of imperfect procedures. But why is this important? Part of the answer is that bearing these things in mind may diminish our expectations regarding the possibilities of perfect procedures. The resulting lack of enthusiasm would be consistent with a chastened conception of citizenship, and it may also forestall a slide into cynicism. Perhaps cynicism is most virulent if we begin with the assumption of procedural perfectibility. Perhaps because we believe that procedures can be perfected, the disappointment and disgust is so great when they fail us. In contrast, political forgiveness requires some understanding of the limitations of imperfect procedures and so is consistent with the skeptical vision of citizenship assumed here.

Political forgiveness also has other advantages over the alternatives. Like forgetting, forgiving permits starting over. Unlike forgetting, political forgiveness requires that the past be recalled and acknowledged. In achieving a state of reconciliation, it is a way for citizens to sustain and understand the debts of the past and move on. Political forgiveness releases institutions from the failures and shortcomings that result from acting in a complex world by achieving a state of reconciliation (something that citizens should be reluctant to do in the case of dirty hands). Like adopting an angle of repose, forgiveness is a kind of weapon that victims can use to reassert their worth vis-à-vis their government. To be able to forgive another implies a form of power that can raise those who have been harmed and lower those who have gained something by doing wrong. Unlike adopting an angle of repose, forgiveness invites a process of reconciliation and restoring civil interactions without the past constantly weighing in. It is this curious attribute of political forgiveness to address and repair wrongs that reveals its potential to restore a civic relationship that is worthy of respect.

Could one argue that political forgiveness is not only a permissible response to the remainders of imperfect governance but also an obligatory response? There are times when citizens should not engage in political forgiveness. Indeed, in the case of dirty hands, I have argued that citizens (understood in a particular way) should be wary of and call into question the claims of necessity advanced by political leaders. Are there occasions, however, when citizens are obligated to forgive? As we saw in chapter 3, it would not make sense to see the obligation as a perfect duty, one that would create a right on the part of government to be forgiven. Nevertheless, a case could be made for seeing the power to forgive as within a general, imperfect duty. In support of such a case, one could argue that the potential goods yielded by forgiveness are great enough to justify according political forgiveness the status of an imperfect duty. The primary potential good when talking about responding to imperfect procedures is sustaining a nearly just government. Political forgiveness accomplishes this end by releasing transgressors from their debts, supplementing justice, and inviting the restoration of a valued political relationship.

As an imperfect duty, nearly just governments would not have a right to forgiveness, but citizens who never forgave would be morally deficient.[9] This argument, however, only applies to cases of procedural imperfections.

9. The discretionary character of the imperfect duty to forgive implies that after meeting the minimal conditions for justice, some wronged citizens may choose to forgive and some

Assuming the dangerous character of claims of necessity, it would not apply to cases of dirty hands. But even within this limitation, doesn't an imperfect duty to forgive still require that we rule out some other alternative (say, forgetting) as being good enough to accomplish the ends set out above? Mustn't political forgiveness be the only way to sustain nearly just political and legal institutions in the long run? I have argued that in the case of responding to imperfect institutions, political forgiveness is superior to an angle of repose and even to forgetting. Although nothing is inherently wrong with forgetting the harmful results of a procedural imperfection, forgetting cannot yield a reconciliatory state. In the case of forgetting (chapter 3), the past could always be resurrected as the basis for future claims against the wrong. In contrast, the point of political forgiveness is to put the past to rest. In addition, the invitation to restore a worthwhile political relationship (assuming that the government is nearly just) is one that would be understood as valuable even for a skeptical citizenry. As an imperfect obligation, however, one could never pressure a victim to forgive a government that had wronged him or her. The importance of justice and of sustaining nearly just institutions supports the conclusion that the political forgiveness of a nearly just government's imperfect institutions is an imperfect obligation.

Appendix: Excuse and Justification

IF IT IS possible either to justify or excuse imperfect procedures or dirty-handed politicians, then the question of political forgiveness need never arise, for those situations. Actually, the problem is less with the notion of justification than with excuse. For justification implies that an actor may have performed the action in question but that no wrong was done.[10] In the case of dirty hands, the possibility for justification exists only if moral dilemmas are denied. For example, realists who subscribe to a strong formulation of reason of state argue that a politician is justified in sacrificing core values if it leads to the survival of the state. Some utilitarians argue that such a sacrifice is justified if the good done outweighs the evil that results.

---

may choose to forget. This is not a problem as long as those who choose not to forgive live up to that duty on occasion, and as long as all citizens understand that any one of them may not forgive on behalf of another.

10. If an action is truly wrong, then justification is ruled out. For justification entails that "we accept responsibility but deny that it [the act] was bad" (Austin 1961, 124).

The phrase "the end justifies the means" implicitly claims that what look like evil means are actually acceptable (given the end). In neither the strong formulation of realism nor under utilitarianism do tragic choices exist.[11] In contrast, I am presuming that politicians do wrong when they dirty their hands. The situation isn't one where the closer we look at the action or outcome the less it will appear wrong, as would be the case under realism or utilitarianism. The assumption that moral dilemmas are real rules out a moral justification for dirtying one's hands.

Similarly, I am assuming that true injustice can be the result of procedures and rules that are themselves just. For example, simply because something has gone through a democratic process does not make it just. We have standards and principles that can be used to judge democratic outcomes, for example, whether the outcome violates individual rights. Only in pure procedural justice does the justification for a democratic process extend to the results of the decision. In the case of imperfect procedures, however, the procedure cannot itself justify the outcome, in a strict sense.

The more difficult issue is whether dirty hands and imperfect procedures can be *excused*. When we excuse, we admit that whatever was done was wrong, but we deny responsibility either in part or in full. For example, I may not be able to keep my promised meeting with you (which is wrong), but my excuse is that traffic was backed up for hours (which is an attempt to relieve me of responsibility). Could the imperfect character of a procedure or institution function as an excuse? Is the imperfection of a procedure like a mistake, an accident, or an intervening event that diminishes or erases responsibility? In the case of dirty hands, does a realm of necessity or the paucity of options excuse politicians who have dirtied their hands?

---

11. The flip side of this denial can be found in idealist positions (or strict deontological positions) that reject the justification or the need to give any weight to claims of necessity. From these perspectives, it is always possible to accomplish just ends through just means. For example, U.S. Supreme Court Justice Davis, in his "thunderously quotable language" (Neely 1991, 176) of *Ex parte Milligan,* set out one of the most eloquent denials of the claims of necessity:

> No doctrine, involving more pernicious consequences, was ever invented by the wit of man than that any of its provisions can be suspended during any of the great exigencies of government. Such a doctrine leads directly to anarchy or despotism, but the theory of necessity on which it is based is false; for the government, within the Constitution, has all the powers granted to it, which are necessary to preserve its existence; as has been happily proved by the result of the great effort to throw off its just authority.

Excusing Imperfect Procedures

If a nervous twitch can excuse my spilling tea on your rug, then perhaps the imperfect character of the institution can excuse an unjust outcome. It is the nature of the beast, one could tell an innocent man who has been convicted of a crime, that sometimes unjust outcomes result. But what is the nature of the excuse here? Clearly, we would be reluctant to say that the jury found the man guilty by accident. Although a mistake has been made (the court has convicted an innocent man), the mistake need not be in the rules and procedures or in their application. Rather, the excuse would have to be that there is no sure-fire procedure for discerning guilt and innocence. But can this imperfection *excuse* the wrong? Is it like a nervous twitch that causes my hand to spill the tea? But why does the twitch excuse? Perhaps because I am not responsible for it: it is not within the realm of my agency; it stands outside my control. There is, in a general sense, some moral distance between me and that bodily activity that diminishes my blameworthiness. To use the language of chapter 6, the twitch is mere behavior; it is not a mechanism that is "my own."

It is possible for the officials, bureaucrats, judges, and lawyers who speak on behalf of the government also to have failures of agency. A judge has a seizure and so fails to consider an important piece of evidence in an appeal. But these failures are not the kinds one is concerned with in talking about imperfect procedures. Rather, they involve the inability of any rule-governed system to be able to encompass every particular situation in meeting its goals. The imperfection is the very fact that institutions use rules and procedures to guide and govern conduct. The imperfection is part of what the institution is in a way that the twitch is not. Because the institution is responsible for the outcome, no separable "imperfection" can bear the weight of responsibility. The imperfect character of an institution cannot excuse the outcome because the imperfection does not lift responsibility off the institution's shoulders.

Ultimately the imperfection of our procedures does not excuse the institution's failings. The knowledge that even in the best of regimes, the innocent will (hopefully rarely) be found guilty and the guilty will be acquitted does nothing to relieve the blameworthiness of those procedures when justice goes awry. It seems that even nearly just institutions will rightly be subject to enormous moral pressures and dissatisfactions. The presumption that no standing justification exists for the wrongful acts resulting from tragic choices or imperfect institutions can now be combined with the claim that no standing excuse is available to imperfect institutions.

Excusing Dirty Hands

In contrast to the case of imperfect procedures, there is something of a tradition of trying to excuse dirty hands, particularly in the conduct of international relations. Appeals to necessity and the representative character of state actors are two kinds of excuses that have been used in cases of dirty hands. Neither is convincing enough to remove responsibility completely for tragic choices.

One excuse common to dirty hands, particularly in the international realm, is that of necessity. But necessity can work as an excuse only if it is understood as inevitability (Walzer 1977, 7–8). Under this conception, dirtying one's hands is much like tripping on a rug and knocking someone else over. Inevitability can work as an excuse because it completely removes human agency and responsibility from the scene. Although fatalists and structuralists would make this claim, few would argue that our policy of nuclear deterrence or the decision of Uruguay to grant amnesty was like tripping over a rug. To the extent that dirty hands imply a choice, necessity looks more like indispensability than like inevitability. It is true that politicians appeal to necessity to impress upon us the indispensability of the means (such as granting amnesty to officials of the ancien régime, suspending the writ of habeas corpus, limiting free speech, or targeting cities with nuclear warheads) or to accomplish a particular end (such as placating the military, securing the union, protecting national security, or preserving sovereignty). But appeals to necessity qua indispensability strongly suggest that the circumstances are such that whatever they do will be wrong. The core of the excuse becomes the realm of necessity itself. In effect, a politician is pleading, "I am not responsible for these alternatives—whichever way I turn, I will do wrong. My lack of responsibility for having only *these* choices surely must diminish the blame for the choice I make." Just as a traffic jam over which I have no control may excuse my absence, the realm of necessity may do the same for politicians.

By being given a set of alternatives that are morally dubious, politicians can, to a degree, be excused for dirtying their hands. The excuse of necessity does diminish blame because of the lack of control over the alternatives but does not remove it altogether. To free these actors completely of blame, the responsibilities of office would have to be irrevocable. Officeholders who are placed in a position in which they must dirty their hands always have the option of resignation. As Michael Walzer notes, the fact that they seek office and desire to hold on to it does imply something about the moral responsibilities that attach to offices (Walzer 1977, 290). The assumption here is that it is not wrong or cowardly to resign rather than do evil. If resignation is a viable moral alternative, then the realm of necessity diminishes but does not eliminate responsibility for dirty hands.

Another excuse common to dirty hands entails shifting responsibility and blame from the government and its officers to those they represent or on behalf of whom they act. We have presumed, however, that nearly just governments can be treated as if they were moral actors in their own right. While this means that governments are blameworthy, it doesn't imply that they bear sole responsibility for what they do. As we saw in chapter 6, the responsibility for governmental wrongs can spill over to the citizenry. As long as governments can be understood as actors, however, this spillover does not entirely shift responsibility onto the shoulders of the citizenry. Chapter 8 considers the problem of applying political forgiveness to ordinary citizens who may also be responsible for wrongful government action.

8
Citizens Forgiving Citizens

CITIZENS, of course, can be wronged not only by their own government but also by other institutions, groups, and individuals. As in the earlier discussion of governmental forgiveness, this chapter brackets the problem of international wrongs. In addition, it defers a discussion of whether nongovernmental groups can be politically forgiven. Such an exploration would require consideration of whether these groups are culpable moral agents.[1] Finally, this chapter also brackets the problem of whether political forgiveness is appropriate if individuals living under an unjust government are wronged by others (whether, for example, political forgiveness would make sense under South Africa's former apartheid regime). Because public acknowledgment of the moral equality of these individuals vis-à-vis each other and vis-à-vis government officials is missing in an unjust regime, political forgiveness cannot have much of a role to play. The concern, then, in this chapter is with citizens who have been wronged by other individual citizens within the context of a nearly just government. Nevertheless, these limitations do not preclude considering whether political forgiveness can be an appropriate response to officials and collaborating citizens of an unjust regime that has fallen. Before raising this difficulty, however, we should explore the lesser harms and injustices that may arise during the reign of a nearly just government.

---

1. In bracketing these discussions, the moral agency of these other entities is left as an open question.

The Lesser Harms of Democratic Governance

Thomas Hobbes noted that the injuries of what he called "popular government" are various and painful. He believed that it was in the character of popular government for an individual "to see his opinion, whom we scorn, preferred before ours; to have our wisdom undervalued before our own faces; by an uncertain trial of a little vain glory, to undergo most certain enmities (for this cannot be avoided, whether we have the better or the worse); to hate and be hated, by reason of the disagreement of opinion; to lay open our secret councils and advices to all, to no purpose and without any benefit; to neglect the affairs of our own family: these, I say, are grievances" (Hobbes 1972, 229–30). The injuries, slights, transgressions, insults, and offenses incurred in the ordinary conduct of democratic politics are plentiful and disheartening. For Hobbes, they are so disheartening and plentiful that they are reason enough to prefer monarchy to popular government. (Hobbes, of course, believed that there were plenty of other reasons to support this preference.) For the sake of argument and without necessarily supporting his conclusions, we may assume that Hobbes is correct—that popular politics will always have this dirty character. Can political forgiveness address the vainglorious misrepresentations, the spiteful exaggerations, and the negative advertisements that seem to be part of the game? Is it appropriate for citizens to forgive other citizens for the way they conduct themselves politically? Is political forgiveness essential to moderate the rough and tumble of political life?

In order not to displace justice, political forgiveness requires that the debt created by the moral infractions be addressed. As we have seen, justice, at a minimum, requires a public acceptance of a common history of who did what to whom. Those who have slandered others or misrepresented their opponents' positions must acknowledge that some offense was committed. Whether more is required in order for political forgiveness to be appropriate depends, of course, on the circumstances and the nature of the offense. If there were an argument against political forgiveness, it would be that in these kinds of offenses justice could be fully met. These lesser harms may be tractable in a nearly just government without excessively burdening the transgressor. If so, there is nothing to forgive; a public apology for a public insult may pay the debt completely.[2] In other instances, where the infraction could not be fully paid back, forgiveness could serve as a supplement.

2. The relationship between political forgiveness and apology is discussed in chapter 4, footnote 12.

Is there an imperfect duty for citizens to forgive these kinds of offenses? Assuming their tractability, the central duty is for the offender to do justice, which would alleviate the necessity of political forgiveness. If, however, some of these wrongs are less tractable, then we would need to consider whether a citizenry that was unforgiving of these lesser harms should be subject to moral condemnation. Once again, however, "unforgiving" is ambiguous: Does it mean that these citizens should forget such offenses, in Nietzschean fashion, or should fall into the cynical state of an angle of repose? Perhaps in these cases, there is an imperfect obligation not to be too cynical of one's fellow citizens. And while this is not the same as an imperfect obligation to engage in political forgiveness, neither does it preclude the possibility of political forgiveness in the interactions of citizens. Hobbes may lead us to be pessimistic about ever getting transgressors to admit to the grating, petty offenses and insults that they commit, but his position does not rule out the pursuit of justice or forgiveness.

Citizens Forgiving Criminals

Not all of the harms perpetrated by one citizen against another are going to be lesser offenses. When they commit crimes, citizens violate the personal or political rights of other citizens. This violation raises the possibility of a *one to one* form of political forgiveness. Crime, as we have seen, also has a political, public dimension. Criminal actions are not merely private matters between the transgressor and the individual; they are also wrongs to the larger political association. In chapter 5, the existence of a public wrong presented the possibility of a *many to one* form of political forgiveness that takes the shape of a pardon. In exercising the power to pardon, however, the actions of the government are separable from the feelings of the individual victim. The existence of these two levels of wrongs raises the question of their connection: Does an official, governmental pardon supersede the right of the individual victim to engage in political forgiveness? In other words, can the victim refuse to engage in *one to one* political forgiveness when the government has pardoned the offender? Alternatively, can the victim engage in political forgiveness when the government refuses to engage in many to one forgiveness?

The public character of governmental political forgiveness commits the government not to discriminate against the offender in public, political interactions. In clearing the transgressor's debt to the political association, the pardon also, through its illocutionary character, invites the restoration of moral equality to the offender, as someone who should be treated no differently than anyone else. And while a pardon proclaims that the criminal is to be officially treated like any other citizen, this does not mean that the victim must free himself of resentment, anger, or disgust toward the offender. Nor does it mean that the offender must be admitted into the victim's private associations or friendships. Indeed, an official pardon may be compatible with a victim's continued pursuit of civil damages against the transgressor. While one effect of the pardon is to invite a larger process of reconciliation, the victim or others may refuse that invitation. Nevertheless, those who refuse the invitation may not impede the pardoned offender's exercise of his personal or political rights without violating the government's restoration of this individual to public life. The fully pardoned offender's freedoms should be protected as vigorously as the victim's.

What would happen if the victim forgave and the government did not? In this case, the victim would have forgiven the transgressor's debt to her, but this performance would be separable from the government's decision to forgive the debt created by the same crime. As long as we assume that crime is a public offense, the victim's invitation to restore the offender need not be picked up by the government (although it is possible that it could be). As far as the victim is concerned, a reconciliatory state may be achieved in which past wrongs do not serve as the basis for future claims. A public expression of forgiveness on the victim's part does not commit the government to any course of action. Just as in the case where a single action wrongs two people, that one has forgiven need not lead the other victim to expect any less from the transgressor. The forgiving victim must be willing to let the other victim make an independent decision regarding the debt.

Citizens Forgiving Citizens Who Have Collaborated

One of the points made by the discussion of governmental culpability in chapter 6 is that moral responsibility can spill over to citizens who were either accomplices in the wrongs or had the knowledge and freedom to prevent or resist them but did not do so. Moral spillover can occur not only when just regimes commit injustices but also when unjust regimes engage in evil or oppressive activities. The scope of this spillover can vary widely, depending on the nature of the wrong and the knowledge and freedom of the citizenry. Under a just government, citizens with the requisite knowledge and power bear some responsibility for their government's actions if they do nothing when the government violates the political or personal rights of others, if they obey a law that violates the principle of equal treatment, if they support officials who appeal to our base instincts, or if they voluntarily agree to serve in the military to fight a clearly unjust war.[3] In oppressive regimes, the number of collaborators may be quite large, even though the avenues for action are narrowed considerably. The question of politically forgiving citizens who collaborated with an unjust regime, however, can arise only after the government has been replaced with a just set of arrangements. Prior to that point, the public acknowledgment of equality among citizens and between citizens and their government is simply not available. In both cases, citizens who did not know or could not freely respond to the wrongs are not responsible. Finally, citizens who are accomplices in evil actions in which the minimal conditions of justice cannot be met should not be politically forgiven by their primary victims. In light of these cases, is it appropriate for citizens to forgive other citizens who collaborated in governmental wrongs?

As in all of these cases, we must first sort through what justice demands of those citizens who have aided, abetted, or refused to resist wrongful government action. The idea that justice requires truth, however, creates an enormous hurdle for political forgiveness in this situation. For rectificatory justice requires knowing who, among those able to act, stood up for the right and who collaborated or said nothing. The victims may, of course, know quite well who actively and passively supported the injustice: who turned down their requests for a ballot, who ordered them to sit in the back of the bus, who served as guards in the internment camps, who informed on them, ignored their cries for help, or joined the party. But this kind of knowledge, by itself, is not sufficient for political forgiveness (however sufficient it may be for private forms of forgiveness). Not only must the victim know what happened, but the offender and the victim must also share a publicly verifiable account of who did what to whom. To engage in political forgiveness prior to this point would short-circuit the minimal requirements for justice.

It is not out of the realm of possibility for those who aided in official injustices to admit publicly their guilt to the victim. Indeed, it may be quite clear that the behavior of the victims and transgressors could be

3. With the exception of the last case, in which non-citizens will suffer the immediate and more serious harms, all of the other cases involve a situation in which some citizens are wronged not only by a government but also by other citizens who should have known better.

verified through the existence of more evidence or through a complete telling of their stories. Such evidence and truth telling could emerge through official commissions or investigations into what had transpired. Once all of this has happened, the first steps toward justice have been taken. Once those steps are taken, then political forgiveness could be a justifiable response by citizens to the wrongful actions of other citizens.

The more difficult question is whether to initiate the pursuit of justice and truth telling when the collaborators are uncooperative or when they sincerely believe that they also stood for what was right and just. White southerners under Jim Crow, Frenchmen under the Vichy government, ordinary Serbians in Kosovo, and corporate officials in apartheid South Africa may be deeply reluctant to discuss, let alone admit, their role in oppression and injustice. Without sufficient cooperation of those who collaborated, it is difficult to see how the pursuit of at least the forensic truth could be undertaken without accusations being recorded, interrogations being undertaken, evidence being collected, and a quasi-juridical apparatus being established. But in many cases, those who did wrong did nothing illegal. In addition, there is always the danger of finding someone guilty merely by association because they subscribed to objectionable ideas or organizations. In short, the danger in such an undertaking is that it would eventually poison the possibilities for civic trust—the sense that one's fellow citizens should be able to participate in public decisions. Clearly, what Shklar called "passive injustice" is the most difficult to rectify because it calls forth mechanisms that intrude on and destroy a sense of moral equality and common enterprise. These mechanisms are more aligned with Robespierre's republic of virtue than with a polity of chastened citizens.

Yet, without truth telling, the possibility for justified political forgiveness evaporates. In addition, without such truth telling, corrective justice is sacrificed. Those who aided or failed to resist a governmental injustice or an oppressive government are "getting off" for the sake of maintaining a veneer of civility and trust among the citizenry. Those who would discourage or prevent such investigations of collaborators could be accused of obstructing the pursuit of justice and committing an additional wrong. Indeed, such a situation looks much like dirty hands where the successor government is standing in the way of getting at the full truth and doing wrong in order to do good. The successor government is creating a situation in which collaborating citizens cannot be forgiven in order to protect or establish a façade of civility. In effect, if the argument of chapter 7 is plausible, the successor government is doing something that is itself politically unforgivable. A similar problem emerges with former officials of the regime.

Citizens themselves, however, may decide that the minimal demands of justice are not worth pursuing; they may not want to know which neighbor had reported them to the secret police, or who had joined the party and who had resigned. Does a desire on the part of individual citizens to let such wrongs slide violate their duty as citizens? It certainly violates the assumption regarding the good of justice. Moreover, under a chastened conception of citizenship, citizens should not let governmental wrongs slide. Is the same true of the wrong done by collaborators? Obviously, much depends on the nature of the wrong and the degree of collaboration. Noncriminal wrongs committed by one citizen against another do not necessarily have the same quality as wrongs committed by a government. As we saw in chapter 7, the skepticism toward government that is part of a chastened conception of citizenship is largely based on a fear of power. Citizens should not let governmental wrongs slide because the government is the perpetrator. If the wrongdoer was one's neighbor, a chastened conception of citizenship wouldn't necessarily lead to a relentless pursuit of justice in the case of collaboration. This is particularly true if the wrongdoer no longer has the potential for exercising power over his fellow citizens. Citizens may decide not to pursue justice in these matters without falling into the kind of self-contradiction that plagues citizens who fail to pursue justice against the government. However, the victim's unwillingness to pursue justice precludes the possibility for political forgiveness. Unless the first steps of justice have been taken, political forgiveness cannot be justified.

Citizens Forgiving Former Officials of an Unjust Regime

The final problem to be considered is the response of victims to officials of a defunct oppressive government. Because these officials bear the full responsibility for their actions, forgiveness in this instance would take a *one to one* form. Nevertheless, in reasoning by analogy, if it is inappropriate to forgive a nearly just government that, to do good, has done wrong (the case of dirty hands), one could argue that surely it could not be acceptable to forgive former government officials who have done wrong to advance their self-interests, ideology, group, or tribe. Given that we are talking about actions which were not the result of tragic choices but simply self-serving and wrong, the culprits should expect to have to meet the full demands of justice: they should be liable to both criminal prosecution and to civil suit. No barrier should be placed before victims trying to secure their due. And if complete justice is not possible, then victims should adopt an angle of repose vis-à-vis their former tormentors; they should neither be trusted nor respected in their civic interactions. Victims should neither forgive nor forget what happened, nor accept their former oppressors as moral equals. From this perspective, it is acceptable to let the wrongs of collaborators slide, but it is not acceptable in the case of former officials. [4]

In chapter 5, I argued that a case could be made for pardoning former officials of an unjust regime (a *many to one* form of forgiveness) if the minimal conditions for justice had been met and other significant values could be advanced, such as stability, peace, or reconciliation. Given the character of political forgiveness, the state should not, as a conceptual matter, officially forgive a wrong that has not been publicly acknowledged by the relevant parties. The central point of the earlier discussion was that demands of public welfare could justify the exercise of the power to pardon and the overriding of demands of justice.

But what would the pursuit of justice entail if individual victims decided to pursue their due against such officials? One could imagine these victims pushing for prosecution and punishment. Alternatively, victims could seek civil damages against the former officials. Failing these alternatives they may seek revenge, appeal to a third party for intervention on their behalf (as Spain attempted to do in the case of Pinochet), or try to obtain public recognition of their plight and the responsibility of the culprits. It is, however, more puzzling to wonder why victims would ever publicly forgive those perpetrators who once held the reins of power, assuming that the wrong done was politically forgivable. In the case of an official pardon, an argument could be made

---

4. In considering the problem of retribution and restitution following the fall of communism in Eastern Europe, Jon Elster has argued that "there is no fixed point from which justice can proceed—only a sea of confusion" (Elster 1995, 568). Among other things, Elster argues that punishing former functionaries and officials would seem to focus on the little fish and not the big fish, whereas offering certain forms of restitution (giving back seized property) appears to advantage some victims at the cost of others. If Elster is correct and post-communist Eastern Europe truly was a sea of confusion, then the oppression there more closely resembled a situation in which political forgiveness would also have no fixed point from which to proceed. Whether Elster's description of the situation is accurate, one could argue that a failure of new governments to address claims of justice would be an injustice. To do nothing, in other words, would be yet another violation of the victim's rights. In doing justice, new regimes may generate new injustices. But this problem simply reinforces the claims regarding the limits of justice. It is not compelling enough to justify proceeding no further.

that some other good more important than prosecution was served. In the case of private individuals, however, it would seem unlikely that such a calculation would be made. Nevertheless, something like this calculation was made in the case of South Africa. In the process of trying to ease the transition to a more democratic state, the Promotion of National Unity and Reconciliation Act established that those who received amnesty would also be protected from the civil suits of victims (Tutu 1999, 55). South African legislators determined that allowing individual victims to seek rectificatory justice would be detrimental to the new government. Although, as Tutu notes, it was "indeed a very high price to ask victims to pay," the pursuit of justice by individuals was seen as a significant threat to stability—apparently no different than the threat posed by official prosecution and punishment.

From one perspective, the prohibition against civil suit may have been the only way to establish the necessary conditions for political forgiveness. If public admissions of responsibility would not have taken place without such a prohibition, then closing down the pursuit of justice through civil action opened the door to political forgiveness at both the individual and state level. That the South African government closed some avenues for redress (civil suit) does not mean that transgressors no longer owed a debt to individual victims. From this first perspective, victims could still forgive. One avenue to achieving a state of reconciliation—the full pursuit of justice—was closed, not all avenues.

That depriving victims of the right to pursue justice opened the door for individual citizens to forgive still leaves unanswered why they would then forgive the debt. After all, victims could choose to forget or adopt an angle of repose or seek justice through other means. But this doesn't mean that there would be no reasons to forgive. Individuals may see an act of political forgiveness as an opportunity to express the virtue of generosity. Or, they may see it as a way to sever the connection to a wrongdoer who remained perversely connected to them as long as a state of reconciliation was not achieved. Or, individuals may do it for the sake of the transgressor, as a way to respond to his or her admission of guilt. In any case, the choice to forgive, forget, or continue to pursue justice would be left to their discretion.

From a second perspective, the need of the South African government to prohibit civil suits paradoxically points to another possible set of reasons for citizens to forgive unjust officials of a previous regime. The action on the part of the government reveals that the response of citizens to individual perpetrators can be a matter of some importance. Without this kind of protection, former officials and wrongdoers were apparently unwilling to support the new regime. The fear of such suits was significant enough to turn it into an issue in the transition. Assume, for a moment, that the new regime granted cooperative offenders immunity from criminal prosecution but not immunity from civil suit. Those who fully participated in the conditional amnesty, having revealed their complicity in various wrongful acts and protecting themselves from criminal prosecution, would also have opened themselves up to civil action by their fellow, injured citizens. Knowing all that they know, the victims could have decided to forgive, and not pursue the matter any further, for any of the reasons set out above. As citizens, however, they could also have believed that the success of the new regime required the continued cooperation of or at least the absence of opposition from these former officials. And while the government would probably not have succeeded or failed depending on whether one victim decided to sue or forgive, they may also have believed that by initiating a process of reconciliation through an act of political forgiveness, they could help the new government take root. In addition, from their perspective, reconciliation would take root in the full disclosure of the wrong and the public knowledge that political forgiveness took place. Although conducted at a level in which the individual effects may be far less significant, this reasoning is analogous to the kind of reasoning the government may perform when deciding to pardon former officials of an unjust regime. In both cases, some important value is achieved by overriding the demands for justice.

The problem with the prohibition against civil suit was that the decision to pursue or forgo the pursuit of justice was taken out of the hands of individual citizens. One may argue, as Tutu does, that it was necessary to do this to obtain the cooperation of all parties. Even though the prohibition did not rule out the possibility for political forgiveness, it was accomplished by sacrificing the rights of victims to receive their due. As mentioned earlier, by dirtying its hands in this manner the South African government committed an act that, from within this theoretical framework, could be understood as politically unforgivable. Perhaps in order to avoid this conclusion Tutu offered the argument of the representative character of the decision. As we saw in chapter 4, however, the failure of this argument raises difficult questions about whether any government, even when led by the most capable, well-intentioned actors, can begin with clean hands.

Putting the South African case aside, citizens could have good reasons for engaging in the political forgiveness of former officials, assuming the minimal conditions of justice have been met. In addition, if former officials are able to demonstrate a willingness to sustain and protect the new, nearly just government, then the case for political forgiveness can be strengthened. Political forgiveness of one's oppressors is not necessarily incompatible with prudence or with the demands of citizenship, although it must be compatible with the minimal demands of justice. If these conditions have not been met and these former officials pose a standing threat to their fellow citizens and the nearly just successor government, the role of chastened citizen would seem to require either a constant call for justice or the adoption of an angle of repose. As long as those former officials pose a threat to the political and personal rights of their fellow citizens, it would seem that they could not expect to achieve a reconciliatory state or participate in a process of reconciliation with their victims.

An irony of this analysis is that because of the public standing of officials, the truth-telling requirements of justice may be more easily met in the case of officials than in the case of ordinary citizens who collaborated. Although the demands of justice should be a good deal more severe in dealing with those who ordered the oppressive acts as opposed to those who collaborated, the possibilities for political forgiveness may be greater in the case of officials than for ordinary citizens. Yet, if truth telling remains an essential component of political forgiveness, it is not clear how one could conclude otherwise. Forgiveness may have a place in politics, but it is not one without bounds.

9

Conclusion

ALTHOUGH political forgiveness may be glimpsed through such practices as financial forgiveness and pardoning, theorizing political forgiveness has entailed trying to understand this concept through a set of conditions. These included (1) the existence of a relationship between at least two parties in which (2) there is a debt owed to one party by the other (3) that is relieved by a party with appropriate standing (4) conveying the appropriate signs or utterances in which (5) the success of the act does not depend on the emotional or internal states of the forgivers, (6) even though it is generally thought good to receive what is due because (7) the effects of settling the past and inviting restoration of the offender or the debtor is somehow also thought to be good.

Understanding these conditions has invited the consideration of governmental and individual responsibility, the relationship between resentment and forgiveness, the prerequisites for the success of political forgiveness as an illocutionary act, the limitations and possibilities for vicarious political forgiveness, the justifications for the authority to forgive collectively, and the appropriateness of citizens to forgive their government and other citizens. Although I have arrived at certain conclusions about each of these concerns, their sum does not add up to a comprehensive theory of political forgiveness, if such an entity is even possible. In undertaking the somewhat more modest project of theorizing political forgiveness, it should not be surprising that a number of avenues remain unexplored and a number of invitations to attend to the assumptions of the argument have been turned down. The former category includes a detailed account of the meaning of financial forgiveness by political institutions, the place of forgiveness in an international context, and the possibility of entities other than citizens and governments engaging in forgiveness. Some assumptions that invite further clarification include the significance of generosity to politics, the coherence of a self-disclosive conception of political life, the full character of collective and individual responsibility, the role of compensation and restitution in meeting the demands of rectificatory justice, and the meaning of what is due. All remain standing invitations for further thinking and exploration.

Despite what has been left unattended, the book does address a set of objections, raised in chapter 1, to bringing forgiveness into political theory. All of these objections have been considered along the way, but it is useful to assemble them here as a way to review the argument. Throughout this book, I have assumed that politics should be more about the content of our actions than the character of our motivations. If forgiveness requires a change of heart or the removal of resentment, then it is incompatible with that conception of politics. In chapter 1, however, I argued that political forgiveness coheres with this view of politics because it is an act of self-disclosure in which the underlying sentiments of the act are irrelevant to its success. It is possible, then, to see political forgiveness as an illocutionary act whose point is to relieve one party's indebtedness to another. This act does not require that the parties cultivate a particular set of sentiments or engage in what was called self-enactment. Political forgiveness is compatible with an agency-based theory of politics.

Having come to some conclusions about the illocutionary character of political forgiveness, perhaps the most significant problem for discerning its place in political theory is in establishing its relationship to justice. In chapter 2, I argued that there would be no theoretical space for political forgiveness if rectificatory justice were understood as complete and capable of trumping all other concerns. In response, I contended that, not only is it possible to conceptualize the intractability of injustice, but there also may be other goods which could override the pursuit of justice. For example, the notion of imperfect procedural justice opened the possibility for political forgiveness when the limits of justice were reached. In addition, the concept of governmental pardoning pointed to the possibility of political forgiveness when other goods overrode the full pursuit of justice. The reconciliatory effect invited by political forgiveness can, on occasion, compete directly with the good of justice. Yet it was postulated that the good of justice was such that political forgiveness should never be a complete substitute. Political forgiveness should not preclude truth telling and the public acknowledgment by all parties of who did what to whom and who owes what to whom. Certain elements of justice remain indispensable conditions for political forgiveness.

A third challenge to theorizing forgiveness in politics was connected to the religious associations that many conceptions of forgiveness possess. This is a problem if one assumes that public life should be able to accommodate a wide diversity of ideas and religious perspectives and that public action should not require subscription to a particular set of sectarian beliefs. Along similar lines, the criticism was raised that forgiveness is frequently associated with a utopian hope in reconciliation in which all things fold back into a greater oneness. As in the case of its theological associations, the objection to this conception of reconciliation was that it would also be incompatible within a diverse, pluralistic society. In response, the reconciliatory effects that political forgiveness achieves and invites are of value to citizens of a nearly just state and not merely to those of one or another religious persuasion. Political forgiveness is able to achieve a reconciliatory state by settling past wrongs and preventing them from serving as a basis for future legitimate claims. In addition, it has the effect of issuing an invitation to initiate a process of reconciliation that restores the civic or social position of debtors and transgressors. These reconciliatory effects do not aim at a greater universal harmony and the elimination of all differences. Political forgiveness does not aspire to the grandest hopes of reconciliation and community.

A Nietzschean argument against forgiveness was also presented as a potential hurdle to theorizing political forgiveness. This argument inverts the connection between forgiveness and resentment and claims that forgiveness, instead of alleviating resentment, actually cultivates it. One advantage of a self-disclosive conception of politics, however, is that by knocking away the importance of self-enactment, it also evades the Nietzschean critique. The point of political forgiveness is not to eliminate or be committed to eliminating the victim's resentment. Whether political forgiveness cultivates resentment is also irrelevant insofar as what counts in successful forgiving are the civil actions of the victim. From one perspective, this position could be seen as compatible with Nietzsche's position because it demands that those who are wronged do not stew in and act on their resentment. From another perspective, however, if Nietzsche is recommending that resentment be purged from the victim in one glorious moment of anger and self-enactment, then this position does not address the corrupting character of resentment in human conduct. More strongly, one could argue that the theory is still trapped in a politics of resentment to the extent that it sanctions an angle of repose as a viable response to governmental wrongs (in the case of dirty hands).

Fully responding to the Nietzschean argument would require examining the coherence of an agency-based or self-disclosive conception of politics, something that I have not taken up here. It is, however, possible to see an angle of repose as part of the economy of resentment that Nietzsche rejects. But the defining condition of an angle of repose is what it is intended to achieve (self-disclosure) and not the sentiment with which it is conducted (self-enactment). Its intent is to allow victims to "keep alive" the wrong that the government and its agents had committed. It is, of course, easier to see how a resentful citizenry could sustain this aim than one for whom such actions are mere expressions of their role as citizens. The argument, however, is not that citizens must generate resentment in adopting an angle of repose; rather, it is that as citizens, they should neither forgive nor forget what the government has done. For those citizens willing to forget the wrong and get on with their lives, the distrust and cynicism conveyed to the government may not be heartfelt, but it is consistent (or so the argument goes) with their role as citizens. Whether resentment attends the action is not relevant to a politics that focuses on self-disclosure.

The conception of political forgiveness presented here is, in many respects, limited. For example, this position could not be plugged into any theory of politics. Theories that view justice as always complete, for example, or that see civic equality as a violation of a natural hierarchy, or that posit the cultivation of certain sentiments as essential for political stability would all be distrustful of this view of political forgiveness. In addition, political forgiveness cannot succeed unless the minimal conditions of justice are met and illocutionary requirements are satisfied. Many acts may be politically unforgivable either because justice is completely impossible or because the message cannot get from the forgiver to the forgiven. In addition, while the goods of reconciliation invited and achieved by political forgiveness are significant, they are not necessarily the highest nor the only goods. The role of a chastened citizenry, the respect due to the experiences of those who have been wronged, the value of governmental stability, and the importance of truth telling may all conflict with and trump the value of reconciliation. While political forgiveness is a generous act, it does not express or contain all that is valued.

In light of these limitations, the question naturally arises of whether an alternative conceptualization of forgiveness would do any better.

The primary competitor, of course, is a view of forgiveness linked to the elimination of negative feelings or a commitment to eliminate them. To some extent, the obstacles to theorizing this form of forgiveness in politics would be more daunting than those entailed by a self-disclosive conception of forgiveness. First, if we assumed a sentiment-based conception of forgiveness, it would appear to apply only to individuals, unless some philosophical sense could be made of the notion of communities or governments feeling resentment and anger. Second, the Nietzschean critique would have to be addressed in a more direct fashion. The complex problem of whether forgiveness cultivates resentment would need to be untangled with greater precision instead of circumvented. Third, Kathleen Dean Moore's claim that forgiveness need not issue in any action would have to be taken seriously by a position that saw forgiveness as essentially a change in attitudes and inner feelings. If no changes in behavior were required, it would be difficult to see how forgiveness could be political. If, on the other hand, the performative character of a sentiment-based forgiveness was emphasized, then attention would have to be given to the illocutionary effects of forgiveness: Does a change in attitude invite a process of reconciliation and achieve a reconciliatory state? Fourth, a sentiment-based conception would have to give an account of how to understand forms of forgiveness that do ordinarily occur in public (pardoning and debt forgiveness) but do not involve forms of self-enactment. Would the proper study of forgiveness in politics, for example, exclude consideration of the international forgiveness of financial debts? Fifth, a sentiment-based vision of forgiveness would also need an account of the relationship between justice and forgiveness. How is rectificatory justice, for example, linked to the presence or removal of resentment? Finally, the boundaries of forgiveness would also need to be established. What could or could not be forgiven? Is there ever a duty to withhold forgiveness? If resentment is a justified attitude to perceived injuries, should it be cultivated politically? Is it appropriate for political institutions to be in the business of cultivating or discouraging certain sentiments on the part of its citizenry? Undoubtedly, some of these issues could be handled more easily than others. Nevertheless, the private character of a sentiment-based vision of forgiveness, its applicability to individuals, and its complex linkages to cultivating that which it seeks to ameliorate all suggest that it would be significantly more difficult, although not impossible, to theorize this sort of forgiveness in politics.

Political forgiveness does have a place in political theory. It is compatible with an understanding of politics that tolerates a wide variety of beliefs and sees injustice as potentially intractable, civic equality as valuable, and self-disclosure as sufficient for political engagement. In the search to understand this concept, however, a role is carved out that may be quite a bit narrower than what would be desired by those who see forgiveness as a central personal and social virtue. But the conditions and assumptions that structure and hedge the concept of political forgiveness also provide its greatest defense against those who would dismiss the concept out of hand. Even if political forgiveness does not live up to our greatest theoretical aspirations, it does address the limitations of justice, point to the importance of generosity in politics, and illuminate the character of political reconciliation.

Bibliography

Adams, Marilyn. 1991. "Forgiveness: A Christian Model." *Faith and Philosophy* 8:277–304.

Albon, Mary. 1995. "Project's Inaugural Meeting." In *Transitional Justice*. Vol. 1. Edited by Neil Kritz. Washington, D.C.: United States Institute of Peace Press.

Arendt, Hannah. 1958. *The Human Condition*. Chicago: University of Chicago Press.

———. 1963. *Eichmann in Jerusalem*. Harmondsworth, Middlesex: Penguin.

Aristotle. 1985. *Nicomachean Ethics*. Translated by Terence Irwin. Indianapolis: Hackett.

Ash, Timothy Garton. July 17, 1997. "True Confessions." *New York Review of Books* 44:33–38.

———. 1997. *The File*. New York: Random House.

Asmal, Kader, Louise Asmal, and Ronald Suresh Roberts. 1997. *Reconciliation through Truth*. New York: St. Martin's.

Austin, John L. 1961. "A Plea for Excuses." In *Philosophical Papers*. Edited by J. L. Austin. Oxford: Clarendon Press.

———. 1962. *How to Do Things with Words*. Edited by J. O. Urmson. 2d ed. Cambridge: Harvard University Press.

Battle, Michael. 1997. *Reconciliation*. Cleveland: Pilgrim Press.

Beardsley, Elizabeth. 1980. "Understanding and Forgiveness." In *The Philosophy of Brand Blanshard*. Edited by Paul Schlipp. La Salle, Ill.: Open Court.

Beatty, Joseph. 1970. "Forgiveness." *American Philosophical Quarterly* 7:246–52.

Benn, Piers. 1996. "Forgiveness and Loyalty." *Philosophy* 71:369–83.

Benn, Stanley I. 1975–76. "Freedom, Autonomy and the Concept of the Person." *Proceedings of the Aristotelian Society* 76:109–30.

Benomar, Jamal. 1995. "Justice after Transitions." In *Transitional Justice*. Vol. 1. Edited by Neil Kritz. Washington, D.C.: United States Institute of Peace Press.

Blandshard, Brand. 1968. "Retribution Revisited." In *Philosophical Perspectives on Punishment*. Edited by Edward H. Madden, Rollo Handy, and Marvin Farber. Springfield, Ill.: Charles C. Thomas.

Boraine, Alexander. 1999. "Alternatives and Adjuncts to Criminal Prosecution." In *When Sorry Isn't Enough*. Edited by Roy L. Brooks. New York: New York University Press.

Braithwaite, John. 1996. "Restorative Justice and a Better Future." *Dalhousie Review* 76:9–31.

Butler, Joseph. [1726]. 1847. *The Whole Works of Joseph Butler*. London: William Tegg.

Calhoun, Cheshire. 1992. "Changing One's Heart." *Ethics* 103:76–96.

Camus, Albert. 1956. *The Rebel*. New York: Vintage.

Card, Claudia. 1972. "Mercy." *Philosophical Review* 81:182–207.

Cassell, Douglass W., Jr. 1995. "International Truth Commissions and Justice." In *Transitional Justice*. Vol. 1. Edited by Neil J. Kritz. Washington, D.C.: United States Institute for Peace Press.

Couper, David. 1998. "Forgiveness in the Community: Views from an Episcopal Priest and Former Chief of Police." In *Exploring Forgiveness*. Edited by Robert D. Enright and Joanna North. Madison: University of Wisconsin Press.

Crocker, David A. 1999. "Reckoning with Past Wrongs: A Normative Framework." *Ethics and International Affairs* 13:43–64.

Dickey, Walter J. 1998. "Forgiveness and Crime: The Possibilities of Restorative Justice." In *Exploring Forgiveness*. Edited by Robert D. Enright and Joanna North. Madison: University of Wisconsin Press.

Digeser, Peter, and Ross Miller. 1995. "Realism, Morality and Liberal Democracy." *Journal of Value Inquiry* 29:331–49.

Dinnen, Sinclair. 1997. "Restorative Justice in Papua New Guinea." *International Journal of the Sociology of Law* 25:245–62.

Downie, R. S. 1965. "Forgiveness." *Philosophical Quarterly* 15:128–34.

Dressler, Joshua. 1990. "Hating Criminals: How Can Something That Feels So Good Be Wrong?" *Michigan Law Review* 88:1448–73.

Duquoc, Christian. 1986. "The Forgiveness of God." In *Forgiveness*. Edited by Casiano Floristan and Christian Duquoc. Edinburgh: Clark.

Elster, Jon. 1995. "On Doing What One Can: An Argument against Post-Communist Restitution and Retribution." In *Transitional Justice*. Vol. 1. Edited by Neil J. Kritz. Washington, D.C.: United States Institute of Peace Press.

Estrada-Hollenbeck, Mica. 1996. "Forgiving in the Face of Injustice: Victims' and Perpetrators' Perspectives." In *Restorative Justice: International Perspectives*. Edited by Burt Galaway and Joe Hudson. Monsey, N.Y.: Criminal Justice Press.

Ex parte Milligan. 1866. 71 U.S. 4 Wall.

EZLN: Documentos y comunicados. 1994. Mexico City: Ediciones Era.

Feinberg, Joel. 1984. *Harm to Others*. New York: Oxford University Press.

Feldman, Lily Gardner. 1999. "The Principle and Practice of 'Reconciliation' in German Foreign Policy: Relations with France, Israel, Poland and the Czech Republic." *International Affairs* 75:333–56.

Finlayson, J. G. 1999. "Conflict and Reconciliation in Hegel's Theory of the Tragic." *Journal of the History of Philosophy* 37:493–520.

Fischer, John Martin, and Mark Ravizza. 1998. *Responsibility and Control*. Cambridge: Cambridge University Press.

Flathman, Richard. 1973. *Concepts in Social and Political Philosophy*. New York: Macmillan.

———. 1976. *The Practice of Rights*. Cambridge: Cambridge University Press.

———. 1989. "Citizenship and Authority: A Chastened View of Citizenship." In *Toward a Liberalism*. Ithaca: Cornell University Press.

Franscona, Joseph L. 1964. *Agency*. Englewood Cliffs, N.J.: Prentice Hall.

French, Peter. 1984. *Collective and Corporate Responsibility*. New York: Columbia University Press.

Gehm, J. R. 1992. "The Function of Forgiveness in the Criminal Justice System." In *Restorative Justice on Trial: Pitfalls and Potentials of Victim-Offender Mediation*. International Research Perspectives. Edited by Heinz Messmer and Hans-Owe Otto. Dordrecht, Netherlands: Kluwer.

Gingell, John. 1974. "Forgiveness and Power." *Analysis* 34:180–83.

Glynn, Patrick. 1994. "Toward a Politics of Forgiveness." *American Enterprise* 5:46–52.

Golding, Martin. 1984–85. "Forgiveness and Regret." *Philosophical Forum* 16:121–37.

Govier, Trudy. 1999. "Forgiveness and the Unforgivable." *American Philosophical Quarterly* 36:59–75.

Gowens, Christopher. 1987. *Moral Dilemmas*. Oxford: Oxford University Press.

Gray, John. 1980. "On Negative and Positive Liberty." *Political Studies* 28:507–26.

Haber, Joram Graf. 1991. *Forgiveness*. Savage, Md.: Rowman and Littlefield.

Hampton, Jean. 1988a. "Forgiveness, Resentment and Hatred." In *Forgiveness and Mercy*. Edited by Jeffrie G. Murphy and Jean Hampton. Cambridge: Cambridge University Press.

———. 1988b. "The Retributive Idea." In *Forgiveness and Mercy*. Edited by Jeffrie G. Murphy and Jean Hampton. Cambridge: Cambridge University Press.

Hardimon, Michael O. 1994. *Hegel's Social Philosophy*. Cambridge: Cambridge University Press.

Harland, Alan. 1996. "Towards a Restorative Justice Future." In *Restorative Justice: International Perspectives*. Edited by Burt Galaway and Joe Hudson. Monsey, N.Y.: Criminal Justice Press.

Hauerwas, Stanley. 1983. "Constancy and Forgiveness: The Novel as a School for Virtue." *Notre Dame English Journal* 15:23–54.

———. 1992. "Why Truthfulness Requires Forgiveness: Commencement Address for Graduates of a College of the Church of the Second Chance." *Cross Currents* 42:378–88.

Hayner, Patricia B. 1995. "Fifteen Truth Commissions, 1974–1993: A Comparative Study." In *Transitional Justice*. Vol. 1. Edited by Neil Kritz. Washington, D.C.: United States Institute of Peace Press.

Hobbes, Thomas. 1972. *The Citizen.* In *Man and Citizen: Thomas Hobbes.* Edited by Bernard Gert. Garden City, N.Y.: Anchor Books.

———. [1651]. 1994. *Leviathan.* Indianapolis: Hackett.

Holmgren, Margaret R. 1993. "Forgiveness and the Intrinsic Value of Persons." *American Philosophical Quarterly* 30:341–53.

———. 1998. "Self-Forgiveness and Responsible Moral Agency." *Journal of Value Inquiry* 32:75–91.

Horsbrugh, H. J. N. 1974. "Forgiveness." *Canadian Journal of Philosophy* 4:269–82.

Hudson, Barbara. 1998. "Restorative Justice: The Challenge of Sexual and Racial Violence." *Journal of Law and Society* 25:237–56.

Hudson, Joe, and Burt Galaway. 1996. "Introduction." In *Restorative Justice: International Perspectives.* Edited by Burt Galaway and Joe Hudson. Monsey, N.Y.: Criminal Justice Press.

Hughes, Martin. 1975. "Forgiveness." *Analysis* 35:113–17.

Huntington, Samuel P. 1995. "The Third Wave: Democratization in the Late Twentieth Century." In *Transitional Justice*. Vol. 1. Edited by Neil Kritz. Washington, D.C.: United States Institute of Peace Press.

Huyse, Luc. 1995. "Justice after Transition: On the Choices Successor Elites Make in Dealing with the Past." In *Transitional Justice*. Vol. 1. Edited by Neil Kritz. Washington, D.C.: United States Institute of Peace Press.

Jaspers, Karl. 1995. "The Question of German Guilt." In *Transitional Justice*. Vol. 1. Edited by Neil Kritz. Washington, D.C.: United States Institute of Peace Press.

Jones, L. Gregory. 1995. *Embodying Forgiveness.* Grand Rapids, Mich.: William Eerdmans.

Kateb, George. 1992. *The Inner Ocean: Individualism and Democratic Culture.* Ithaca: Cornell University Press.

Kolnai, Aurel. 1977. "Forgiveness." In *Ethics, Value, and Reality: Selected Papers of Aurel Kolnai.* London: Athlone Press.

Krog, Antjie. 1999. *Country of My Skull: Guilt, Sorrow, and the Limits of Forgiveness in the New South Africa.* New York: Times Books.

Lang, Berel. 1994. "Forgiveness." *American Philosophical Quarterly* 31:105–18.

———. 1996. "The Holocaust and Two Views of Forgiveness." *Tikkun* 11:42–45.

Levi, Primo. 1988. *The Drowned and the Saved.* New York: Vintage Books.

Lewis, Meirlys. 1980. "On Forgiveness." *Philosophical Quarterly* 30:235–45.

Locke, John. [1690]. 1980. *Second Treatise of Government.* Indianapolis: Hackett.

Louw, Johannes P. 1993. "Forgiveness." In *The Oxford Companion to the Bible.* Edited by Bruce M. Metzger and Michael D. Coogan. New York: Oxford University Press.

Martin, Ralph P. 1981. *Reconciliation.* Atlanta: John Knox Press.

May, Larry. 1987. *The Morality of Groups.* Notre Dame: University of Notre Dame Press.

———. 1993. *Sharing Responsibility.* Chicago: University of Chicago Press.

McCold, Paul. 1996. "Restorative Justice and the Role of Community." In *Restorative Justice: International Perspectives.* Edited by Burt Galaway and Joe Hudson. Monsey, N.Y.: Criminal Justice Press.

McElrea, Frederick W. M. 1996. "The New Zealand Youth Court: A Model for Use with Adults." In *Restorative Justice: International Perspectives.* Edited by Burt Galaway and Joe Hudson. Monsey, N.Y.: Criminal Justice Press.

McGary, Howard. 1989. "Forgiveness." *American Philosophical Quarterly* 26:343–51.

Messmer, Heinz, and Hans-Owe Otto. 1992. "Restorative Justice: Steps on the Way toward a Good Idea." In *Restorative Justice on Trial: Pitfalls and Potentials of Victim-Offender Mediation.* International Research Perspectives. Edited by Heinz Messmer and Hans-Owe Otto. Dordrecht, Netherlands: Kluwer.

Miller, David. 1987. "Justice." In *The Blackwell Encyclopedia of Political Thought.* Edited by David Miller, Janet Coleman, William Connolly, and Alan Ryan. Oxford: Basil Blackwell.

Mills, Jon K. 1995. "On Self-Forgiveness and Moral Self-Representation." In *Journal of Value Inquiry* 29:405–6.

Minor, Kevin I., and J. T. Morrison. 1996. "A Theoretical Study and Critique of Restorative Justice." In *Restorative Justice: International Perspectives.* Edited by Burt Galaway and Joe Hudson. Monsey, N.Y.: Criminal Justice Press.

Minow, Martha. 1998. *Between Vengeance and Forgiveness: Facing History after Genocide and Mass Violence.* Boston: Beacon Press.

Moore, J. J. 1991. "Problems with Forgiveness: Granting Amnesty under the Arias Plan in Nicaragua and El Salvador." *Stanford Law Review* 43:733–77.

Moore, Kathleen Dean. 1989. *Pardons: Justice, Mercy, and the Public Interest.* New York: Oxford University Press.

Morgan, Edmund S. Dec. 3, 1998. "The Big American Crime." *New York Review of Books* 45:14–18.

Morris, Herbert. 1968. "Persons and Punishment." *Monist* 52:475–501.

———. 1988. "Murphy on Forgiveness." *Criminal Justice Ethics* 7:15–19.

Murphy, Jeffrie G. 1982. "Forgiveness and Resentment." *Midwest Studies in Philosophy* 7:503–16.

———. 1988a. "A Rejoinder to Morris." *Criminal Justice Ethics* 7:20–22.

———. 1988b. "Forgiveness, Mercy, and the Retributive Emotions." *Criminal Justice Ethics* 7:3–15.

———. 1998. "Jean Hampton on Immorality, Self-Hatred, and Self-Forgiveness." *Philosophical Studies* 89:215–36.

Murphy, Jeffrie G., and Jean Hampton. 1988. *Forgiveness and Mercy.* Cambridge: Cambridge University Press.

Neblett, William. 1974. "Forgiveness and Ideals." *Mind* 8:269–75.

Neely, Mark E. 1991. *The Fate of Liberty.* New York: Oxford University Press.

Neier, Aryeh. 1995. "What Should Be Done about the Guilty?" In *Transitional Justice.* Vol. 1. Edited by Neil Kritz. Washington, D.C.: United States Institute of Peace Press.

Newman, Louis E. 1987. "The Quality of Mercy: On the Duty to Forgive in the Judaic Tradition." *Journal of Religious Ethics* 15:155–72.

Nietzsche, Friedrich. [1887]. 1956. "The Genealogy of Morals." In *The Birth of Tragedy and the Genealogy of Morals.* Translated by Francis Golffing. New York: Doubleday.

———. [1888]. 1968. *Twilight of the Idols / The Anti-Christ.* Translated by R. J. Hollingdale. London: Penguin.

North, Joanna. 1987. "Wrongdoing and Forgiveness." *Philosophy* 62:499–508.

Oakeshott, Michael. 1975. *On Human Conduct.* Oxford: Clarendon Press.

O'Shaughnessy, R. J. 1967. "Forgiveness." *Philosophy* 42:336–52.

Pankhurst, D. 1999. "Issues of Justice and Reconciliation in Complex Political Emergencies: Conceptualizing Reconciliation, Justice, and Peace." *Third World Quarterly* 20:239–56.

Parfit, Derek. 1984. *Reasons and Persons.* Oxford: Oxford University Press.

Peachy, Dean E. 1992. "Restitution, Reconciliation, Retribution: Identifying the Forms of Justice People Desire." In *Restorative Justice on Trial: Pitfalls and Potentials of Victim-Offender Mediation.* International Research Perspectives. Edited by Heinz Messmer and Hans-Owe Otto. Dordrecht, Netherlands: Kluwer.

Pion-Berlin, David. 1995. "To Prosecute or to Pardon? Human Rights Decisions in the Latin American Southern Cone." In *Transitional Justice.* Vol. 1. Edited by Neil Kritz. Washington, D.C.: United States Institute of Peace Press.

Pitkin, Hanna Fenichel. 1969. "The Concept of Representation." In *Representation.* Edited by Hanna Fenichel Pitkin. New York: Atherton Press.

Rawls, John. 1971. *A Theory of Justice.* Cambridge: Harvard University Press/Belknap Press.

———. 1999. *The Law of Peoples.* Cambridge: Harvard University Press.

Raybon, Patricia. 1996. *My First White Friend.* New York: Penguin.

Retzinger, Suzanne M., and Thomas J. Scheff. 1996. "Strategy for Community Conferences: Emotions and Social Bonds." In *Restorative Justice: International Perspectives.* Edited by Burt Galaway and Joe Hudson. Monsey, N.Y.: Criminal Justice Press.

Richards, Norvin. 1988. "Forgiveness." *Ethics* 99:77–97.

Roberts, Robert C. "Forgiveness." 1995. *American Philosophical Quarterly* 32:289–306.

Rousseau, Jean-Jacques. 1988. *Rousseau's Political Writings*. Edited by Alan Ritter and Julia Conaway Bondanella. New York: W. W. Norton.

Sa'adah, Anne. 1992. "Forgiving without Forgetting: Political Reconciliation and Democratic Citizenship." *French Politics and Society* 10:94–113.

Sandel, Michael. 1982. *Liberalism and the Limits of Justice*. New York: Cambridge University Press.

Searle, John, and Daniel Vanderveken. 1985. *Foundations of Illocutionary Logic*. Ithaca: Cornell University Press.

Seneca, Lucius. 1928. "On Anger." In *Moral Essays*. Vol. 1. London: Heinemann.

Shklar, Judith N. 1990. *The Faces of Injustice*. New Haven: Yale University Press.

Shriver, Donald W. 1995. *An Ethic for Enemies: Forgiveness in Politics*. New York: Oxford University Press.

Smart, Alwynne. 1968. "Mercy." *Philosophy* 43:345–59.

Smart, J. C. C., and Bernard Williams. 1973. *Utilitarianism: For and Against*. Cambridge: Cambridge University Press.

Smiley, Marion. 1992. *Moral Responsibility and the Boundaries of Community*. Chicago: University of Chicago Press.

Snow, Nancy E. 1993. "Self-Forgiveness." *Journal of Value Inquiry* 27:75–80.

Soyinka, Wole. 1999. *The Burden of Memory, The Muse of Forgiveness*. New York: Oxford University Press.

Strawson, P. F. 1974. "Freedom and Resentment." In *Freedom and Resentment and Other Essays*. Edited by P. F. Strawson. Oxford: Methuen.

Talbott, Thomas. 1993. "Punishment, Forgiveness, and Divine Justice." *Religious Studies* 29: 151–69.

Tavuchis, Nicholas. 1991. *Mea Culpa*. Stanford: Stanford University Press.

Tennyson, Alfred. [1860]. 1969. "Sea Dream." In *The Poems of Tennyson*. Edited by Christopher Ricks. London: Longmans, Green.

Thomas, Christopher. August 14, 1995. "Kwai Victims to Make Peace with Guards; VJ-Day Commemorations." *London Times*.

Trollope, Anthony. [1870]. 1988. *The Vicar of Bullhampton*. Oxford: Oxford University Press.

Tutu, Desmond Mpilo. 1999. *No Future without Forgiveness*. New York: Doubleday.

Twambley, P. 1975–76. "Mercy and Forgiveness." *Analysis* 36:84–90.

Van Ness, D. 1989. "Pursuing a Restorative Vision of Justice." In *Justice: The Restorative Vision*. Edited by P. Arthur. Issue no. 7 of New Perspectives on Crime and Justice. Akron, Penn.: Mennonite Central Committee Office of Criminal Justice.

Verwoerd, Wilhelm. 1999. "Justice after Apartheid?" In *When Sorry Isn't Enough*. Edited by Roy L. Brooks. New York: New York University Press.

Waldron, Jeremy. 1984. *Theories of Rights*. Oxford: Oxford University Press.

Walzer, Michael. 1977. *Just and Unjust Wars*. New York: Basic Books.

——. 1979. "Political Action: The Problem of Dirty Hands." In *Political Theory and International Ethics*. Edited by Charles R. Beitz. Princeton: Princeton University Press.

Weber, Max. 1946. "Politics as Vocation." In *From Max Weber: Essays in Sociology*. Edited by H. H. Gerth and C. Wright Mills. New York: Oxford University Press.

Weiner, Brian. 1996. "Political Forgiveness." Presented at the annual meeting of the Western Political Science Association, San Francisco.

Wiesenthal, Simon. 1976. *The Sunflower*. New York: Shocken Books.

Wright, Martin. 1991. *Justice for Victims and Offenders*. Philidelphia: Open University Press.

Yancey, Philip. 1993. "Holocaust and Ethnic Cleansing: Can Forgiveness Overcome Horror?" *Christianity Today* 37:24–29.

Young, Iris Marion. 1990. *Justice and the Politics of Difference*. Princeton, N.J.: Princeton University Press.

Zalaquett, José. 1995. "Confronting Human Rights Violations Committed by Former Governments: Principles Applicable and Political Constraints." In *Transitional Justice*. Vol. 1. Edited by Neil Kritz. Washington, D.C.: United States Institute of Peace Press.

Zehr, Howard. 1997. "Restorative Justice: The Concept." *Corrections Today* 59:68–71.

Index